DRIFTING TOGETHER

The Political Economy of Canada-US Integration

John N. McDougall

broadview press

To all the students I have taught over the years.

© 2006 John N. McDougall

Library and Archives Canada Cataloguing in Publication

McDougall, John N.
    Drifting together : the political economy of Canada-US integration / John N. McDougall.

Includes bibliographical references and index.
ISBN 1-55111-780-0

    1. Canada—Foreign relations—United States. 2. United States—Foreign relations—Canada. 3. Free trade—Political aspects—Canada. 4. Free trade—Social aspects—Canada. 5. Free trade—Canada. 6. Free trade—United States. I. Title.

FC249.M38 2006   327.71073   C2006-901396-9

Broadview Press is an independent, international publishing house, incorporated in 1985. Broadview believes in shared ownership, both with its employees and with the general public; since the year 2000 Broadview shares have traded publicly on the Toronto Venture Exchange under the symbol BDP.

We welcome comments and suggestions regarding any aspect of our publications—please feel free to contact us at the addresses below or at broadview@broadviewpress.com.

North America
PO Box 1243, Peterborough, Ontario, Canada K9J 7H5
PO Box 1015, 3576 California Road, Orchard Park, NY, USA 14127
Tel: (705) 743-8990; Fax: (705) 743-8353
email: customerservice@broadviewpress.com

UK, Ireland, and continental Europe
NBN International, Estover Road, Plymouth, UK PL6 7PY
Tel: 44 (0) 1752 202300; Fax: 44 (0) 1752 202330
Email: enquiries@nbninternational.com

Australia and New Zealand
UNIREPS, University of New South Wales
Sydney, NSW, Australia 2052
Tel: 61 2 9664 0999; Fax: 61 2 9664 5420
email: info.press@unsw.edu.au

www.broadviewpress.com

Broadview Press gratefully acknowledges the financial support of the Government of Canada through the Book Publishing Industry Development Program for our publishing activities.

Typesetting by Aldo Fierro.

Edited by Betsy Struthers.

PRINTED IN CANADA

CONTENTS

ACKNOWLEDGEMENTS

I would like to express my thanks to my good friends and colleagues, Leon Surette, Professor Emeritus of English, for his astute reading and editing of several chapters, and Bob Young, who made helpful comments on early versions of the theoretical chapters. My new and valued colleague Radoslav Dimitrov also read and commented helpfully on most of the manuscript. Greg Yantz and Michael Harrison of Broadview Press provided much encouragement and constructive advice, and comments from the appraisers they provided were challenging, but very useful. Betsy Struthers's copy editing was invaluable and extremely efficient.

I am also grateful to several journals and publishers who gave me permission to reproduce or draw heavily upon portions of some of my previous publications, as follows:

"The Long-Run Determinants of Deep/Political Canada-US Integration," in folio no. 7 of *Thinking North America*, edited by Thomas J. Courchene, Donald Savoie, and Daniel Schwanen, *The Art of the State*, Vol. 2 (Montreal: Institute for Research on Public Policy, 2004).

The Politics and Economics of Eric Kierans: A Man for All Canadas (Montreal: McGill-Queen's University Press, 1993) 156-68.

"European and North American Integration: Some Implications for Transnational Democracy" in Bruce Morrison, ed., *Transnational Democracy in Critical and Comparative Perspective: Democracies Range Reconsidered* (Aldershot: Ashgate, 2003) 121-30.

"North American Integration and Canadian Disunity," *Canadian Public Policy* 17, 4 (December, 1991): 399-402.

LIST OF ABBREVIATIONS

AIT	advanced information technology
BCNI	Business Council on National Issues (Canada)
CBC	Canadian Broadcasting Corporation
CAP	Common Agricultural Policy (EU)
CMA	Canadian Manufacturers Association
CPR	Canadian Pacific Railway
CRIC	Canadian Centre for Research and Information
CRTC	Canadian Radio-Television and Telecommunications Commission
EU	European Union
DFAIT	Department of Foreign Affairs and International Trade (Canada)
FIRA	Foreign Investment Review Agency (Canada)
FTA	Canada-US Free Trade Agreement
FTC	Free Trade Commission (Canada-US-Mexico)
G7	Group of Seven (major industrial countries)
GATS	General Agreement on Trade in Services
GATT	General Agreement on Tariffs and Trade
GDP	gross domestic product
IGO	international governmental organizations
IPI	international political integration
ISI	import substitution industrialization
ITO	International Trade Organization
MNC	multinational corporation
NAFTA	North American Free Trade Agreement
NATO	North Atlantic Treaty Organization
NDP	New Democratic Party (Canada)

NEP	National Energy Program (Canada)
NGO	non-governmental organization
NORAD	North American Aerospace Defense Command
NTBs	non-tariff barriers
OAS	Organization of American States
OECD	Organization for Economic Cooperation and Development
PACE	Pacific Corridor Enterprise Council (Canada-US)
PNWER	Pacific Northwest Economic Region (Canada-US)
R&D	research and development
ROC	rest of Canada (outside of Ontario)
ROW	rest of the world (outside of Canada)
TCE	trans-Canadian economy
TNR	transnational relations model
UN	United Nations
US	United States of America
USCS	US Central Sector
WP	world politics model
WTO	World Trade Organization

INTRODUCTION

If it was not clear before the second American war with Iraq, it is almost universally recognized today that the United States (US) is, by a wide margin, the most powerful country in the world and, possibly, the most powerful nation the world has ever seen. It goes without saying, therefore, that it is overwhelmingly the superior power on the North American continent, both politically and economically. Moreover, American business and political leaders are increasingly conscious of their country's global dominance. In turn, many Canadians are coming to realize that Americans' awareness of their new status—paradoxically in combination with an enormous sense of vulnerability to terrorism—has placed Canada's relationship with the US in an entirely different context from the one that prevailed for most of the late twentieth century. In particular, American anxieties about the security of its borders has underscored for Canadians the degree of their country's economic dependence on the US, as well as their political and economic vulnerability to the consequences of American policies and actions, both at home and abroad. In these circumstances, it is a significant question whether intensified economic integration with the US is compatible with Canada's own independence and long-term prosperity. Moreover, in a world now dominated by a single superpower, Canadians share this question with people all over the world who, in comparable ways, confront the challenge of maintaining their economic well-being and political autonomy despite increasing pressures that arise out of the US's dominance of global politics and economics. This book, therefore, attempts to weigh the overall political effects of Canada's economic integration with the US in a manner that illuminates the relationship between economic interdependence and political autonomy across the globe.

Most people consider the terrorist attacks in New York City and Washington, DC[1] on September 11, 2001 (9/11) to be a major turning point in world affairs. The attacks certainly had a significant impact on the relationship between Canada and the US. However, as this book will demonstrate, the ensuing War on Terror provoked changes in the Canada-US relationship that, while certainly significant, do not truly constitute a change in direction. Rather, they amount to an acceleration or amplification of profound changes that have been going on for at least a decade. These earlier changes were associated less with threats to the physical security of Canadians and Americans than with the adoption of free trade by the two countries in January 1989. However, the consequences of the 9/11 terrorist attacks dramatized the deep impact of free trade. Immediately after the towers of the World Trade Center collapsed, huge lines of waiting trucks formed at all major Canada-US border crossings. Almost as rapidly, many Canadians developed deep anxieties over the longer term economic price they might pay if Americans' concerns over the security of the border became a new fact of life with which Canadians would have to contend. The almost instantaneous consensus among Canada's government and business leaders, one widely shared by the general public, was that Canada must do everything in its power to restore the smooth functioning of the border or lose the benefits of free trade.

This fear, which approached the level of panic, has become the dominant political philosophy of Canada's economic and political power-holders, who now seem to give absolute political and economic priority to preserving a smoothly functioning border with the US. In order to maintain the flow of goods and people between the two countries at its normally high rate, Canada has had to reassure Americans that an open border will not put the US at risk and, more generally, that they can trust Canada to be an asset rather than a liability in the

---

[1] From now on, the capital city of the US will be referred to simply as "Washington." References to the State of Washington will be either so designated or otherwise qualified.

campaign against international terrorism. Accordingly, Canada has had to comply with a wide variety of American demands and expectations, among them revising its immigration policies, placing a battle group under American command in Afghanistan in the winter of 2002, agreeing to establish a Canada-US Planning Group to examine increased Canada-US land and maritime military cooperation, and committing Canadian forces to a tour of duty in Kabul in the fall of 2003.[2]

However, the government of Jean Chrétien stopped short of joining the American-led attack on Iraq in early 2003, insisting instead on United Nations (UN) approval of any strong sanction against the Iraqi president, Saddam Hussein. With this exception, many major adjustments in Canada-US relations since 9/11 can only be regarded as an erosion of Canada's domestic and foreign policy autonomy. This is not a new departure, merely an intensification of a process of economic and political integration that has been under way for many years, even decades. In this sense, the political compromises that Canada has made over the past several years in order to keep its exports moving across the American border provide a dramatic revelation of the overwhelming degree to which the Canadian economy depends on access to the American market.

This dependence—which has grown steadily since the 1950s when both the flow of American direct investment into Canada and the shift in Canada's exports toward the American market accelerated substantially—created a condition in which Canadians dare not stray very far from the economic and political path set by the US. Until recently, Canadian governments (both federal and provincial) focused on maintaining American investment. The flow of goods across the Canada-US border was—with a few notable exceptions—taken for granted (cf., the countless times over the years that Canadian and American officials have referred in speeches to "the longest undefended border in the world," a description that more

---

[2] See Elinor Sloan, "The Road from September 11: Canada-U.S. Defence Relations in the Terrorist Era," in David Carment, Fen Osler Hampson, and Norman Hillmer, eds., *Canada Among Nations 2004: Setting Priorities Straight* (Montreal and Kingston: McGill-Queen's University Press, 2005) Ch. 10.

recently can hardly be stated without qualification). Today, however, the price of an open border for goods is that Canadian governments abandon or refrain from policies in any area of national life that Americans might perceive as raising the risk to their physical security.

As a result of this preoccupation with access to the American market, Canadians face an "autonomy/prosperity trade-off" that is both latent in their economic dependence on the US and is now more starkly apparent than ever before. Viewed most broadly, this trade-off derives from the fact that the national priorities that help to bind Canadians together as a distinct and independent political community are frequently at odds with the seamless economic integration with the US upon which Canada's economic fortunes depend. In its immediate, more practical sense, this trade-off means that Canadians may no longer be free to significantly stray from American norms and values—for example, by decriminalizing marijuana—without paying an economic price in the form of closer, time-consuming inspections at the border.

The publication of the C.D. Howe Institute's "Border Papers" was a clear sign that Canada's economic and political elites had become very concerned about preserving and even extending the seamlessness of the Canada-US trade and investment relationship. The Institute commissioned a series of studies to explore the "specific policy challenges Canada faces as it moves toward deeper Western Hemispheric integration, beginning with the United States."[3] Significantly, the framers of these studies expected them to show that economic and physical security were complementary, rather than antagonistic, and that Canada and the US (and Mexico) "can achieve greater physical and economic security without loss of sovereignty and the erosion of the distinctive political and cultural institutions the people of each country hold dear."[4] However, as the first study in the series made clear, it may be a tall order to sustain an acceptable balance between national sovereignty and intensified North American integration, that is, to maintain autonomy without abandoning prosperity.

---

[3] See the insert ("Box 1") at the beginning of the first commentary in the series: Wendy Dobson, "Shaping the Future of the North American Economic Space: A Framework for Action," *C.D. Howe Commentary* 162 (April 2002): 2.

[4] Dobson.

In the first of the Border Papers to be published, Wendy Dobson argued that, given the American preoccupation with heightened security following 9/11, the Canada-US border could once again become a major trade barrier and that "reinforcing North American self-protection and being seen to do so is in the Canadian interest."[5] Thus, Canada should weld the goals of physical and economic security together in a "strategic bargain" aimed at achieving deeper overall integration.[6] Such a "big idea" was necessary, according to Dobson, because an agenda of piecemeal negotiations was unlikely to attract sufficient American attention in the fog of war that had settled on Washington. In other words, given its current preoccupations, a bold initiative involving a large package of linkages and trade-offs might catch the attention of the American government that ad hoc, issue-by-issue negotiations probably would not.[7]

Many of the individual recommendations presented in Dobson's analysis deserve consideration on their merits, but it is difficult to see how her "big idea" can prevent the loss of Canada's sovereignty and distinctive political and cultural institutions. Although her commentary reiterates with mantra-like insistence that its proposals would not undermine Canada's political independence, most of her suggested initiatives involve the kinds of joint policy formation and/or cooperative institutional arrangements that are generally associated with a loss of political autonomy.[8] Similarly, many of the policy

---

[5] Dobson 1.

[6] Dobson 1 and 19-20.

[7] Dobson 30.

[8] See Dobson 25-29, for proposals for joint measures in border management; bilateral working groups, possible common training programs, and mutual recognition of policies in immigration; mutual recognition of labour-market policies; joint planning in the energy sector; similar joint planning for other national resources such as water; new, more advanced levels of joint military planning and operation; a common competition policy; a joint commission on the formation of a possible customs union; and a North American Commission to map out steps toward deeper integration. A more recent study in the series examines the prospects for a customs union between the two countries, which would reduce Canadian autonomy substantially in several areas of trade and economic policy. See Danielle Goldfarb, "The Road to a Canada-U.S. Customs Union: Step-by-Step or in a Single Bound?," *C.D. Howe Commentary* 184 (June 2003).

changes adopted by the Chrétien government following 9/11 involved an increased emphasis on the bilateral Canada-US relationship. This reorientation has been reinforced by a shift of responsibility for Canada-US relations within the structure of government away from the Department of Foreign Affairs and International Trade (DFAIT) to the office of the deputy prime minister (and hence the Prime Minister's Office). Prime Minister Paul Martin took the further significant step of creating a Cabinet Committee on Canada-US Relations, which he chairs.

Recent studies of the overall effects of the 9/11 attacks on the Canada-US relationship are addressed in some detail in Chapter 10. However, it is interesting to note that one of the first academic papers distributed in their aftermath stated that the early changes combined the "shock of the new" with "the hold of the familiar."[9] The new element, according to this formulation, is the explicit recognition that Canada-US border issues had become the "main game" of Canadian foreign policy. Much of the last years of Lloyd Axworthy's term as minister of foreign affairs (1996-2000) were heavily committed to multinational coalition-building around a "human security" agenda that often excluded, if not opposed, the US on such issues as landmines and an international criminal court. This legacy is rapidly giving way to "more effective 'management' techniques aimed at ensuring access to the American market."[10]

At the same time, according to this source, some of the long-standing traditions of Canadian foreign policy remained discernible in the Canadian government's approach to the Canada-US relationship. For example, Canadian decision-makers resisted the rebranding of the border as a continental perimeter; maintained an emphasis on incrementalism (as opposed to sweeping changes); rejected the trilateralization of border issues to include symmetry with American-Mexican border arrangements; and continued to promote foreign policy objectives

---

[9] See Andrew F. Cooper, "Canadian Foreign Policy after September 11: A Preliminary Analysis," paper presented to the Annual Conference of the Canadian Political Science Association, Toronto, 31 May 2002.

[10] Cooper 1.

apart from North American trade and the terrorism agenda, such as the New Partnership for African Development.[11] Even the single most concrete change to come out of Canada-US negotiations following 9/11—the "Smart Border" declaration of December 2001—had strong roots in earlier steps to improve the functioning of the border, including (among other developments) the Canada-US Partnership agreement of 1999.

It is truly remarkable, however, how prevalent most of these discussions were even prior to 9/11. There is, in fact, a growing literature on what might be called "the emergence of a North American community." Most of this literature acknowledges that North American political integration is unlikely to take the same form as it has in Western Europe with the formation of the European Union (EU), but it also stresses that economic and political integration are becoming increasingly interconnected. At the very least, a "continental mindset" appears to be developing in parallel with the increasing intensity of cooperative efforts among the three members (Canada, the US, and Mexico) of the North American Free Trade Agreement (NAFTA). These cooperative efforts need not involve the formal transfer of national sovereignty required by the Treaty on European Union (commonly called the Maastricht Treaty, the founding document of the current EU). Nevertheless, it appears that a change is taking place in the Canadian government's operational definition of sovereignty. For example, former Prime Minister Chrétien felt that Canada's sovereignty would remain intact so long as "the laws of Canada [are] passed by the Parliament of Canada," a definition that threatens to become increasingly hollow and symbolic if the policies adopted by Canadian governments are based in fact more on what partnership with the US and Mexico requires.[12]

The stark reality for Canadians, then, is that the only way for Canada to keep the border as open as is necessary to support its prosperity is to do everything the US requires in order for that country to

---

[11] Cooper 2 and 4.

[12] See Shawn McCarthy and Campbell Clark, "Canada will make its own laws, PM vows," *Globe and Mail*, 20 September 2001.

feel secure. In concrete, practical terms, this means that Canadians must accept American standards and priorities with respect to such matters as immigration controls and airport and seaport security or, at the very least, must win American approval of Canada's approaches to these matters. It also means a much higher Canadian priority on strengthening its military forces in order to play a more active part in the preservation of overall North American security. As J.L. Granatstein put it in the second of the C.D. Howe Border Papers, "If we do not provide a credible military to help defend North America and the values of freedom, democracy, secularism, and pluralism we share with the United States, the Americans will do it for us—because they must."[13] As high as the price of doing this may appear to some Canadians, Granatstein argues, it is not as high as the price of an ineffectual and irrelevant Canadian foreign policy that will result from allowing the Canadian armed forces to continue to languish in its current understaffed and underequipped condition.

Of course, it remains to be seen whether a majority of Canadians will agree with Granatstein that they must more than double their spending on defence within ten years, join the Northern Command and a National Missile Defence, and abandon the "Pearsonian internationalism" that has marked much of their post-Second World War foreign policy. Nonetheless most commentators to date seem to agree that the economic risk of a failure to do so is very high. In the meantime, as the C.D. Howe Institute's Border Papers demonstrate, it is indeed important for Canadians to approach the post-9/11 agenda with a fuller and more accurate understanding of the present and possible future state of the Canada-US relationship.

Americans, as well as students of American foreign policy everywhere, may also find the US's relationship with Canada a valuable case study of the ways in which its enormous economic and military

---

[13] J.L. Granatstein, "Friendly Agreement in Advance: Canada-US Defense Relations Past, Present and Future," *C.D. Howe Commentary* 166 (June 2002): 17. According to Granatstein's estimates, the price of this new priority will not be cheap: $2.5 billion more than the current budget of $12 billion in 2003, $3.5 billion the year after, $4.5 billion in 2005, $5.5 billion in 2006, $6.5 billion in 2007, and $1.5 billion each year after that for at least the next five years.

power can affect much of the rest of the world in the age of unipolarity. For one thing, as this book aims to show, a plausible argument can be made that Canada-US relations illustrate the process of globalization in microcosm. For another, they demonstrate that even the strongest allies and best friends of the US will be wary of its power in the world and become resentful when American foreign and domestic actions cause them harm or constrain their choices. Its friends can be frustrated by the ability of the US to alter the agenda of multilateral and bilateral negotiations across a broad range of issues simply by acting as it sees fit and leaving the rest of the world to "take it or leave it."

As Lloyd Gruber has pointed out in *Ruling the World*, the US benefits enormously from its capacity to create a "new status quo" through its unilateral actions, which then alter the context within which all other countries—friends and foes alike—must redefine their priorities. This usually means going along with American preferences even though it may be costly for them to do so.[14] By learning more about their relationship with Canada, which is replete with instances of such asymmetries of power and consequence, Americans might become more mindful of the difficulties they can cause their best friends and neighbours, even when they do not intend to do so. Beyond this, the Canada-US relationship also holds lessons of interest to people all over the world, especially those who share borders with larger, more powerful neighbours and/or are attempting to strike a balance between the economic benefits and political costs of intense interdependence.

Finally, it must be acknowledged that Americans are unlikely ever to fully appreciate the depth of Canadian anxiety about the possible loss of independence. In fact, the disparities between the two countries are so great that it is not clear that anything could give Canadians complete confidence that their national survival is not in question. Thus, despite the emphasis placed here upon the balances that pervade the relationship, there is one fundamental asymmetry—or imbalance—that needs to be underscored because it

---

[14] See Lloyd Gruber, *Ruling the World: Power Politics and the Rise of Supranational Institutions* (Princeton, NJ: Princeton University Press, 2000) 7.

underlies the essential dynamics that inform a wide spectrum of issues and interactions. That fundamental asymmetry is that Canada is perpetually worried about how its foreign policy can preserve or enhance its independence of the US. There is no counterpart to this in American foreign policy.

The rest of this book, therefore, examines in detail the theory, history, and future prospects for Canada-US economic and political integration. For example, the main point of the Chapters 3, 4, and 5, which are devoted to economic history, shows how the superior performance of the American economy for over 300 years laid the groundwork for the steady progress of economic integration between Canada and the US during the twentieth century. Another important theme in these chapters is the major differences in the development of the Canadian and American economies, including the greater de-gree and scope of national government intervention in the Canadian case and the greater economic dynamism and diversification in the American. Meanwhile, Chapters 1 and 6 examine the Canada-US relationship in theoretical terms, with special attention to theories of international interdependence and integration. Most such theories suggest that high levels of economic integration promote political integration or, at least, policy harmonization. Thus, these chapters examine the extent to which, in conformity with this theoretical model, the close interdependence of the Canada-US economic rela-tionship that developed in the second half of the twentieth century is leading toward political integration.

Both the history and the theory presented in the book are designed to help the reader understand the content and significance of NAFTA, which was signed by Canada, the US, and Mexico in 1992 and which came into force on January 1, 1994. The discussion in Chapters 7, 8, and 9 sets out a fundamental conflict in Canadian policy priorities. While NAFTA formalizes the long process of Canada-US economic integra-tion described in earlier chapters, it also represents a clear break with the long history of Canadian attempts to avoid political union with its southern neighbour. On the one hand, the implementation of NAFTA represents continuity with the past, an extension and consolidation of the economic dimension of the relationship; on the other, the policy harmonization it promotes is a major departure from some traditions in the politics of the relationship, at least for Canada.

Chapter 10 places Canada's economic *and* political integration with the US in a global context, since much of what is taking place politically and economically in North America is also taking place in other parts of the world, notably in the EU and the Asia Pacific region, in the process many observers refer to as "globalization." The Conclusion asks how and to what extent North America can be regarded as a microcosm of globalization and to what extent Canadian attempts to cope with Americanization may help us understand the challenges that globalization represents to nation-states all over the world.

chapter 1
THE ANALYSIS OF CANADA-US INTEGRATION: THEORY, KEY CONCEPTS, AND SCOPE

This book examines the effects of North American free trade on Canada-US relations beyond the dimensions of trade and investment flows. Specifically, its chapters trace the impact of the two free trade agreements—the Canada-US Free Trade Agreement (FTA) of 1989 and the North American Free Trade Agreement (NAFTA) of 1994—on Canada's own cultural policies, communications regulations, cross-border regional interactions, social policy, defence and security policy, and foreign policies. Distinctively, the study sets the transformation of Canada-US relations resulting from free trade against the backgrounds of both economic history and theories of economic and political integration. In doing so, it argues the case that, while the members of NAFTA are highly unlikely ever to undertake the form of political integration adopted by the EU, Canada is already engaged in a process of policy harmonization with the US that amounts to political integration by stealth. Thus, the "integration question" in North America is, for Canada, essentially a question of preserving its democracy.

This argument involves several key conceptual and empirical questions, including the nature of both economic and political integration and, more importantly, the relationship between the two. Of course, conceptual relationships aside, the fact of the convergence of the Canadian and American economies must be established, something this study does by examining the evolution of the two economies and the manner in which their respective evolutionary paths have led almost unavoidably to the adoption of free trade. Moreover, following the formal economic integration of the two countries with the two free trade agreements, pressures toward political integration have increased, in part as a matter of advances in the rationalization of the corporations conducting the major part of the trade and investment flows between the two countries, but also as a consequence of the significant increase in Canada's trade dependence on the American market and the economic vulnerabilities associated with that heightened level of dependence.

This book makes the case that the conversion of economic integration into political integration is largely disguised by the distinctive character of political integration in North America and its major differences from political integration in the EU, where the process has been characterized by a high degree of institutionalization and centralized decision-making. By contrast, political integration in North America, though substantial and growing, is confined to a less visible and clear-cut process of policy harmonization and coordination between Canada and the US (and, to a lesser extent, Mexico). Accordingly, the book inquires into the degree to which Canadian and American policies are, in fact, converging across the spectrum of issue areas identified in the first paragraph of this chapter. It also addresses both the degree to which Canadian and American values may be converging and the role of converging values in the political integration process.

On the question of value convergence, two possibilities may be considered, both of which promise more advanced levels of political integration in the form of even greater policy harmonization. On the one hand, Canadian and American values may converge among both the economic elite and the general public, with the result that economic integration will be converted into political integration at a fairly swift pace. On the other, the values of Canada's economic elite may fuse with their American counterparts, while those of the general public remain more distinct, in which case (depending on how responsive the Canadian political system is to the values and preferences of its general population) political integration will come more slowly. (The argument assumes that no political integration will take place if the values of neither the economic elites nor the general population support it—the condition Canada was in until after the Second World War.)

Before these questions are discussed, some central concepts and questions of interpretation require attention. These include the conceptual differences between independence, political autonomy, and sovereignty, as well as the relationship between all three of these concepts and the democratic expression of national will. The North American and global developments that may shift the existing balance between interdependence and autonomy toward greater, and perhaps more formal, political integration also need discussion. The rest of this chapter examines the literature on each of these questions to discover the degree to which it supports the argument that free trade is leading toward political integration with the US, possibly despite the reluctance of a majority of Canadians.

CANADA-US RELATIONS AND THE THEORY OF INTERNATIONAL POLITICAL INTEGRATION

If there were no relationship between economic and political integration, this study would be beside the point. However, the fairly voluminous literature that explores the relationship between the two processes can be taken as evidence of, at least, the plausibility of its existence. Of initial interest is that, apart from any analytical or theoretical debate, the question of whether or not economic integration leads to political integration has been a persistent and sometimes central issue in Canadian politics. Since before Confederation, Canadians have been consistently torn by the tension between the economic gains and political costs of continental integration.

Kim Nossal has portrayed the essence of this long-standing issue as a dialogue between what he calls the "economic nationalists" and the "integrationists." Economic nationalists are convinced that Canadian integration with the American economy is not in Canada's political interest and that a viable nation-state must keep foreigners from owning its resources and industries and should generally avoid dependence: "a nation should strive to forge a distinct economic unit to safeguard its political, cultural and social separateness."[1] On the other side stand the integrationists, whom Nossal expressly declines to describe as "continentalists" because he does not believe their views endorse the ultimate absorption of Canada into a single North American political entity. Instead, integrationists favour expanded economic links with the US, stressing their benefits and downplaying their political costs.[2] In an interesting twist of the economic nationalist argument, the integrationists claim that their approach to economic development does an even better job of promoting the political values that the nationalists hold so dear: by enriching the country, economic integration with the US means that Canadians can better afford to pay for the social, cultural, and foreign policies that differentiate them from Americans.[3]

After a careful analysis of the arguments and evidence assembled by both sides, Nossal concludes that the economic nationalists succeed in making the point that economic integration does lead to a loss of political autonomy. However, in his view this does not mean that Canada must lose its status as a sovereign state or that it will lose an independent and indigenous state apparatus capable of making authoritative decisions on behalf of the country. Nevertheless, "the cumulative effects of trade and investment patterns have indeed placed considerable constraints on the achievement of Canadian autonomy in numerous domains by creating patterns of dependence on the economic relationship with the United States."[4] He notes in passing that this is not the same as domination by the US, since the dependence is self-generated. It is not even the case that Canadians are incapable of changing this condition, but they are constrained from

---

[1] K.R. Nossal, "Economic Nationalism and Continental Integration," in Denis Stairs and Gilbert R. Winham, Research Coordinators, *The Politics of Canada's Economic Relationship with The United States*, Vol. 29, Royal Commission on the Economic Union and Development Prospects for Canada (Toronto: University of Toronto Press, 1985) 56.

[2] Nossal, "Economic Nationalism," 56-57.

[3] Nossal, "Economic Nationalism," 43.

[4] Nossal, "Economic Nationalism," 85.

doing so by the high costs of reversing the extent of the economic ties that have developed.

Nossal argues further that, in contrast to economic nationalists, integrationists fail to make a convincing case for their argument that the deep-seated fears of Canadians about losing their political autonomy are based on ill-founded emotionalism and that in the joint management of a free trade area "the government of Canada *will* be able to maintain maximum independence." Rather, he concludes,

> those who argue for closer economic integration with the United States are unable to show that, in the long term, a future generation of Canadians *will not* find themselves so integrated into the American economy that it will make more sense to submerge their national identity into some form of continental federalism.[5]

Whether or not Nossal is correct in his assessment of these contending schools of thought, his analysis helps to make clear their opposite positions on the validity of the theoretical proposition that economic integration promotes political integration. As Nossal puts it, the integrationist argument (somewhat ironically) rejects this proposition on the basis of liberal economic theory, which posits a fundamentally apolitical view of transborder movements of capital and goods. As their label suggests, they favour *economic* integration because they believe it can be kept *politically safe*. In contrast, the economic nationalists espouse integration theory by insisting on the opposite claim that economic interdependence must have political consequences. Nossal finds the latter argument the more convincing one, although he cautions that loss of autonomy is not to be confused with the disappearance of sovereignty or complete cultural assimilation.

According to the communications approach to international political integration associated (most notably) with Karl Deutsch, Nossal's economic nationalists are probably right.[6] In bare outline,

---

5 Nossal, "Economic Nationalism." Emphasis in the original.

6 Karl W. Deutsch, *Nationalism and Social Communication: An Inquiry into the Foundations of Nationality*, 2nd ed. (Cambridge, MA: The MIT Press, 1966).

the Deutschian theory of integration posits that the intensification of transactions of all kinds between two or more societies will, over time, bring about a positive political reorientation of those societies toward one another in the form of increased mutual responsiveness and support for the advancement of common goals. (An important intervening variable in this causal relationship is the level of mutual trust between the people of the two societies, a dimension that will be considered later.) By this measure, the process of Canada-US integration began with the increasing flows of trade, investment, people, and ideas between the United States of America and British North America during the second half of the nineteenth century. Similarly, the major turning point was the period during which the volume of such transactions between Canada and the US first overtook those between Canada and the UK and then began to dominate.

This given, it seems at least plausible to proceed on the assumption that, to the degree that Canada and the US have integrated economically beyond some critical threshold, the pressures toward some form of political integration should exist and at least some preliminary manifestations of it should be evident. However, the fact of economic integration remains to be established, and Chapters 3 and 4 of this book are devoted to this task. For the moment, it is sufficient to note that the historical evolution of the American and Canadian economies established two fundamental realities. First, the American economy has always been more highly developed than the Canadian one, to the extent that by the middle of the twentieth century its market, capital, and technology had begun to play a critical role in Canada's economic development. Second, and obversely, the relative weakness of the Canadian economy meant it increasingly has depended upon American imports, capital, and technology.

The precise extent of this economic integration will receive more detailed discussion in later chapters. For now, it should be sufficient to note that, for most of the last half of the twentieth century, each was the other country's largest trading partner, and Canada was the world's largest, single recipient of American direct investment. Countless Canadian subsidiaries of American corporations depended on their parent firms for almost all of their research and development, and daily and annual flows of people back and forth across the border were the highest in the world. In fact, on almost every accepted measure of economic integration, there was at least as much—and probably more—integration between Canada and the US than there was between any two countries in Western Europe between the 1950s and 1990s, when Europe was well on its way to becoming the economic union we know today. Nevertheless, by some definitions, the EU is taken to be the most advanced instance of regional economic and political integration yet seen, which raises a question as to why economic integration has produced significant political integration in Europe but not in North America. The key to this question is the role of institutionalization in the process of political integration.

The most significant difference between the European and North American processes of economic and political integration is that the Europeans have accepted large-scale transfers of authority from the national level to the "supranational" level. Today's EU—like its predecessor the European Economic Community, established in 1957—has relied on the creation of major, state-like institutions to conduct the common affairs of the integrated partners.[7] Because it is possible to imagine a future in which this institutional structure comes to be invested with all the powers associated with the central government of a fully sovereign, federated state such as the United States of America, the EU has generally been regarded as having the potential to evolve ultimately into a new sovereign state—perhaps the "United States of Europe." If this degree of institutional centralization is taken as the hallmark of political integration, then the Canada-US relationship is nowhere near it. So far, the countries of North America have relied upon only a small number of minor institutions to manage and promote their moves toward economic integration, and it would be stretching the definition to refer to NAFTA as a "supranational" organization of any sort.

---

[7] The principal examples are the European Commission, which is essentially a European-wide bureaucracy; the Council of Ministers, which is the equivalent of a national cabinet, or executive; the European Parliament, which is elected by, and legislates on behalf of, a European-wide electorate; and a European Court of Justice, which acts as a supreme court.

There are two possible explanations for this difference. The first is that there is no necessary link between economic and political integration after all; Canada and the US represent a disconfirming case of the theory that the former leads to the latter. The second, contrary, explanation is that Canada-US economic integration is in fact leading to political integration, but in a non-institutionalized form that substitutes various modes of policy harmonization and political accommodation for region-wide, state-like institutions. The answer hinges upon whether political integration must assume the institutional form it has taken in Europe.

This book calls into question the institutional model, making the case that Canada and the US are undergoing a form of political integration that is dissimilar to that of the EU only in that it does not rely on central, state-like institutions. A strong case for this interpretation, and some clarification of what it might mean in the present context, can be found in Peter Katzenstein's meticulous application of the Deutschian framework to the case of German-Austrian integration. Katzenstein refers to this relationship as a "disjoined partnership," which he defines as two countries that are so close to one another in so many ways that it is hard to understand why they continue to remain separate.[8] Disjoined partnerships thus comprise countries—such as Canada and the US—that are substantially integrated with one another culturally, socially, and economically, yet remain politically autonomous.

The most important aspect of Katzenstein's analysis of German-Austrian relations for this argument is that his definition of political integration does not focus on institutions. Rather, he understands political integration and disintegration as "different degrees of the purposeful coordination of political behavior in the achievement of common tasks."[9] In other words, political integration is identified principally (though not exclusively) with the harmonization and standardization of the national policies of participating states.

---

[8] Peter J. Katzenstein, *Disjoined Partners: Austria and Germany since 1815* (Berkeley, CA: University of California Press, 1976) 16.

[9] Katzenstein 14.

Support for this interpretation can be found in the way Katzenstein describes the nature of German-Austrian relations during the period between the First and Second World Wars. On the one hand, the interwar period created the conditions for "an extensive and effective coordination of policies and a considerable erosion of Austria's political autonomy." Yet, on the other hand, "Austria and Germany stopped short of establishing a full-fledged political community," owing principally, first, to the prevailing structure of the international political system between the wars and, second, to prevailing domestic political circumstances which were not conducive to unification.[10] Later, he underscores the point that "short of the unification of the political institutions of the two countries," the "assimilation of Austrian to German political practices went far beyond anything witnessed [previously]."[11]

Another key point that Katzenstein's book makes very clear is that the process of political integration is a probabilistic, not a deterministic one. It involves "co-pressures" toward, as well as "counter-pressures" against, outright political union, even at the highest levels of socio-economic integration.[12] Moreover, the key factors determining which pressures are in ascendance during any particular period in an international relationship are (to paraphrase Katzenstein) the pressures bearing on the integrating countries from the current state of the international system; the relations between the two countries' elites; the relations between the elites and masses within each of them; and the prevailing state of domestic political party competition.[13] In short, from the viewpoint of the individual members of an

---

[10] Katzenstein 132-33.

[11] Katzenstein 148.

[12] Katzenstein, Ch. II.

[13] It should be noted that Katzenstein's case study has been extrapolated to a comparison with Canada-US relations. See Henry J. Jacek, "Unequal Partners: The Historical, Political, Economic and Cultural Dimensions of The Austrian-FRG/Canadian-U.S. Dyads," in Harold von Riekoff and Hanspeter Neuhold, eds., *Unequal Partners: a Comparative Analysis of Relations Between Austria and the Federal Republic of Germany and Between Canada and the United States* (Boulder, CO: Westview Press, 1993) 27-45. Jacek does not adopt Katzenstein's label of "disjoined partners" for the Canada-US relationship, preferring the more familiar term "unequal partners" to cover the same category of relationships, but Katzenstein's book is the first work he cites.

integrated relationship, the determination of whether it becomes unified or remains a disjointed partnership lies in a combination of international conditions and the options provided by the domestic political system.

Katzenstein's model deserves close attention because it underscores some of the critical differences between the integration processes taking place in Europe and North America. It does this by establishing the importance of domestic politics to the varying degrees of political integration attained during different phases of the German-Austrian relationship, as well as the importance of the relationship between elites and masses within the domestic politics of the partners, especially the smaller one. Studies of the integration project in Europe generally agree that it has been an elite-driven process, but no one suggests that economic and political leaders in Europe have driven their general populations in a direction they were determined not to go. (However, results of the French and Dutch referendums on a new constitution for the EU seem to promise new lessons on the relations between elites and masses over the question of deeper and wider political integration.[14]) In the case of North America, it is pretty clear that neither the elites nor the general populations of Canada, Mexico, or the US are pressing the case for political integration in the full-fledged form of political *unification or even of advanced forms of institutional integration*. However, the case of political integration in the form of *policy harmonization* is more ambiguous.

Some of this ambiguity may be unresolvable, mostly because it does not represent a clear-cut political choice, in contrast to political unification, which is absolute. The formal transfer of sovereignty from member states to the government of a newly created union has either taken place or it has not. In this sense, the EU is misnamed, given that—despite its high degree of centralization—its members retain their status as sovereign states. Policy harmonization, in contrast, is relative; it proceeds (or recedes) by degrees. Put somewhat differently,

---

[14] See Norman Barry, "Dutch Join French in Rejecting EU Constitution," 2 June 2005; Foundation for Economic Education website: <http://www.fee.org/vnews.php?nid=6944>.

political integration as political unification is a question of "either/or"; political integration as policy harmonization is a question of "more or less." The importance of this form of ambiguity to the present analysis is that it opens up the possibility that—in the extreme case—a national population could be subjected to a government that harmonized itself into extinction, or at least irrelevance, without ever choosing that fate or even being aware of it.

Apart from any political threat this possibility might actually hold for Canadian independence, it severely complicates the application of Deutschian integration theory to the Canada-US case—particularly with respect to the role of attitudes and values in the political integration process—in two major ways.

First, the ambiguities surrounding policy harmonization point to the importance of specifying whose values matter—those of economic and political elites or of the general public. To the degree that those who influence and run national governments are able to operate without the informed support of the public, it is possible that advanced degrees of policy harmonization could take place, regardless of whether or not the relevant attitudes and values of the populations concerned actually favour such accommodations. This means that public opinion surveys attempting to discover whether or not, or to what extent, the values of Canadians and Americans are converging are largely beside the point. There may be no real advantage, for example, in attempting to validate Michael Adams's recent and widely discussed claim that Canadians "embrace a different hierarchy of values. Moreover, the differences ... are increasing rather than decreasing with economic integration."[15] As a result, Adams— rather like Nossal's integrationists—holds out the possibility of

> economic integration and strategic interdependence without
> the loss of cultural integrity and political sovereignty. This, I
> would argue, is because Canada's founding values, historical
> experiences, and political institutions are very different from

---

[15] Michael Adams, *Fire and Ice: the United States, Canada and the Myth of Converging Values* (Toronto: Penguin Canada, 2003) 142.

those in the United States and have a greater influence on Canadians' contemporary values than the much vaunted forces of globalization.[16]

Nevertheless, at least one other recent and comprehensive study of Canadian and American values points to extensive and deep-seated similarities between the two countries and remains essentially agnostic on the question of future divergence or convergence.[17]

Second, and similarly, the ambiguity surrounding policy harmonization renders almost irrelevant the question of the "capacity for choice" that Canadians may or may not retain under the current free trade regime. If support for political integration is greater among elites than among the broader population, and if those elites can prevent non-integrative policy options from being fairly represented on the electoral agenda, then policy harmonization between Canada and the US could substantially increase without Canadians ever explicitly adopting it as a policy. It is true that several studies of "policy convergence" published during the past five years claim that there is little evidence of such convergence taking place or that free trade is responsible for any convergence there has been.[18] This finding, however, does not rule out the possibility that economic integration between the two countries may impose long-term constraints on the choices that their political system makes available to their populations.

However, in reviewing the individual arguments that lead to this possibility, some key conceptual issues have not yet received the attention they require if the full implications of that scenario are to be fully understood and substantiated. To them the discussion now turns.

---

[16] Adams 143.

[17] Edward Grabb and James Curtis, *Regions Apart: the Four Societies of Canada and the United States* (Don Mills, ON: Oxford University Press, 2004) Ch. 12.

[18] George Hoberg, Keith G. Banting, and Richard Simeon, "The Scope for Domestic Choice: Policy Autonomy in a Globalizing World," in George Hoberg, ed., *Capacity for Choice: Canada in a New North America* (Toronto: University of Toronto Press, 2002) Ch. 9. This study will receive more detailed attention below in the discussion of "policy autonomy."

CORE CONCEPTS AND DEFINITIONS

Since a principal focus of this investigation of the Canada-US relationship is the effects of continental free trade on Canada's capacity
to maintain or adopt distinctive policies across a wide range of issue
areas—that is to say, on Canadian autonomy—it is important that the
analysis address directly the cluttered conceptual terrain surrounding the inter-related notions of independence, interdependence, and
dependency; of national sovereignty; and of political autonomy. Giv-
en that, in some respects, this entire book is an exploration of the
exact meaning and significance of all of these concepts and the interrelationships among them, the following discussion of such concepts
is not intended to be exhaustive, but rather to stipulate the meanings
attached to them for purposes of this study.

Independence, Interdependence, and Dependency

Among the most fundamental of various key concepts informing
in the process of integration is the notion of *interdependence*. Two or
more countries are considered to have become interdependent when
they rely on one another for some goods or services that they value
and would prefer not to give up. (One observer has defined interdependence as a relationship that would be costly for both sides to
break.) This draws attention to the fact that international interdependence and integration grow out of exchanges, transactions, and
communication between two countries, both of which believe them
to be beneficial. It also means that national *independence*—which,
as we shall see in the next section, is often and inaccurately confused with *sovereignty*—is here defined residually as one country's
lack of reliance on other countries for its economic and physical
well-being. By these definitions, therefore, no country in the world
at present is completely independent, and most—including some of
the most powerful—are heavily interdependent.

Numerous complexities surround the political significance of various kinds of mutually beneficial exchange relations, most of them

concerning the different degrees of mutual *vulnerability* involved. Relationships are rarely exactly equal—one of the two countries in a relationship will need the exchanges taking place more than the other, giving the "less dependent" partner a degree of leverage over the more dependent one. Although measuring the different degrees of dependence and vulnerability between two or more countries is a difficult exercise, generally speaking the country with more alternatives to a given relationship—say, a variety of different trading partners—will be less vulnerable, because the loss of one partner can be compensated by an increase in trade with one or more of the others. Most of the members of the G7, for instance, trade with all the other members of the G7 and a variety of less developed countries. In contrast, a typical Third World country in Africa, Asia, or Latin America will conduct most of its trade with only one or two of the G7 countries and perhaps with a scattering of other less developed states, creating a condition of vulnerability to those partners.

This last example introduces the notion of *dependence*, which (for reasons that will not be examined here) some observers prefer to call "dependency." Unlike interdependence, which implies at least some degree of equality and mutuality in a relationship, dependence suggests severe disparities in status, wealth, and power. Therefore, in keeping with the definition of interdependence introduced a moment ago, dependence might be defined as a relationship which *only one side* would find it costly to break. A Third World country in a trading relationship with only one G7 country, and with no other countries either developed or undeveloped, would find it very damaging to sever that relationship; the vulnerability runs only one way. Such dependent relations are generally not regarded as instances of integration (or at least not voluntary integration) and are frequently analyzed as relations of domination and subordination.

Sovereignty

As noted, independence is often confused with sovereignty. Perhaps the most promising point of departure in navigating this difficult landscape is Stephen Krasner's comprehensive exploration, which distinguishes four major usages of the concept of sovereignty:[19]

1. domestic sovereignty, referring to the organization of public authority within a state and to the level of effective control exercised by those holding authority;
2. interdependence sovereignty, referring to the ability of authorities to control transborder movements;
3. international legal sovereignty, referring to the mutual recognition of states or other entities; and
4. Westphalian sovereignty, referring to the exclusion of external actors from domestic authority configurations.[20]

As already mentioned, there are those who argue that the adoption of free trade has not significantly diminished Canadian sovereignty, and there are others who argue that free trade has even reinforced sovereignty by bringing Canada and other countries together to regulate at the intergovernmental level global forces that have escaped the bounds of national regulation. Such analysts appear to be addressing a combination of Krasner's Westphalian and domestic categories of sovereignty. Typically, they emphasize the fact that Canadian authorities continue to exercise exclusive authority to make the laws that govern the lives of Canadians and that neither the FTA nor NAFTA (or the WTO and other multilateral trade agreements) have created a level of authority above that of the Canadian Parliament to make rules for Canadians.[21] This argument is far from conclusive, however, because both reasons given are contestable, and, moreover, they are all largely beside the point, even if true. The central concern with political autonomy and/or

---

[19] Stephen Krasner, *Sovereignty: Organized Hypocrisy* (Princeton, NJ: Princeton University Press, 1999) 9–25.

[20] Krasner 9. "Westphalian sovereignty" derives its label from the Peace of Westphalia (1648), which is generally regarded as having laid the foundations of the modern European state system.

[21] As Hoberg, Banting, and Simeon put it conclusively, "Canada has formidable capacities for domestic policy choices in a wide range of sectors. It is up to Canadians and their elected officials to choose how to exercise that freedom of choice" (291).

the policy capacity of national governments is not who ultimately holds the power "to decide" (whatever that may mean in these circumstances), but who or what determines the constraints within which such decisions are made.

International actors and forces can affect the choices that national governments make both from inside and outside their national borders. A classic example of an international actor influencing a government from within the state are the subsidiaries of multinational corporations that—as members of the domestic society and as perfectly legitimate participants in national policy-making processes—attempt to ensure that decisions of the Canadian government promote the economic and political interests of their foreign parents and/or the countries within which the parent companies reside. Another very significant example of an actor influencing a government from outside the state today is the ability of the US to define the terms, conditions, and processes of international agreements and institutions and to oblige smaller states in the system to "take it or leave it." Lloyd Gruber argues that it is a mistake to regard as "free" the decisions of smaller states to "take" such arrangements if the only reason they have for doing so is that the larger power can make it even more costly to reject them.[22]

Krasner's category of interdependence sovereignty connects these points about the international forces affecting governments with another constraint on Canadian political autonomy, one that stems from some recent developments in the Canada-US relationship. NAFTA has begun to detract from Canada's freedom of action in relation to the US by the very fact of the increased levels of exports it has promoted. Since exports to the US comprise over 80 per cent of total Canadian exports worldwide and generate over 30 per cent of Canada's total gross domestic product (GDP), Canada's ability to continue to export to the American market arguably represents the country's most vital national interest. This massive dependence on exports to a single foreign market has transformed earlier, quantitative levels of trade interdependence into a qualitatively new condition that

---

[22] Gruber 47-50.

verges on export dependency. (The imbalances involved are unmistakable: Canada accounts for less than 20 per cent of American exports and less than 3 per cent of its GDP.) In multiple senses of the phrase, Canada simply cannot afford to see the border close or even its efficiency of operation much disrupted. Yet, Canada's capacity to prevent such closures or disruptions by the US is practically non-existent. As a consequence, there is not likely another country on the planet whose interdependence sovereignty is as vital and yet so asymmetrical.

   With all this in mind, we will reserve the term "sovereignty" to Krasner's notion of legal sovereignty. This is the only one of his four categories that remains completely untouched by free trade.[23] As the preceding discussion has argued, Krasner's other three categories have been compromised to some extent and so will be kept distinct as far as possible throughout this book. Reductions in governments' "room for manoeuvre" or their capacity to regulate effectively will be referred to here as the erosion of policy capacity and/or political autonomy. Meanwhile, the notion of the erosion of independence will be restricted to a dearth of economic options, such as a reduced selection of trading partners or potential investors, and the inability to regulate information flows and immigration.

   Nevertheless, the foregoing analysis does not deny that free trade agreements can, in a roundabout manner, promote national independence and enlarge the scope for effective government action when compared to attempts to contend with globalizing pressures on a stand-alone basis. Moreover, free trade agreements certainly need not detract from Canada's (or any country's) legal status as a recognized member of the community of sovereign states. In fact, national sovereignty can be enhanced, rather than diminished, through

---

[23] This contention directly contradicts a view expressed by some prominent Canadian commentators on the Canada-US relationship under free trade, who speak of "constitutionalization" by trade agreements. See, for example, Stephen Clarkson, *Uncle Sam and Us: Globalization, Neoconservatism and the Canadian State* (Toronto: University of Toronto Press, 2002) esp. 53-58. In Krasner's terms, however, I believe such arguments address a loss of domestic and interdependence sovereignty, given that such agreements do not touch on Canada's legal status within the international community.

membership and participation in international governmental organizations (IGOs). Two ways in which this is true will be elaborated
briefly here. The strong way in which belonging to IGOs can "increase"
sovereignty is through the proliferation of the arenas within which an
individual state is accepted as a full and equal member, thus increasing the number of other states which extend recognition to it and
expanding the range of issues and activities over which that status is
operational. The weaker way is to reinforce the capacity of the state to
retrieve control of problems—think of global warming and the ozone
layer—which have escaped the capacity of any single state to remedy on
its own, through combined efforts with other states.[24] To this extent,
IGOs might be argued to promote interdependence sovereignty by
(ultimately) restoring a state's capacity to regulate what crosses its
own borders, although purists might also point out that it correspondingly erodes Westphalian sovereignty by sharing with "external" authorities some control over how it behaves within its borders.

Policy Autonomy

Let us now consider the vexed question of the degree to which economic
integration brings about a decline in the policy autonomy (sometimes
referred to as "policy capacity") of participating countries. One major
Canadian study of North American integration has made a strong case
that no such decline takes place, or at least is not nearly as pronounced
as many feared at the time that free trade was adopted (and as some
continue to claim).[25] Paying particular attention to several aspects of
social and environmental policy, Hoberg, Banting, and Simeon conclude that there has been very little convergence between Canadian

---

[24] For a careful discussion of this interpretation, see Kal Raustiala, "Rethinking
the Sovereignty Debate in International Economic Law," *Journal of International
Economic Law* 6, 4 (December 2003): 9-11 and *passim*.

[25] See Hoberg, Banting, and Simeon, Ch. 9. Their chapter is reviewed in greater detail
in Chapter 9 of this book, which is concerned with the convergence of Canadian
and American values and policies.

and American policies in these areas since the adoption of the FTA in 1989 and that where convergence has taken place it is not clearly attributable to the effects of economic integration or it has taken the form of superior, not inferior, standards of performance in Canada. Many instances of the adoption of common or similar policies, they argue, are more likely to result from parallel domestic pressures than from international constraints stemming from the liberalization of trade and investment flows.[26] Moreover, with regard to the notion that market liberalization must, as some would put it, "shrink that state," Hoberg, Banting, and Simeon cite several studies to the effect that—whether in Canada itself or across the OECD—average corporate taxation rates have not converged toward levels lower than they were several decades ago and have not become more uniform.

This is not the place to undertake a critical review of Hoberg, Banting, and Simeon's work. However, much of the rest of this book can be seen as an inventory of the ways in which economic integration between Canada and the US—particularly in the form of trade dependency on a single market and networking among the affiliates of multinational corporations—is affecting a wide range of non-economic aspects of the relationship, contrary to the position they take. It is sufficient for present purposes to highlight some of the factors that cast doubt on their findings. There is a vast and still growing literature on the ways and extent to which globalization is bringing about massive adjustments in state policies almost everywhere. (Some argue that globalization *is* such adjustment.) It seems implausible to suggest that Canada-US relations over the past 20 years or so have been immune from these developments or that they are not simply a North American version of them. Second, the fact that Hoberg, Banting, and Simeon found little convergence in social and environmental policies attributable to international constraints may be a consequence of the policy fields they examined and therefore may not be very representative. Among other issue areas are various industrial policies, including regulations specifically singled out in NAFTA as candidates for harmonization and

---

[26] Hoberg, Banting, and Simeon 253-54.

standardization under the auspices of the agreement's multiplicity of working groups and committees. Finally, Hoberg, Banting, and Simeon pay little attention to the manner in which economic integration alters the players and modes of Canada's domestic policy processes. International economic integration—including that embracing the North American continent—is at least as much about investment as it is about trade, and foreign direct investment is not simply a matter of capital flows but involves the exercise of power and influence within the host economy.

A NOTE ON MEXICO'S PLACE IN THIS ANALYSIS

It should be clear from the theoretical issues discussed here why—given the role of NAFTA in the current dynamics of integration in North America and Mexico's equal standing with Canada and the US within the NAFTA framework—Mexico has been largely omitted from the analysis. While Mexico is a part of the North American continent and is engaged in some of the processes of economic and social integration we are examining, Mexico and the US (much less Canada and Mexico) have not acquired the status of "disjoined partners" and likely never will. Moreover, there are only a few areas where knowledge of Mexico is necessary to achieve a clear and comprehensive understanding of how NAFTA is affecting Canada-US relations. In those few areas where this is the case, the Mexican side of the equation is addressed.

Second, and more specifically, given the role of integration theory in much of the following discussion, the economic and increasingly political integration taking place between Canada and the US has occurred, and continues to occur, without any connection to Mexico, either directly or indirectly, and there is no reason to assume that this will not continue to be the case. Even though some forms of integration are deepening between the US and Mexico, practically none are doing so between Canada and Mexico or among all three countries at once. Moreover, relations between the US and Mexico seem unlikely ever to become as close or achieve the scope of those that have developed between Canada and the US.

Without attempting to make an exhaustive case for this conclusion, the principal justifications for it can be briefly summarized. First, Mexico and the US do not share the same language, while Americans and most Canadians do. (To the chagrin of most Quebec nationalists, even many French-speaking Canadians speak English as well.) Second, Canada and the US have in common a legacy of British legal and political traditions that makes each of them much closer to one another than either is to Mexico. Third, and finally, partly because of the violence that marked earlier phases in their history, and partly because of the disparities in their levels of development and overall power economically and politically (which are substantially more significant than those between Canada and the US), Mexicans are even more wary of becoming too close to the US than most Canadians are. In a word, the level of mutual trust between the people of the two countries—a critical factor in the process of political integration—is significantly lower than that between Canada and the US.

This being said, there are a few areas of the Canada-US relationship that cannot be adequately addressed without paying attention to Mexico. This is especially true of those aspects of NAFTA that involve all three countries equally, which sometimes means that Canada and the US have to act differently toward each other than they otherwise might, either because the agreement requires that they treat Mexico equally or because they need to accommodate particular Mexican interests. For instance, the standardization of trucking regulations under NAFTA probably would be farther advanced if the US and Canada were dealing exclusively with each other. Also (as discussed below), the perceived obligation of the US to treat each of its NAFTA partners as equally as possible has complicated some aspects of border security and management.[27]

---

[27] For numerous examples of this, see Bradley J. Condon and Tapen Sinha, *Drawing Lines in Sand and Snow: Border Security and North American Economic Integration* (Armonk, NY: M.E. Sharpe, 2003).

GLOBALIZATION, THE END OF THE COLD WAR, FREE TRADE, AND CANADA-US RELATIONS

Globalization, the end of the Cold War, and continental free trade have all figured largely in the last 30 years of the Canada-US relationship.[28] However, the possible connections between these three developments are problematic, making it difficult to isolate the independent role of any one of them in transforming the relationship over that period, especially given that they all took place more or less simultaneously. This presents an analytic challenge: How does the analyst separate the effects of these three sources of change on Canada-US relations?

In some respects, the most difficult job of sorting out degrees of influence pertains to the respective roles of globalization and continental free trade, partly because the latter can be argued to be a regional manifestation of the former. Both, for example, are heavily associated with the removal of barriers to the flow of goods and investment between countries. Both have also been significantly advanced by the technological developments in telecommunications and by regulatory changes toward the telecommunications sector itself. Given such similarities, it might seem simplest and most advantageous to conflate the two developments for the sake of analysis. However, this strategy would largely foreclose one important dimension of understanding: How has global trade liberalization—especially the US role in it—affected Canada-US trade liberalization?

---

[28] There is a huge and still growing literature on globalization, and no attempt will be made here to summarize the core claims of these studies or even to provide a single definition of what globalization means. In the present context, it is sufficient to say that most discussions of the economic aspects of globalization define it as a process of deepening international economic integration that is driven primarily by 1) declining communications and transportation costs; 2) advanced information technologies; 3) huge increases in the speed and volume of world financial transactions; and 4) new forms of rationalization in the production and marketing practices of multinational corporations. For an excellent review of the range of (contested) definitions of the subject, see Jan Aart Scholte, *Globalization: A Critical Introduction* (New York: Palgrave, 2000) Ch. 1.

It is first necessary to understand the extent to which the effects of globalization on Canada-US relations should be interpreted as the effects of the end of the Cold War or, more precisely, the collapse of the Soviet Union and the end of bipolarity. (We will see that this event marked the transition from Phase II to Phase III in Chapter 2's overview of the Canada-US relationship.) The possibility that the consequences of these two developments might be confused for one another is quite high because they occurred at roughly the same time. Most commentators agree that full-blown globalization reached significant momentum in the early 1990s; the Soviet Union began to implode in the late 1980s and passed into history in 1991. The suggestion, then, is that at least some of the changes in the world economy that people want to attribute to globalization as an essentially economic and technological phenomenon, are perhaps more directly the result of the rise of the US to the strategic status of the world's only superpower.

There are three main reasons for identifying the effects of globalization with those of today's unipolarity. First, the international capitalist system, whose expansion into previously unpenetrated regions is also part of globalization, is centred on the American economy. While European and Japanese corporations have increased in prominence over the past 30 years, a substantial portion of the world's transnational corporations are still headquartered in the US. More important than that, much of the growth and dynamism of the economies and firms of Europe and Asia depend, at least in part, on access to sales in the American market. Finally, whereas—again—the American lead in technological development has been significantly reduced from what it was in the period immediately following the Second World War, that lead is still a factor. In short, the international capitalist system may not be synonymous with American capitalism, but its spread is, in a real sense, an extension of American capitalism. The collapse of the Soviet Union created significant opportunities for that system to expand more rapidly and more widely.

Secondly, the disappearance of the Soviet Union and the associated discrediting of the Soviet model has weakened political opposition to the spread of capitalism and American influence. The most obvious case here, of course, is that of avowedly Marxist (or even simply socialist) governments that previously had maintained formal ties with the Soviet Union or were dependent upon it both militarily and economically, such as most of Eastern Europe, parts of the Middle East and Africa, and Cuba. To be within the Soviet sphere of influence was to stand outside of (and often in opposition to) the capitalist trading and investment system. In addition, many other governments created so-called mixed economies that amounted to a blend of free markets and national economic policies such as government ownership, state subsidization of business activity, tariffs, and protective regulations. Many had begun to move away from these policy instruments before the collapse of the Soviet Empire, but nearly all have abandoned them since. The decline in restrictions against foreign investment across most of the developed and underdeveloped world is perhaps the most significant and widespread change along these lines.

Thirdly, and finally, the disappearance of the Soviet Union and the end of the Cold War has affected relationships between the US and its principal allies in Europe and Asia. In the absence of the Soviet threat, the ties among the Western nations are being transformed as American strategic leadership wanes, much as its economic dominance eroded during the 1970s and 1980s. This development requires more careful analysis and measurement to be firmly established; it should not be forgotten that the US still represents by far the world's most powerful combination of economic and military power. However, it remains true (and more than a little ironic) that for some purposes the US's standing with respect to its allies has diminished as it has taken on its current status of the world's only superpower.

The main reason for this decline in American leadership, of course, is that the power of the US is less vital to the security of its allies now that they are no longer threatened by Soviet expansion or communist meddling. Moreover, the US's partners are much more inclined than they used to be to attend to their own present and future position in the global power structure and to promote their individual strategic interests. Even its allies are not warm to the idea of American domination. Meanwhile, the US is wary of the emergence of a new global rival, and neither Japan or Germany can be casually struck from the list of future contenders. In sum, the collapse of the Soviet Union served to bring to the surface the underlying differences among the security interests of the US and its allies, especially in Europe and Asia.

This last reason also explains why there is so much concern that the post-Cold War economic era might see genuine multilateralism give way to rivalry among the world's three most prosperous economic regions centred on Germany, the US, and Japan—what observers sometimes refer to collectively as the "triad" and respectively as the euro, dollar, and yen "zones" or "blocs." It is also the reason that has the most relevance to Canada's relationship with the US in two ways. First, the apparent move toward regional economic integration in Europe and, to a lesser extent, in Asia was one of the reasons why the government of Canada and the Canadian business elite began to give serious thought to free trade with the US in the mid-1980s. Clearly, the collapse of the Soviet Union was not a factor at this time (for the good and sufficient reason that it had yet to happen), and the Canada-US FTA cannot be attributed to post-Cold War developments. Nevertheless, even the degree of regional protectionism that was evident in the 1980s was enough to convince many Canadians that they had to find shelter against intensifying global economic rivalries by moving under the same trade and investment roof with their most obvious economic partner. (A common observation in those days was that, without the FTA, Canada would be the only major industrial country—or G7 member—without unrestricted access to a market of over 100 million people.) History aside, the contemporary relevance of this development is that if the triadic structure of the global economy were to consolidate, Canada's opportunities for trade diversification would become even bleaker than they already are.

The collapse of the Soviet Union and the exacerbation of economic regionalism did play a direct role in the creation of NAFTA in 1994, although this time it worked at first on the calculations of the American, not the Canadian government. The interest of the government of President George Bush, Sr. in North American and possibly

Western Hemispheric free trade was rooted in concerns about international economic rivalries and the growing reluctance of key economic partners to accept American leadership in the world economy. Earlier American interest in the FTA had been partly driven by a desire to remind reluctant partners in the General Agreement on Tariffs and Trade (GATT) that the US could cultivate a bilateral alternative to multilateral bargains which were proving to be slow, messy, and unsatisfactory; a similar calculus was a factor in bringing Mexico into NAFTA. As well, the Enterprise of the Americas Initiative (a predecessor of the planned Free Trade Association of the Americas) was floated by the same American leaders at the same time, invoking the prospect of a Western Hemispheric bloc.

All this said, it is still not clear whether or not globalization would have become as powerful a force in international relations if the world had still been dominated by the Cold War rivalry between the US and the Soviet Union. It is even less clear that there would be much difference in the Canada-US relationship with or without the continued existence of a powerful Soviet Union. Certainly John Kirton believes that the Canada-US relationship could not possibly avoid a major transformation after a change in the international political system as enormous as the collapse of the Soviet Union and the end of the 50-year-long Cold War.[29] When such a major change takes place in the environment of a relationship, and therefore in the foreign policies of both partners to it, it is hard to see how the relationship itself could be left unaffected.

So much for globalization and the end of the Cold War. Much less will be said here of the difficulty of factoring continental free trade into the analytic mix just discussed. Given that the collapse of the Soviet Union and the adoption of the FTA were almost simultaneous, the condition of unipolarity should rarely be completely out of the reader's mind when assessing many of the arguments presented below on the impact of free trade on the Canada-US relationship. The

---

[29] John Kirton, "Promoting Plurilateral Partnership: Managing United States-Canada Relations in the Post-Cold War Period," *American Review of Canadian Studies* 24, 4 (Winter 1994).

US then as bipolar rival and the US now as unrivaled hyperpower are, so to speak, two very different countries and are therefore two very different neighbours and two very different trading partners. Just how different is essentially the subject of the remaining chapters. However, it seems safe to say in summary fashion that free trade with the US would almost certainly have occurred sometime before the end of the twentieth century in the absence of either the end of the Cold War or global trade liberalization, but that the presence of both has given a special turn to the *consequences* of free trade for the relationship, especially in the aftermath of 9/11.

chapter 2
CANADA-US RELATIONS AT
THE TURN OF THE CENTURY

We begin our review of the Canada-US relationship by assessing how it altered through the twentieth century, especially during the last decades, and how it stands at the beginning of the twenty-first century. As we shall see below, the pivotal events of the previous century were the First and Second World Wars, and it is important to appreciate how these global convulsions laid the foundations for the early construction of the expanding North American "partnership."[1] Strictly speaking, the relations between Canada *as Canada* and the US did not begin until the so-called "interwar" years (1919-39) because, until then, Canada's diplomatic relations were subject to the final authority of Britain. In 1931, the British Statute of Westminster finally gave Canada independent control over its own foreign policy. However, soon after winning this autonomy, the Second World War forced Canada's relations with the US into a hot-house of military, economic, and diplomatic cooperation aimed at the defeat of their common enemies. Following the war, the emerging American-Soviet rivalry consolidated many of the modes of Canada-US wartime cooperation into an even more dense set of interconnections that, by the late

---

[1] Charles F. Doran, for one, describes the relationship explicitly in these terms in *Forgotten Partnership: US-Canada Relations Today* (Baltimore, MD: Johns Hopkins University Press, 1984).

1970s, had earned the label of "complex interdependence."[2] For four decades, the Cold War thus moulded both the contours of Canada's foreign policy and the place of its relationship with the US within that foreign policy.

However, that mould first cracked and then disintegrated in the final ten or twelve years of the twentieth century, forcing a major and fairly rapid transition in both the global and domestic contexts of Canada-US relations. Two developments in particular were of major significance. The first was the widening scope and quickening pace of international economic integration (commonly referred to as "globalization" and discussed in Chapter 1) as embodied in the FTA of 1989. The second was the collapse of the Soviet Union and the consequent end of the Cold War. Both these events, although in very different ways, set the context for the present state of Canada-US relations by intensifying Canada's economic interdependence with the US while at the same time increasing pressures on Canada to align more closely with American foreign policy, pressures that intensified after 9/11.

This chapter provides a broad historical and analytical overview of the Canada-US relationship. The first section breaks down the history of the relationship into four major phases: from European settlement to the early 1940s; the Cold War (1947-89); the New World Order (1990-2001); and the War on Terror (2001 to the present). The second section summarizes more recent changes. Following these historical and empirical explorations of the relationship as a whole, the chapter concludes by describing historical American perspectives on Canada and exploring where Canada fits into American foreign policy.

THE FOUR PHASES OF THE CANADA-US RELATIONSHIP

Demarcating any human domain into discrete segments can never be entirely accurate, given the number of commonalities that the various segments inevitably share, and is always somewhat arbitrary, given

---

[2] Robert O. Keohane and Joseph S. Nye, *Power and Interdependence: World Politics in Transition* (Toronto: Little, Brown and Co., 1977) 167-72.

the difficulty of specifying exactly what distinguishes one segment from another. However, the segments (or "phases") of the history of the Canada-US relationship discussed in this section do seem truly different from one another, although the precise point of transition from one to the next may not always be evident. This lack of clarity is partly the product of the impact of extra-North American circumstances; the character of all four phases is much more a consequence of changes in the configuration of world power than of more stable conditions within the two countries. If nothing else, this volatility serves as a useful reminder that nothing in the present condition of the relationship is necessarily permanent and that, all things considered, neither party—either alone or in concert—is likely to possess sufficient capacity to control the direction it may take next.

Phase I: From European Settlement to the Early 1940s

During the era of European settlement, the North American continent was simultaneously host to three European empires. Spain occupied what today is Florida, the American west and southwest, and Mexico. France held sway over Atlantic Canada, the St. Lawrence River, much of the Great Lakes, and most of the Mississippi River watershed. Britain—prior to the American War of Independence and disregarding the territory chartered to the Hudson's Bay Company—occupied the Thirteen Colonies, which were lodged between the Atlantic seaboard and the mountain ranges to the east of the Mississippi River and which stretched from present day Maine in the north to Georgia in the south. (All three empires held various highly prized islands in the Caribbean as well, over which they were almost constantly fighting.) This early political landscape was most significantly altered by (in chronological order) the conquest of Quebec by the British in 1759; the transformation of the Thirteen Colonies into the United States of America between 1776 and 1783; the Louisiana Purchase in 1803 (according to which former French territories not taken over by the British were purchased from France by the US); and a sequence of American acquisitions (by war or purchase) of Spanish-held lands between 1810 and 1853.

As already noted, prior to the British Statute of Westminster in 1931, there was no Canada-US relationship to speak of, since much of Canada's foreign policy was officially part of British imperial policy, a product of the history of the British North American provinces (see Chapters 3 and 4) after the fall of Quebec and the American War of Independence.[3] This meant that, apart from commercial relations, the most serious diplomatic disputes involving the US and "Canada," including several highly contentious struggles over where exactly to locate the boundary between them, were conducted between the American and British governments. More significantly, even to the limited extent it is possible to speak of Canadian foreign policy during the years between the First and Second World Wars, there is not a great deal to say about Canada-US relations during this period because both countries were essentially "isolationist" in orientation. That is, both Canada and the US, although for slightly different reasons, emphasized the insularity of North America and its distance, both physical and psychological, from the machinations of the European balance of power and world politics generally. Canada's desire to do this was fed by its determination to both establish and exercise its growing independence from Britain. The US, meanwhile, more or less ignored Canada as a distinct political player, assuming that, regardless of Canada's legal foreign policy independence after 1931, Britain still spoke for its former imperial possessions with respect to key aspects of their foreign relations. In any case, as Fox has summed up these years, "In the days of isolationism, there were no security issues perceived in either Washington or Ottawa as matters for coordinating decision-making."[4]

---

[3] The exception to this was Canada's conduct of its own foreign commercial relations, including the negotiation—if not the final ratification—of trade treaties. For a succinct account of Canada's early conduct of foreign commercial relations, as well as its later acquisition of complete foreign policy independence, see Kim Richard Nossal, *The Politics of Canadian Foreign Policy*, 3rd ed. (Scarborough, ON: Prentice Hall, 1997) 235-39 and 147-50, respectively.

[4] William T.R. Fox, *A Continent Apart: The United States and Canada in World Politics* (Toronto: University of Toronto Press, 1985) 80.

Of course, close *economic* relations had existed between the two countries since the early nineteenth century, but the key players in these relations were firms and individuals, not governments. However, the deepening of these economic ties, both during the two world wars themselves and over the period of peace between them, had political consequences. For example, it tended to reinforce Canada's increasing separation from Britain at the same time as it established a platform for the much closer political association between Canada and the US that developed after 1945. In fact, it might be said that, during the first half of the twentieth century, Canada moved from political and economic dependence upon Britain to economic dependence upon the US, a process discussed in greater detail in Chapter 4.

In sum, despite these tightening economic ties, and despite (or possibly because of) a common aloofness from the European high politics of the interwar years, American and Canadian politics had little of consequence to do with one another. Perhaps the best illustration of how politically separate the two countries were during this period was the response each made to the outbreak of war at the end of it: Canada was more than two years ahead of the US in going to war against Germany. A comparable degree of disconnectedness was not seen in the second phase of the relationship which closely followed that war.

Phase II: The Cold War (1947-89)

The Cold War rivalry between the US and the Soviet Union created a combination of circumstances that opened up the space necessary for Canada to pursue a foreign policy relatively independent of the US. The massive devastation of the Second World War had severely weakened the former great powers in Europe at the same time as it had strengthened both the US and the Soviet Union militarily and both Canada and the US economically. As the rift between the two emerging superpowers deepened, it became clear that the US and Canada had a common, though not identical, foreign policy agenda, one driven by a shared interest in countering the threats posed by the communist adversary.

Fox summarizes this agenda as one of joining together to promote North American security, cooperating in aiding the security of Western Europe, preventing the spread and/or use of nuclear arms, and avoiding a third world war.[5] It is worth noting that the first of these objectives was well served by both the spirit and the modes of co-operation that had developed between the two countries during the Second World War. As early as 1940, the Canadian and American governments recognized that an attack on one of them was tantamount to an attack on the other. Planning against this contingency led to the Ogdensburg Agreement between Prime Minister Mackenzie King and President Franklin Roosevelt, which provided for the creation of a Permanent Joint Board on Defence in order to coordinate the military protection of the "north half" of the western hemisphere.[6] Moreover, under this institutional umbrella, the two countries adopted an array of economic and military arrangements aimed to meet the threat posed to North America by the German and Japanese military. Many of these agencies became templates for deepening forms of cooperation occasioned by the common cause against the Soviet Union after the war ended.[7]

More important than these institutional and procedural precedents, however, was the fact that they were consistently based on the notion of North America as a "security unit," a perception that also drove much Canadian-American collaboration during the Cold War. Arguably, this mentality reached a high-water mark in their joint response to the threat of a nuclear attack from the Soviet Union over the Arctic. For both governments, the protection of Canadian airspace became a vital security interest, and both also understood that anything Canada was unable or unwilling to do to provide that protection, the US would do for themselves (a realization that echoes in the recent debate over Canada's participation in the American plan

---

[5] Fox 80.

[6] As quoted in John Herd Thompson and Stephen J. Randall, *Canada and the United States: Ambivalent Allies* (Montreal and Kingston: McGill-Queen's University Press, 1994) 152.

[7] For an overview of such joint arrangements and agencies, see Thompson and Randall, Ch. 6.

for national missile defence). The most conspicuous institutional expression of this idea was the creation in 1958 of the North American Air Defence Command (NORAD, known since 1981 as the North American Aerospace Defence Command), which provided for joint Canada-US command of continental air defences.

A similar notion of North America as a security unit explains the fact that both Canada and the US contributed to the protection of Western Europe from the Soviet Union through their participation in the North Atlantic Treaty Organization (NATO). For much the same reasons, neither North American country wanted to gaze across the Atlantic Ocean at a European continent controlled by Moscow. However, this common willingness to contribute to Western European security, precisely because it involved territory outside North America as well as the interests of a variety of other major players, often led to differences between the two North American partners. More precisely, disagreements between the US and one or more of its European allies could also give rise to disputes between Canada and the US about the best way to resolve them. To some extent, this very circumstance created opportunities for Canada to play a distinct and at least partially independent role in trans-Atlantic relations.[8]

The problem of exactly how to prevent the huge Soviet military forces in Central and Eastern Europe from overwhelming West Germany, France, Italy, and Britain was rarely one that yielded unique solutions, and the very fact of political disagreement over the best solution to this problem—between the Americans and the Europeans, among the Europeans themselves, and between the Canadians and the Americans—created ample scope for disagreements among all the allies. (The central strategic question of whether or not the

---

[8] As Kim Richard Nossal has pointed out, during the Cold War era, the mediating role Canada played in "intra-bloc" relations may have been more pronounced than its complementary role in "inter-bloc" relations. It is worth noting, however, that in either case, he emphasizes that the function of intermediation—getting in-between—represents a more substantial grounding for Canada's status as a "middle power" than does Canada's location in the power ranking of states. See Nossal, *Politics of Canadian Foreign Policy* 53-70.

Americans should pledge a nuclear response to a purely conventional military attack on NATO's European members is an example of a contested issue.) These disagreements also meant that Canada had to work out how the Canada-US relationship fit within its wider foreign policy. Beyond any of the specific foreign policy goals Canada pursued during the course of the Cold War, it was unavoidably preoccupied with its overarching determination to preserve, as far as possible, its independence of the US.

Canada's European partners in NATO shared a similar preoccupation, despite acknowledging the primary role of the US in defending the West against the East. (The most dramatic instance of this was France's withdrawal from NATO's integrated command structure in the 1960s.) Apart from complicating the adoption of NATO strategies, this qualified acceptance of American leadership further widened the scope for Canada's occasional role in NATO as an "interpreter" and intermediary in the trans-Atlantic dialogue among the major players. Meanwhile, and in addition, Canadian participation in NATO contributed to Canadian independence because important aspects of its security relations with the US were embedded, as it were, in a multilateral forum rather than concentrated in the bilateral and highly unequal North American forum.

Canada's penchant for multilateralism reached beyond the protection of Western Europe through NATO to a wider set of international commitments—especially its active support of the UN—as an extension of its strategy of embedding as far as possible its bilateral partnership with the US in a matrix of international governmental organizations. Efforts to prevent nuclear war by preventing proliferation of nuclear weapons provide a good example of this. Canada understood that its ability to influence the American stance on these issues was probably greater as part of a multitude of nations' expressions of concern before UN agencies than it would be in bilateral discussions with American officials. In fact, on its own, Canada had no "standing" to address the American Departments of State or Defense on questions of nuclear deterrence, non-proliferation, or disarmament; as a member of the international community, however, it could legitimately and effectively be heard at the multilateral level.

A further extension of the logic of multilateralism in the service of Canadian independence was its relations with the Third World. Here, Canada was able to carve out a unique, if modest role in placing life-and-death Cold War issues in the broader context of international justice and development. This often involved initiatives that the Americans either could not or would not undertake for themselves, either because their immense economic and military power made underdeveloped countries wary of them as partners or because their primary focus on the "high politics" of managing the superpower rivalry left much of the "low politics" of international development off its agenda. Unlike most other members of NATO, Canada had neither an imperial past nor a neo-imperial present, a degree of innocence that enabled it to bring its resources and status as one of the world's leading economies into a more comfortable dialogue with countries of the developing world on economic and social issues. At the same time, Canada could claim that its actions served the long-term security of the US by contributing to political stability in regions of the world that might otherwise be even more contentious zones of Cold War competition.

In sum, Phase II in the Canada-US relationship—the first phase in which the two countries engaged directly with one another as equally independent partners—was marked primarily by the Canadian desire to expand the relationship beyond its exclusively North American setting to embrace Western Europe, much of the Third World, and, on some issues, the entire community of nations. This strategy rendered the stark imbalances in the bilateral relationship less palpable. It also garnered multilateral support for some of Canada's desired departures from a strictly American course of action and provided space for some "Canadian only" initiatives, especially in the context of the UN and the Third World. None of these strategies is entirely comprehensible outside the context of Canada's desire to remain as independent as possible of the US. A means to that end was to create an independent foreign policy in that wider cause, a goal that was becoming more urgent in the light of the two countries' growing economic interdependence in the second half of the twentieth century. But, as we shall see, Canada's capacity to pursue a distinct foreign

policy in the wider cause of national independence was much diminished by the new circumstances of a unipolar international order.

Phase III: The New World Order (1989-2001)

The third phase in the Canada-US relationship permitted much narrower scope for the exercise of a distinctive Canadian foreign policy
in the service of strengthening Canada's overall independence. Phase
III occupies a relatively brief period bounded by the destruction of the
Berlin Wall in 1989 and the 9/11 terrorist attacks. The unification of
Germany, the withdrawal of Soviet troops from Eastern Europe, and
the disintegration of the Soviet Union itself were all parts of a massive
transformation of the structure of the international political system.
Stated simply, the world left behind the bipolar order that had marked
the Cold War standoff between the two superpowers and entered a
new unipolar order of only one superpower (or "hyperpower").While
the full ramifications of this transformation still remain to be seen,
what is already clear is that this New World Order is no longer as
conducive as the previous one to many of the foreign policy strategies
that Canada pursued during Phase II.

Many of Canada's most successful strategies had involved mediating between the US and countries allied to it (such as other
members of NATO) and cooperating with countries who wanted to
keep their distance from it (such as many countries in Africa, Latin
America, and Asia). The very structure of a unipolar world, dominated and pervaded by the economic, political, and military might
of a single country, and the corresponding end to the dynamics of
the superpower rivalry that characterized the Cold War, meant that
there was much less space "in between" the US and other countries
within which Canada could define a distinct role. Consequently,
Phase III was marked instead by (1) the substitution of economic for
diplomatic interests as foreign policy priorities; (2) a smaller relative
emphasis on multilateral relations and organizations relative to bilateral and trilateral ones; (3) a greater emphasis on the countries of the
Western Hemisphere rather than the British Commonwealth and

la Francophonie[9] as primary venues for relations with Third World countries; and, finally, (4) an explicit commitment to join with the US in its declared mission to spread democracy and market-based economies worldwide. The direct or indirect consequence of these shifts in emphasis was to bring Canadian foreign policy "closer to home" and, in that sense, closer to the foreign policy objectives and processes of the US.

Furthermore, according to an overview written in the mid-1990s by Bruce Doern and John Kirton, Canadian foreign policy was becoming "internationalized" in response to three forces: globalization, free trade agreements, and the end of the Cold War. Doern and Kirton acknowledged that "it makes little sense to speak of the internationalization of foreign policy" in that foreign policy is by definition the conduct of the country's relations with the rest of the world.[10] Their point, however, was that, to a greater or lesser extent, various foreign (or foreign-connected) influences were playing an important role in formulating Canada's foreign policy. They also noted that trade agreements between the US and Canada "virtually create[d] a fourth pillar to the Canadian constitution," along with the three established pillars of parliamentary government, federalism, and the Charter of Rights and Freedoms.[11] Their theme was that the advent of Canada-US free trade, along with the collapse of the Soviet Union and globalization in general, was blurring the distinctions between the internal and external domains of Canadian government policy and between the domestic and foreign influences that bear on the conduct of Canada's international relationships.

To make their case, Doern and Kirton noted four major changes in Canadian foreign policy during the 1990s, each of which either represented, or contributed to, a blend of national and international elements:[12]

---

[9]   An international organization of French-speaking organizations and governments.
[10] Bruce Doern and John Kirton, "Foreign Policy," in G.B. Doern and B. Tomlin, eds., *Border Crossings* (Toronto: Oxford University Press, 1996) 239.
[11] Doern and Kirton 255.
[12] The rest of this paragraph is a condensation of Doern and Kirton's own introductory summary of their four main themes; see Doern and Kirton 240-41.

1. the increasing prominence of economic foreign policy concerns, including active promotion of free trade liberalism in Canada's external relations;

2. the increasing dependence of Canada's DFAIT on other federal government departments for expertise, budgetary resources, and legislative authority;

3. the increasingly direct involvement in the conduct of foreign policy, especially in relation to the formation and implementation of trade agreements, by business, social, immigration, and environmental interest groups, all of whom had growing international ties; and

4. the expanding links between the Canadian government and IGOs, which reflect the fact that more and more areas of government that were once primarily (if not exclusively) domestic were now bound up in Canada's relations with other countries and international institutions.

The first of these four changes is particularly important, in that many of the commitments and undertakings Canada has negotiated with other governments as part of the free trade agenda have required changes in Canada's domestic policies and regulations. The policies agreed to in order to open up national markets have not simply required change "at the border" between Canada and the rest of the world; rather, they have demanded a rebalancing between state and society within Canada itself. The insistence that the government of Canada, along with all the other national governments that sign such economic agreements, "level the playing field" between foreign and domestic investors and producers demands that these governments give priority to a wide range of domestic reforms. This reality has become clearer as, among other indicators, the World Trade Organization (WTO) carries forward negotiations over the General Agreement on Trade in Services (GATS), which are almost completely preoccupied by the degree to which foreign service-providers will be allowed to offer services—including health, education, and even water supply—that have been the domain of domestic (often government) agencies.

In short, the global trade and investment agenda has been simultaneously a domestic social, economic, and political agenda. This has meant that Canada's participation in the international processes promoting economic change and cooperation has become part and parcel of internal governance and not just a foreign policy concern. Similarly, the coming together of the two countries over the FTA added new elements to the bilateral relationship. Traditional military/security and trade/investment issues were replaced by "smaller bilateral trade, transportation and cultural issues, larger challenges of multilateral institution-building and intervention, and debates over domestic social priorities." [13] Moreover, Kirton adds, there was a "continuing movement toward integration and cooperation, through a further opening of the border between the two countries already among the most densely and diversely interdependent of any in the world."

At the same time, the end of the Cold War resulting in the US's rise to global pre-eminence meant that Canada had to come to terms with a much deeper change in American priorities. According to Kirton, following the collapse of Soviet power, it became the objective of the US to forge a partnership with Canada so that the two countries would "lead as partners" in a process of "global engagement" which had four primary focal points (all of which will be discussed in detail in Chapter 10):

1. combating economic stagnation within the core market democracies;
2. enlarging the community of democratic market economies through conversions of the former communist countries;
3. isolating states outside this circle; and
4. conducting humanitarian interventions more selectively and through multilateral organizations.[14]

More recently, of course, cooperation with the US and many of its allies in the War on Terror has expanded even further the list of areas

---

[13] Kirton, "Promoting Plurilateral Partnership" 453.
[14] Kirton, "Promoting Plurilateral Partnership" 463.

in which Canada and the US work actively together. However, none of this new activity has displaced the agenda items identified above; it has only added to them.

Phase IV: The War on Terror

It seems reasonable to say that 9/11 and the ensuing War on Terror did not usher in changes in the international political system as momentous as those introduced by the end of the Cold War. In fact, so far, most of the distinctive features of the War on Terror represent a consolidation of the unipolar power structure that underpinned Canada-US relations during Phase III. We can anticipate, therefore, that Phase IV will not introduce much that is new and distinctive, but will merely deepen and intensify already apparent trends. This seems particularly true with respect to the increasing prominence of economic interests in Canada's foreign policy, the deepening concern with the degree of trade dependence Canada has developed with its immediate southern neighbour compared to the rest of the world, and the degree to which this trade dependency on a single foreign market undermines Canada's capacity to maintain autonomous policies in other areas, including foreign policy. Meanwhile, the New World Order has coincided with an increasingly assertive and explicit unilateral strategy on the part of the Bush administration in the US.

It is true that Canada under Prime Minister Jean Chrétien did not follow President George W. Bush in his campaign to transform the War on Terror into a war in Iraq. Nonetheless, the War On Terror continues to complicate the proper functioning of the Canada-US border for trade purposes. The need for close collaboration on border issues may make Prime Minister Paul Martin's government more sensitive than his predecessor's to American military and security priorities, even though he appears, at least temporarily, unwilling to make Canada a full participant in the development of continental missile defence. There are signs of such heightened sensitivity in his government's most recent budget, which promise significant increases in spending on the military.[15] Meanwhile, one of Canada's most prominent busi-ness associations joined counterparts in the US and Mexico in releas-ing a study that called for the creation of a North American "secu-rity perimeter, the consolidation of NAFTA into a customs union, a strategic plan to further integrate continental energy production and distribution, and the increased harmonization of border controls for both goods and people."[16] Of course, only time can confirm the plau-sibility of these proposals, but it is worth noting that—based on the trends already visible in the evolution of the Canada-US relationship from Phases II through what we have already seen of Phase IV—such economic and political developments will further reduce the capacity of Canada's foreign policy to remain distinct from the US.

With these proposals in mind, it is important to cast some light on the likelihood of their implementation from the perspective of the US itself. (If that country does not deem them to be in its own interests, the chances of seeing such developments are probably as close to zero as things get in international relations.) From its very beginnings, the US has pondered the possibility of taking over the territory to its north, and it has occasionally—though not for a long time—taken military steps toward that goal. More importantly, however, it has reckoned that the balance of considerations weighed in favour of permitting Canada's continued sovereignty.[17] An intriguing combination of ele-ments has sustained this assessment for a long time and seems likely to do so for the foreseeable future. No account of the Canada-US relationship could be complete without some attention to this balance of considerations bearing on American policies toward Canada.

---

[15] Daniel Leblanc, "Ailing Forces Get Big Boost," *Globe and Mail*, 24 February 2005: F2.

[16] Paul Koring, "Task Force Urges Joint Security Perimeter," *Globe and Mail*, 14 March 2005: A1.

[17] See Sean M. Shore, "No Fences Make Good Neighbors: The Development of the US-Canada Security Community, 1871-1940," in Emanuel Adler and Michael Barnett, eds., *Security Communities* (Cambridge: University of Cambridge Press, 1998) Ch. 10. Shore's analysis presents an interesting application of Karl Deutsch's work on international security communities to the evolution of the Canada-US relationship, and the volume in which his chapter appears is a useful exploration of this aspect of Deutsch's work on international political integration. For reasons that will not be elaborated here, the present author felt that, on balance, following Peter Katzenstein's application of the Deutschian framework to the German-Austrian case was a superior adaptation of it for the purposes of this book.

AMERICAN PERSPECTIVES ON CANADA
AND CANADIAN FOREIGN POLICY

Viewed from the American side of the border, the existence of a separate country to the north has often seemed a geographic, economic,
and political anomaly. From time to time, various solutions to this
condition were either encouraged or eagerly awaited, such as by making provision in the Declaration of Independence for the provinces
of British North America to join the Union; invading them periodically, either to encourage their populations to throw off British rule
in favour of unification or to discourage the British enough to induce
them to give the colonies up; or by allowing sufficient time for "Manifest Destiny" to make the Americans masters of the entire continent. The fact that, in 2005, divided sovereignty still persists over
North America is obvious evidence that none of these approaches
did the job, and it seems important to establish why they did not, or
why even more determined and forceful actions were never taken.

According to Fox, a combination of factors—some of which reso-
nate today—explains the American failure to embark on a concrete,
as opposed to a declaratory, campaign to take over the British North
American provinces. First, the annexation of Canada would have
achieved no more security for commercial interests in the US than
they already enjoyed, since prior to Canada's Confederation, there
were almost no impediments to the movement of people, trade, and
investment. Second the general expectation in the US was that its
"Manifest Destiny" would eventually give it possession of all of North
America and that there was no need to go to war to achieve a foreor-
dained outcome. Third, through most of the nineteenth century, the
US was preoccupied with "winning the west," that is, expanding effective possession and control of the territory it had acquired from
France and Spain. Fourth, the incorporation of the British North
American provinces as full political players in the Union would have
upset some delicate political balances concerning key issues it already
had on its agenda, such as the deep divide between "free" and "slave"
states. Fifth, in the aftermath of the Civil War (1861-65), there was
more interest in the demobilization of American military forces than

in directing them toward a fresh campaign against a domain still under British protection.[18]

A combination of abstract reasoning and common sense practicality may provide an explanation for the American willingness to accept Canada's ongoing independence. Fox, for example, feels that the simplest explanation for the fact that Canada and the US share their portion of the North American continent as separate sovereignties rather than as a single nation is the absence of a viable alternative. As he puts it, "Nobody is proposing it, a federation of the two federations would not work, and a proposal to create a colossal federation of fifty states and ten provinces seems even more far-fetched than a federation of federations."[19] Further, the gross imbalance of power between the integrating units is enough for him to rule out a European style of economic and political union. He therefore concludes:

> The absence of a feasible alternative is the negative explanation for the present pattern of Canadian-American relations. More positively, the interests of the two countries are in major respects perceived as enough alike or so compatible that they do not strain a power imbalance that otherwise would be irksome to Canadians and tempting to Americans. Both countries benefit from treating the security of North America as an indivisible whole. Both benefit also from the complementarity of their economies, which makes a high degree of informal [private sector] integration appropriate.[20]

Fox's closing reference to the complementarity of the two economies resonates strongly with another American perspective on the delicate balances that mark the relationship. Also writing in the mid-1980s, Doran concluded that the foundation of the Canada-US relationship has been an "implicit quid pro quo" whereby the US tolerated Canada's less than proportional contribution to continental

---

[18] Fox 35-39. A more detailed overview is ably provided in Shore 338-44.
[19] Fox 82.
[20] Fox 83. Note that Fox was writing before the first free trade agreement was signed.

security in exchange for relatively open access to Canada's resources and markets.[21] Thus, he considered that Canada's National Energy Program (NEP) of 1980 was a severe test of this tacit understanding, precisely because the policy preferences it extended to Canadian-owned oil and gas companies, and withdrew from American ones, represented a major departure from the principles of economic non-discrimination that had previously been understood as Canada's half of the "grand bargain" between the two countries.

At this fundamental level, Fox and Doran—both, by the way, American scholars—share several major points of agreement in their respective assessments of the definitive trade-offs in the Canada-US relationship. While the vocabulary they employ to make their points is not identical, their accounts spell out the essential, if mostly tacit, terms of the mutual understanding that has evolved between the two countries in a similar way:[22] the US has to tolerate Canada's need to assert independence (sometimes in ways that seem completely unnecessary from the American perspective) so long as these assertions do nothing to threaten the US's own security and long-term economic interests. On the Canadian side, this understanding means that Canada must neither take actions that the Americans believe could represent such a threat nor adopt positions different from those of the US simply for the sake of being different or, worse, simply to appear more "righteous."

Furthermore, Canada needs to acknowledge that a preoccupation with power relations and the global distribution of power is inherent in the role of a superpower, even a dominant one. One consequence of superpower status is that some of the causes dear to nations with less responsibility for world order cannot be adopted or perhaps even acknowledged. Correspondingly, the US needs to recognize that smaller countries such as Canada are wary of the superpower tendency to exaggerate the possible threats to their status and to caution it that excessive reactions to such challenges can create unnecessary confrontations.

---

[21] Doran 263-65.
[22] Cf. Fox, Ch. 6, and Doran, Ch. 2.

Given these more thematic evaluations of the "American stake" in Canada's independence, it is possible to construct a balance-sheet listing both the costs and the benefits to the US of Canada's status *as a separate country* and sovereign actor in world politics.[23] First consider the following benefits:

- an ongoing demonstration to the rest of the world that the US is not an imperial power or, at least, not a conventional imperial power, precisely because it has not seen fit to employ its power advantage to seize for itself and on its own terms all the benefits referred to in note 23;
- as with the previous point, an ongoing demonstration to the world that the values that the US shares with its allies—such as freedom, democracy, equality, and respect for the sovereign rights of other peace-loving nations—truly do govern American foreign policy and will not be sacrificed for the sake of the narrowly de-fined self-interest of the US;
- consistent access to judgements and policy evaluations from a "trusted critic" of its foreign policy;
- periodically, the achievement by Canada of some international goals that the US could not attain at all, or at least not as effec-tively, on its own; and
- avoiding the prospect of politically "digesting" Canadians as citizens and existing Canadian jurisdictions as players in the American political process.

---

[23] Note that there is a difference between the benefits the US receives from Canada's independent status—which by definition it could not possess if the two became one country—and the benefits it receives from Canada's *existence* (its presence on the border as a territory endowed with rich resources and occupied by over 30 million, highly skilled, liberal, peace-loving, and relatively prosperous people). The benefits to be listed therefore exclude the following ways in which Canada's existence and characteristics are valuable to the US: a proximate and secure source of raw materials, including oil and natural gas during an era of growing and unwelcome American dependence on less dependable sources elsewhere; the exploitation of those resources by American-based firms which have earned substantial revenues from their Canadian subsidiaries; and continuing enjoyment of an economic relationship that unmistakeably contributes to American prosperity generally and, more particularly, to the continuing success of a range of powerful American firms.

On the other side, consider the disadvantages:

> putting up with complaints about the manner in which the US acts to meet its responsibilities as a world leader, especially when they come from a country that consistently refuses to carry its fair share of the costs of doing so;
> facing hard, focused, well-informed criticism of American foreign policies from a country that is often listened to with respect by many other countries across the world, as well as by many influential Americans;
> living with the additional uncertainties and risks that Canada is a weak "link in the chain" of both Homeland Security and the War on Terror;
> living with at least some limits on access to resources, markets, and investment opportunities that would not exist if the two countries were entirely integrated economically, which they clearly would be if they were a single country and clearly are not yet under NAFTA's terms; and
> having on occasion to fine-tune American domestic and foreign policies to accommodate Canadian interests and sensitivities for the sake of overall harmony in the partnership.

One impression created by the cumulative effect of both lists is that the Canada-US relationship is very much a matter of striking a wide range of sometimes highly delicate balances—including some attention to maintaining an overall balance among the balances! This impression is reinforced by two further fundamental facts. The first is that the relationship touches just about every aspect of both domestic and foreign policy in both countries, although this is probably more true of Canada than of the US. The second is that the relationship "isn't going to go away" for either country. Despite these hard facts, however, the relationship is subtle, and its subtleties cannot be ignored. Finally, for both countries, understanding this reality in principle does not in itself say anything about how these balances are to be struck in practice. Changing times and circumstances, especially changing personalities holding office, demand refinements in the precise manner in which these fundamental balances can be achieved or even whether or not they will be sought, as recent impasses between American presidents and Canadian prime ministers remind us.

As one example of changing time and circumstance, it is worth remembering that the New World Order not only altered the basic power calculations founding the foreign policies of every country on the planet, but it also arrived 40 years after the start of the Cold War. As Handelman has pointed out, generational differences matter. Some of the instinctive accommodations that eased the Cold War relationship between American decision-makers and their Canadian counterparts flowed from their common experience of the Second World War, an experience no longer available to those in positions of authority today.[24] Similarly, the gradual shift in the centre of both economic and political power in the US away from the northeast, which shares a border with Canada, to the south and southwest, which does not, has created a psychological distance between the two sets of leaders.

Having said this about the gradual transformation in some foundations of the relationship, no analysis would be complete without a reminder of its enduring and possibly indelible strengths. Among these, the first and foremost has to be the overwhelming scale of the commercial relations among private individuals and firms in the two countries, together with the quasi-institutional linkages among industrial sectors, governments at all levels, and a host of voluntary associations. Finally, there are travellers, shoppers, and families crossing the border in world-record volumes every year. Add to this the bedrock similarities provided by shared social, economic, and political values, and it becomes difficult to predict that the two countries will not always find their way back to one another, not only because they cannot ever leave one another. This is one of the reasons why Americans may have an interest in learning more effectively "to make the best it," that is, learning more about Canada and Canadian

---

[24] Stephen Handelman, "The Rise of North America Inc.: A Perspective from the United States," *isuma: Canadian Journal of Policy Research* 1, 1 (Spring 2000): 19-20.

foreign policy and how it can either augment or detract from their own capacity to promote their interests in the wider world.

The US may from time to time be concerned about how its wider interests may be advanced or hindered by actions taken by Canada, but it has no need to worry that they might undermine its status as an independent country. Of course, no great power, not even a superpower such as the US, is completely immune from concerns about how particular foreign policy decisions in the present can—by provoking adverse reactions by other states—subsequently affect their scope for independent action in the future. (For example, it is not a foregone conclusion that military campaigns, such as in South Vietnam in the 1960s or in Iraq currently, promote rather than impede the US's ability to realize broader and longer term foreign policy goals.) However, the US has no concern that actions it takes in the wider world today will undermine its independence of Canada. For Canada, in contrast, it is scarcely possible to imagine a foreign policy decision that is absent of any bearing on its long-term capacity to maintain its independence of the US.

chapter 3
THE EVOLUTION OF THE
NORTH AMERICAN ECONOMY I: THE US

The economic history of North America is essentially a story of the gradual integration of the entire continent. The process began among some of the British North American colonies before the American War of Independence (1776-83); its engine was the economic growth of the main colonies of the northeastern coast (what we today think of as Massachusetts, Rhode Island, Connecticut, New York, Pennsylvania, and Maryland). Not coincidentally, these early economies all centred on major ports, and the commerce of each was largely based on the North Atlantic fishery off the coast of Newfoundland. As this hub of prosperity diversified into agriculture and manufacturing, it undertook a long period of expansion into the interior of the continent.

The economic integration of the US was pretty much complete by the mid-twentieth century. At the same time, the integration of the US economy with the Canadian and Mexican economies was well underway. Through much of the nineteenth century, both Canada and Mexico had developed in the shadow of the successful and powerful American northeast and its quest for its "Manifest Destiny" to control the entire continent. In the face of this challenge, the governments of the two weaker countries adopted a variety of defensive policies to fend off total absorption. Nevertheless, neither country could resist the potential advantages of trade and investment relations with the US and they both began to show signs of economic schizophrenia:

open to American capital and trade in some ways; closed, or at least guarded, in others.

The gradual absorption of the Canadian and Mexican economies by the US was primarily the result of the latter's more rapid industrialization and diversification in contrast with the formers' expansion along a more fixed and narrow path (a condition they shared until very recently with the states of the American south). In these different patterns of economic progress, it is possible to see the earliest origins of today's North American free trade regime. Stated briefly, by the last quarter of the twentieth century, the long-term evolution of the Canadian and Mexican economies had placed both countries in a condition of severe vulnerability. With their increasing awareness of this vulnerability, neither country could see any viable alternative to signing free trade agreements with the US and thus creating a new trade regime that formalized their access to, but also their dependence on, the American market.

This deepening integration of the economies of North America, however, is not simply a result of the fact that the American economy is so much more powerful than the Canadian or Mexican ones. It has also come about because, though not perfect, American institutions and government policies have proven over two centuries to have been conducive to a more dynamic process of economic development. Because of this proven superiority, it will be extremely difficult from now on for the leaders of either Mexico or Canada to resist pressures to bring their own economic policies more closely into line with more successful American approaches. Thus, policy harmonization in the direction of the American model is likely to be the hallmark of North American political economy in the early twenty-first century.

As this process of policy integration moves forward, it has behind it the momentum of many decades' worth of gradual economic integration. It is therefore important to understand the origins and evolution of this process, as well as to appreciate the fundamental differences between the American, Mexican, and Canadian economies and how trade liberalization may, over time, work to reduce those differences.

CONTRASTING PATTERNS OF GROWTH AND DEVELOPMENT

We begin by introducing some general comparisons between the Canadian, American, and (to a limited extent) Mexican economies. These comparisons are largely based on the comprehensive history of the evolution of North American economy presented by Canadian economic historian W.T. Easterbrook (with some help from other sources on particular points).[1] According to Easterbrook, the American northeast enjoyed a number of distinct economic advantages that gave it a greater capacity for prosperity and self-sustaining development than either Canada or Mexico, advantages that stemmed from several more fundamental differences among the three North American societies.

These "deep differences" are the long-term effects of what Easterbrook calls the "initial conditions" prevailing within the three colonial societies: the social, political, and economic characteristics that were "imported" from their respective colonizing powers—England, France, and Spain—at the time that they were founded. A further set of differences flowed from what he calls the "uncertainty response" of the various colonial administrations to the general climate of economic security (or insecurity) that surrounded the earliest development of the colonies themselves.

For Easterbrook, the one true success story in the New World was the economy of the northeastern US, or "the US Central Sector" (USCS). He sums up the major differences between it and the economies of Canada, Mexico, and the American south by differentiating between the *genuine development* of the first and the *mere growth* of the latter three, a distinction that parallels what he terms the "transformation" of the USCS and the "persistence" of the other regions.

---

[1] W.T. Easterbrook, *North American Patterns of Growth and Development: The Continental Context* (Toronto: University of Toronto Press, 1990). Easterbrook's analysis owes a great deal to his teacher at the University of Toronto, the great Canadian economic historian Harold Innis (who also taught and inspired communications guru Marshall McLuhan). Innis is strongly identified with the "Laurentian Thesis" of Canadian economic development, which in broad outline is represented as the foundation of Easterbrook's account.

In short, the economy of the USCS experienced earlier and more rapid industrialization than the rest of North America.

Regarding Canada and the US, specifically, the contrast Easterbrook describes can be summarized as follows: the USCS was more

- freely competitive;
- innovative;
- dynamic;
- open and democratic;
- independent of government; and
- secure and confident.

Meanwhile—on the opposite side of all of these coins—the Canadian economy was more

- highly concentrated;
- rigid, conservative, and protective;
- persistent and locked into early patterns of expansion;
- heavily regulated, centralized, and government-directed;
- traditional, authoritative, and bureaucratic; and
- insecure and defensive.[2]

We will now turn to a more detailed look at two of the factors that, according to Easterbrook, largely account for the deep differences between the two largest North American economies.

---

[2] Some readers may notice that most of the differences just itemized strongly resemble the comparisons that economic commentators often draw between the "Anglo-American" model for economic growth and the "Continental European" model. Moreover, when Canadian commentators use these terms, they often make the point that the market/state relationship in the Canadian economy of today stands somewhere between the American/British model and the Continental European model. This is consistent with Easterbrook's argument that, to this day, many of Canada's economic characteristics can be attributed to the fact that Canada originated as a colony of a continental European state, France.

Initial Conditions and "Path Dependency"

The English-speaking colonies in North America inherited a more favourable legacy from the home country than New France inherited from France. Moreover, after Britain took possession of Quebec from France in 1759, many of the weaknesses of the French colony continued to limit the economic development of what was to become Canada. Thus, the first chapter in the long story of Canada's economic subordination to the US concerns the basic flaws in the legacy of French imperial rule. Among other things, this is a powerful demonstration of the influence of a phenomenon known as "path dependency." This concept is so central to appreciating the force of Easterbrook's analysis of North American economic and political evolution that it is worth taking some time to be clear about what it means.

Path dependency may be generally defined as a tendency for the consequences of initial social choices to limit the range of choices available in the future. It is a term economic historians and other social scientists use to account for the durability (or long-term stability) of many aspects of social, political, and economic life. Most of human existence is governed by various kinds of formal and informal institutions and constraints—the family, social mores, customs, courts, legislatures, departments of government, and regulatory agencies, among others; these institutions tend to persist for considerable periods of time in the forms in which they were initially created.

The structures of state authority within a society seem particularly resistant to significant and sudden changes, even when changes in other aspects of social life appear on the surface to be major and swift. As a recent example, the liberation of the countries of Eastern Europe from Soviet domination and their conversion from communist societies to market democracies has had a much smaller effect on their government processes (and especially their administrative practices) than one might have expected. In fact, Russia itself has so far failed to erase many of the traces of former Communist Party rule.

There are a number of reasons for the persistence of institutions, even when their inefficient performance might be expected to promote their replacement or significant reform. One is their "public goods" character: the benefits that might arise from reforming them cannot be directly and exclusively captured by those who make the attempt. (Only idealists, or the completely desperate, can envisage any personal gain from the energy expended in promoting change.) Another is the large economies of scale associated with the production of institutional outputs. This means that, at the margin, the cost of additional "units"—which in any case can be compared only against some imaginary alternative supplier—are so small that the inefficiencies of the existing system are hard to detect. Yet another is the fact that most social institutions are networked with other institutions and their outputs, which means that individual changes can be made (if at all) only at the price of revamping the entire system at the same time and that any incremental changes are therefore unlikely to have much tangible effect.

Finally, institutions are often created to provide solutions to problems of social coordination, rather than more deeply seated conflicts of interest. That is, many important institutions were initially designed to solve problems—comparable to deciding which side of the road to drive on—where the superiority of one option over another is not obvious as long as everyone agrees to do the same thing. Moreover, having been adopted, any such coordinating mechanism is automatically (and often permanently) perceived to be superior to any of its alternatives: once one solution is adopted, it becomes easier (that is, less costly for all actors) to maintain support for the existing arrangement than to organize a consensus around one of many possible alternatives to it.

For reasons such as these, there is an intrinsic plausibility to Easterbrook's argument that the imperial legacies of the colonizing empires in North America laid down the paths that significantly conditioned their colonies' subsequent economic, social, and political evolution. Moreover, as we shall see in the next section, imperial legacies begin at home, in the sense that what is "transplanted" to the colonial setting must first be present in the economy, society, and political institutions of the colonizer. For example, as a colonizer, Britain in the late 1600s exhibited a limited government with both a thriving free-hold agricultural sector and dynamic commercial and manufacturing sectors with increasing overseas interests. Other advantages that Britain passed on to the Thirteen Colonies included a tradition of decentralized administration, English common law, and—for most of them, especially in the northeast—Protestantism.

However, the main point about these basic differences in the beginnings of the American and Canadian economies is not that Britain was a better colonizer than France. In fact, it is truer to say that, from the beginning, the primary difference between the two cases was that the British state was less substantially involved in the creation and development of its first colonial possessions in North America than the French state was with its. For example, the New England colonies were settled by religious dissidents without state support. Maryland was state-supported, but neither it nor the other New England colonies were established to extract commodities such as fish, fur, and timber for the sake of the home country. However, these forms of imperial exploitation were present in the case of what became Canada (except for Acadia, which was also a self-supporting agricultural settlement similar to New England).

In short, one of the most fundamental differences in the initial conditions affecting the European penetration of North America is that New France developed according to a central design (or state plan) and that some of the key elements of this plan continued to dominate the development of early Canada long after the centre of colonial authority shifted from France to Britain. Thus, the central argument of Easterbrook's book can be summed up as the proposition that the Canadian economy has been more "persistent" (or path dependent) than the American economy. It may be worthwhile, therefore, to examine more fully what this means and what accounts for it.

Decentralized Administration

Britain, of course, has never been a federation on either the American or Canadian models, but it did have different levels of jurisdiction or "divided government." As American economist Barry Weingast has argued,

[t]hough the British do not use the label *federalism* ... 18th-century England was a de facto federal system. First, the national and local governments were important and distinct sources of political authority. Second, by the beginning of the 18th century, the national government was limited in its ability to regulate the domestic economy (though international trade was heavily controlled). The constitutional changes during the 17th century abolished, greatly restricted or granted jointly to Parliament and the Crown many of the powers of the Stuart kings.[3]

Weingast claims that these reforms set England on the road to a "market-preserving federalism" that helped to foster economic growth during the emerging industrial revolution in two major ways:

First, limits on the national government's authority to regulate economic activity prevented it from responding to efforts by established economic interests to provide national controls that would have effectively prevented many of the new industrial activities. Second, the induced political competition among local jurisdictions implied that some localities were willing to take on the extra burdens in exchange for the prospect of generating new forms of economic activity, local employment and taxes.[4]

Given this, it is not surprising that much of the early industrialization in the US was regulated, if at all, at the state and local levels, thus

---

[3] Barry Weingast, "The Economic Role of Political Institutions: Market Preserving Federalism and Economic Development," *The Journal of Law, Economics and Organization* 4, 1 (December, 1994): 6-7.

[4] Weingast 8. Earlier (on page 3), Weingast points out that for most of the last 300 years, "the richest nation in the world has had a federal structure: the Netherlands from the late 16th century to the mid-17th century, England from the late 17th or early 18th century through the mid-19th century, and the United States from the late 19th century to the late 20th century." However, it should be noted that the "federalism" involved in these three cases involved quite different governing institutions. Weingast is essentially stressing what he sees as the virtues of constitutionally constrained central governments. Of course, in reference to the US, it was precisely the attempt to reassert central imperial control—and taxes—over the American colonies that led to the American War of Independence in 1776.

helping to "preserve the market" there once the process of industrialization spread across the Atlantic Ocean.

It is worth noting, as we shall see more clearly in the next chapter, that the fur trade conducted in New France was marked by the exact opposite of such decentralizing characteristics. Increasing commercial pressure from the English colonies to the south and the Hudson's Bay Company to the north forced the trade centred on Montreal to engage in major expenditures on military posts and other defensive measures that created a drain on the finances of New France and France itself. The result was increased centralized control of the former by the latter, and the paternalism of old France was reinforced. As Harold Innis summed this up, "Centralized control as shown in the activities of the government, the church, the seigniorial system and other institutions was in part a result of the overwhelming importance of the fur trade."[5]

Common Law

Easterbrook argues that, in the US, the central state played a neutral, or "permissive" role in relation to business and the economy in general. Property rights were legislated and enforced, meaning that the national government was undoubtedly involved in the economy, but many of the laws guaranteeing these rights were either taken directly from established British practices or were based on British precedent. It might therefore be said that it was "the law" rather than "government" that regulated the American economy, whereas in New France and later in British North America, the colonial governments tended to use much more intrusive instruments of government.

---

[5] Harold A. Innis, "The Importance of Staple Products in Canadian Development," in Daniel Drache, ed., *Staples, Markets and Cultural Change: Selected Essays* (Montreal and Kingston: McGill-Queen's University Press, 1995) 11. Pointing to similar developments, Easterbrook (59) adds that they "created in the process a framework of centralized control within which later expansion under British auspices was continued."

Of particular importance in this connection was the British common-law tradition respecting the "fee-simple ownership" of land.[6] When combined with the other early American initiatives with respect to the sale and distribution of public lands, this tradition gave an enormous boost to American agricultural productivity, which provided a well-laid foundation for later commercial and industrial undertakings.

Protestantism

This is not the place to review the long and tortured debate about the relationship between the Protestant faith and the origins of capitalism (or, for that matter, the relative merits in general of the Protestant and Roman Catholic branches of Christianity). One of the most controversial books in all of the social sciences is Max Weber's work on this subject, *The Protestant Ethic and the Spirit of Capitalism*.[7] Only one significant point will be considered here, namely, the ways in which the Protestant Reformation both promoted individualism and spread literacy. The emphasis of nearly all the Protestant denominations, including the Puritans who landed in New England and the Quakers who settled Pennsylvania (not to mention the Dutch who founded Manhattan), is on the unmediated relationship between the individual and God. If the individual believer is not to receive the word and will of God indirectly *via* priest, bishop, or pope, then he or she must discover them directly by consulting the "Book of God," that is, by reading the Bible or having it read aloud by somebody else (but in the community's language, not Latin!).

As a consequence, areas dominated by the Protestant religion tended to place a high value on public education. Within a few generations of their foundation, the colonies of the USCS through their own local initiative and investments began to develop some of the

---

[6] Fee-simple ownership means that there are no government restrictions on the sale or transfer of land from one individual to another.

[7] Max Weber, *The Protestant Ethic and the Spirit of Capitalism*, trans. Talcott Parsons with a forward by R.H. Tawney (London: G. Allen and Unwin, 1930).

most literate and highly educated societies in the world. As we shall see, this fact had a salutary effect on the adaptation and dissemination of both agricultural and (later) industrial innovations, which in turn drove most of the American economy to unprecedented rates of economic growth.

Settlement

Easterbrook further argues that, overall, Britain's colonizing efforts did much more to promote agricultural development in the New World than those of France. However, even Britain did not build its empire to acquire basic food for its population (with the partial exception of the cod fisheries off the shores of Newfoundland) but rather to exploit the commercial potential of an imperial trading system. This system involved exporting British manufactures to its colonies and importing from them a variety of exotic foods—such as sugar, tea, and cocoa—that were not available at home.

This strategy led to the creation of a triangular trading system across the North Atlantic. British colonies in North America either sold food to the British Navy or exported it to the slave-based plantations in the West Indies; the sugar, spices, and other tropical foodstuffs of the West Indies were exported from there to Britain; and British manufactures were exported to the North American colonies. The USCS's participation in this structured set of trade relations allowed its farmers to profit from their emerging agricultural surpluses. When combined with New Englanders' exploitation of the Grand Banks fishery, this trade also laid the foundation of an active commercial sector.

New France afforded no comparable opportunities for settlement and agricultural exports. Initially, the French interest in North America was limited to cod. Religious restrictions on eating meat helped to create a heavy demand for cod for both consumption in France itself and for export to the rest of southern Europe. Meanwhile, the large sun-dried salt deposits available to many fishing ports in France prompted its fishery to adopt an on-board, salt-cured method for preserving fish for the trip home. Consequently, unlike the British, who instead dried the cod on the shores of Newfoundland, the French fishing fleets showed little interest in establishing land bases on North American soil. Thus, the earliest French economic interest in North America did not encourage settlement. As we shall see in the next chapter, the fur trade, which followed the cod fishery as the focus of French interest in North America, provided no greater incentives for the permanent settlement of the interior than the fishery had provided toward the settlement of the coasts.

In addition to the imperial influences that discouraged the rapid settlement of New France, the colony faced further commercial disadvantages in comparison with the British Atlantic colonies. Most of these had to do with its location. The shores of the St. Lawrence River proved fertile enough for self-sufficient family farms, but few farms developed far from the river itself, limiting the overall extent of arable lands. More importantly, the valley of the St. Lawrence was much farther from exploitable markets for foodstuffs (such as the West Indies) than were the northeastern British colonies and suffered the additional disadvantage of being ice-bound for significant parts of the year.

The combined effect of all these influences has been well summarized by Marc Egnal in an interesting study of the "divergent paths" of economic development followed by Quebec, on the one hand, and Britain's northern and southern colonies in North America, on the other. For Egnal, the wide differences in the rates of growth among these three regions can be best measured against the benchmark of the mid-eighteenth century, when the economic characteristics of all the North American colonies were remarkably similar in nature. As he succinctly states, "[i]n 1750 the North, South and French Canada had much in common. They had a similar standard of living. And they took the same approach—called the 'household economy'—to economic activities."[8] He cites figures showing grain output per acre—the most significant data allowing for a direct comparison of

---

[8] Marc Egnal, *Divergent Paths: How Culture and Institutions Have Shaped North American Growth* (New York: Oxford University Press, 1996) 4.

early Quebec with the USCS—to make the important point that the productivity of the two areas was very similar. In fact, at that time, the annual rates of growth were scarcely distinguishable (at 0.5 per cent).[9]

In sum, by the mid-eighteenth century, there was little to differentiate the family farms that populated all of the settled regions of North America. There was, however, a huge difference in the total number of such units in each territory, and consequently the overall size of their respective populations differed enormously. To quote Egnal again:

> In 1750 the North had 660,000 people, the South 510,000 and New France only 50,000. New France had a tragic flaw—its weak growth in numbers—that cost it dearly in the imperial wars of the eighteenth century. But it was not backward in its standard of living or pace of development.[10]

Moreover, largely owing to these differences in population base, the similarities among these regions did not last for long. One hundred years later, as measured by income per person and agricultural income per worker, the standard of living in the northeastern American states had risen to a level roughly double that of what is now Quebec.[11] Thus, New France was not only smaller to begin with, but it grew considerably more slowly during the years after 1750. In other words, the differences in their initial conditions had significant economic consequences over time.

Responses to Uncertainty

The last point to be made about the early development of Canada and the US concerns the very different levels of overall security (or

---

9 Egnal 5.
10 Egnal 7.
11 Egnal, Tables 1.3 and 1.4, 18-19.

insecurity) each faced. Easterbrook defines this factor as the varying degrees of "uncertainty" that entire societies experience with respect to their economic and political fortunes over time. (It is therefore not the same as the quantifiable "risk" that surrounds the investments of an individual or firm.) Almost from the moment of their union with one another, and particularly following the final defeat of Napoleon by the combined European powers in 1815, the American states enjoyed an unusual degree of security from foreign intervention. From that same moment on, the Canadians and Mexicans, by contrast, had to worry that the growing power of the US might someday be directed against them.

Ironically, given the fact that the British presence in North America was more and more at risk, the British were one of the keys to the US's own safety. The possibility that the US might fight another war with Britain seemed increasingly remote as the nineteenth century progressed, and Britain's command of the high seas meant that no other serious threat to the US could come from across the Atlantic. Meanwhile, on the other side of the Pacific Ocean, Japan was quiescent, while China was in thrall to various colonial powers. The rest of the western hemisphere was weak or in disarray.

This absence of external threats gave an even greater impetus to the American states' growing preoccupation with westward expansion in the era of manifest destiny. But more than that, it meant that this expansion was carried out primarily by private enterprise and without major strategic intervention on the part of the American government. It is true that the Louisiana Purchase—through which the new government of the US acquired the "American" portions of the colony of New France that it had not already taken over in the course of the War of Independence—should not be overlooked as a major intervention by the central government. However, this act, along with further instances of territorial acquisition from the Spanish that followed it, simply involved the central state in the expansion of territory; it did not necessarily include an ongoing, centrally determined plan for the economic development that subsequently took place in that territory. Where private enterprise alone did not suffice, it was primarily the individual state governments that carried forward initiatives for further development. The opening of the American west (the "Wild West") was, therefore, more or less spontaneous and largely free of central-state intervention.

Planned or not, the very dynamism of the American assault on the interior of North America represented a threat to the other, slower developing societies on the continent. Canada, Mexico, and even the American southern states all began to fear, and ultimately feel, the growing economic might of the USCS as it spread westward and southward. Canada experienced the War of 1812, the Annexationist movement and, just prior to Confederation in 1867, the Fenian raids. For Mexico, the Mexican-American War of 1846-48 resulted in the US gaining most of what are now Texas, New Mexico, and California. The south was definitively defeated by the north during the American Civil War of 1861-65 (the example of which, it can be said, frightened the leaders of the British North American colonies into uniting two years later). Thus, all the other societies in North America were to develop under the shadow of the most successful one—the USCS—and they did so increasingly within its economic orbit. For Canada and Mexico, this meant that their national governments played a much more extensive managerial role in the development of their economies than it had in the US. As a result, the balance they struck between private enterprise and bureaucratic entrepreneurship leaned toward central planning and control, and their economic development was largely defensive in nature.

LATER SOURCES OF AMERICAN ECONOMIC SUPERIORITY IN NORTH AMERICA

As we have seen, as early as the mid-1700s, the British colonies in the northeast of today's US possessed a bundle of political, social, and economic characteristics that endowed them with unparalleled economic potential. Not only that, but almost immediately following independence from Britain in 1783, the new United States of America began a long process of expansion into the heart of a continent with staggering opportunities for rapid and diversified economic development.

These included most of North America's fertile land and the best of its climate; immense forest, mineral, and coal reserves; and an abundance of navigable rivers. From the vantage-point of the twenty-first century, however, it is possible to discern several other social, political, and economic characteristics that help to explain how the US managed to make the most of this potential and to amass enormous economic power during the ensuing 200 years.

There were four principal keys to this success. The first was the accumulated size of the American population, which helped the US to become the largest single internal market on earth. The second was the relative decentralization, openness, and flexibility of the American economy and political institutions. The third was the supportiveness (as opposed to intrusiveness) of American laws and regulations bearing on the economy, especially with respect to the emergence of a new form of business enterprise—the large-scale, vertically integrated corporation. The fourth was the extraordinarily highly developed system of public and private universities, which throughout the period provided advanced post-secondary education and publicly accessible research and technology.

It will be easier to understand not only the arrival, but the precise form of North American free trade in the 1980s and 1990s if the nature and consequences of these sources of American continental and global pre-eminence are more fully appreciated.

Large Internal Market

If a large population were all it takes to achieve high levels of economic prosperity, then China and India rather than the US would be today's economic giants (although current growth rates suggest the former may well become tomorrow's economic giant). As the contrast between New France and the American colonies has already illustrated, a large population does appear to be a necessary, though not sufficient, condition for a country to rise to the rank of a leading economic power, but the population also has to be highly skilled and efficiently mobilized for overall economic activity to expand rapidly. Moreover, the larger the market, the greater degree of diversification and specialization within that market, promoting still further levels of efficiency. This is because, other things being equal, the more refined and specialized the division of labour in an economy becomes, the lower the cost of producing its aggregate output. As the total size of the market increases, even narrowly specialized producers can become large and achieve lower unit costs of production (that is, achieve economies of scale).

If there were no national barriers to trade (as opposed to natural ones, such as transportation costs), these effects could occur practically anywhere in the world. All countries, big or small, would simply achieve specialization and economies of scale by doing more and more of what they do best and exporting that to other countries. (This is the strategy through which tiny Singapore and Hong Kong, using increasingly open world markets, have reached high levels of economic prosperity.) However, in a world in which national territorial boundaries generally restrict the access of foreign producers to national markets, the achievement of high degrees of specialization and full economies of scale typically must depend on the size of the producer's own economy, since that is the only market to which it has unrestricted and duty-free access. (Future progress toward the global liberalization of markets may gradually reduce the importance of home markets, but the world is still a long way away from a single global market.) Thus, until recently, any one country's ability to achieve efficiency has been contingent on the size of its economy overall.

By the outbreak of the Second World War, the US had already enjoyed more than 100 years as one of the world's largest industrial economies. (Canada did not achieve this status until *after* the Second World War and largely because of it). It had thus been in a position for some time to reap fully the advantages of both specialization and economies of scale, as well as a highly developed research and development (R&D) establishment. Not only did it have one of the largest populations among industrialized countries, but the income per person in the US became the highest in the world.

A good illustration of the benefits of a large and prosperous market can be found in the recent American domination of the motion-picture industry, to the point where Hollywood movies have come to displace locally produced films from most of the national markets in the industrialized world. It is hard to believe that countries such as Britain, France, Germany, or Japan—all of whom once had thriving movie industries of their own—cannot provide the skills and resources necessary to sustain successful motion-picture industries, and most of them still do produce many good films. However, their own markets are comparatively small, while at the same time the limited interest of most Americans in watching movies made elsewhere effectively shuts these foreign film producers out of the American market. Meanwhile, Hollywood producers can write off the high costs of producing their movies against the huge sales they achieve at home. Not only that, but with those costs initially written off, American producers can further afford to distribute their movies in foreign markets for a fraction of the cost of the local product, thus edging foreign movie-makers out of the theatres in their own countries.

What is true of artistic (or entertainment) innovation is just as true of industrial innovation. Industrial R&D certainly is dependent upon the availability of high-quality and low-cost inputs for leading technological industries. However, the capacity of a national economy to achieve and maintain overall technological superiority (or even long-term competitiveness) also depends upon the ability to write off development costs against very large sales of final products. The same applies to the cost of providing the best intermediate goods and services (or "infrastructure"). No national economy can achieve high levels of productivity without support from strong and efficient national networks of transportation and communications, but not all countries can do so cheaply. Because they tend to require large amounts of sunk capital and other overheads, which lead to high ratios of fixed-to-variable costs, smaller markets often fail to permit the realization of full economies of scale in such industries.

As we shall see in the next chapter, the interplay between the high costs of infrastructure and the potential size of the national market has proven to be one of the most important single factors differentiating the American and Canadian economies. Unlike their European and Asian competitors in the late nineteenth century, the American and Canadian economies were destined by their geography and history to develop on a continental scale, requiring massive investments in sepa-rate national systems of continent-wide infrastructure. The Americans did this on the strength of an economy roughly ten times the aggregate size of the Canadian economy. This was a significant factor both in the greater efficiency of the transportation and communications indus-tries which spanned the American portion of the continent and in the greater productivity of the economy they were built to serve.

Neutral *versus* Strategic Uses of the State

The absence of a strategic role for the central government of the US did not mean that there was no important role for government in the economy. Certain national legislation, such as laws of incorpo-ration and intercorporate ownership, played a vital part in helping the private sector gradually construct a continental economy, first in the US itself and then throughout the entire continent. This legis-lation, however, tended to be permissive rather than interventionist in character. The American government encouraged the success of business and entrepreneurship and subsidized the creation of some national infrastructure, but it did not attempt to marshal business to a national plan for economic development.[12] (Easterbrook goes so far as to encapsulate the differences between Canadian and American economic development as "Plan or no Plan."[13])

There are four good examples of the neutral uses of the state in support of American economic success. One was the basic approach

---

[12] Even after its victory in the American Civil War, and on the verge of a massive westward expansion of the Union, the federal government of the US declined to expand the economic role of the central government much beyond the role of suppressing local regulatory barriers to interstate trade and investment. Thus, the key economic agency of the central state was the judiciary, "the very model of lean administrative organization." See Richard Franklin Bensel, *Yankee Leviathan: the Origins of Central State Authority in America, 1859-1877* (New York: Cambridge University Press, 1990) 20, fn. 20.

[13] Easterbrook 82. He elaborates on this difference as one between "a program of control exercised by a conservative elite dedicated to orderly and directed growth, or, alternatively, a formula based on the dispersion of power in investments free of central control."

to the acquisition and possession of land, which was based on the inherited British tradition of secure property rights. Another was the
support for a near-universal system of public education and a univer-
sity-based system of R&D. A third was the willingness of the American
government to allow failing businesses to disappear altogether in the
face of superior competition from more efficient or innovative firms,
rather than propping them up with subsidies or favourable regulation.
A fourth was the evolution of legislation governing the formation and
acquisition of business corporations. In addition, it is striking that, to
the extent that Americans did use government to promote economic
development, state rather than federal governments had the more
significant practical role, a further demonstration of the characteristic
preference of the American system for decentralized, and even competitive, exercise of the powers of government.

Land Policy

A useful summary view of the role of land policy in the acceleration
of the growth of the American economy has been provided by North
and Thomas:

> Questions surrounding the disposal of public lands contin-
> ued as a subject for debate throughout the nineteenth century.
> Endless arguments centered on the influence of land policy on
> economic growth, and pressure was continuous for reduction
> in the minimum price per acre and for changes in the credit
> terms. In perspective, it appears that the disposal policy as
> carried out accelerated both the westward movement and the
> over-all growth of the American economy, and that it encour-
> aged the inpouring of capital as well as of labor from other
> lands and from the eastern United States.[14]

---

[14] Douglass C. North and Robert Paul Thomas, *The Growth of the American Economy to
1860* (Columbia, SC: University of South Carolina Press, 1968) 182-83.

As indicated in this brief account, the price and terms according to which land was transferred from the public domain to private individuals varied over time (roughly in keeping with the rise and fall of the economic rents accruing to the settlement of new lands in different regions of the country). However, the more important point is that land was transferred from public ownership, usually at very low cost.

According to one source:

> In 1785, the first public land disposal legislation was passed. It not only set minimum acreage to be sold and its price, but it also laid out the township system of land division that has characterized American surveying ever since.... Prior to 1862, the general system of land distribution was to put the lands up for auction. If no one bid above the set minimum, the land was not sold. After 1862, distribution was based mainly on development of the land.[15]

These policies did not always lead to an efficient rate of settlement or optimal land use, but they were almost entirely free of discriminatory allocation: they were not harnessed to any master strategy for American economic development. They did not even prohibit holdings by foreigners, which was a strong inducement to settlement and foreign railway investment in the mid-nineteenth century.[16] It is true that lands were occasionally granted for specific public purposes, such as warrants to war veterans and land grants to colleges and railways. However, with the exception of federal support for railways, these forms of subsidy were not elements in national economic planning. Most canal, road, dam, and railway construction did involve goverment subsidies, but such subsidies came predominantly from the states.

---

[15] Douglass C. North, Terry L. Anderson, and Peter J. Hill, *Growth and Welfare in the American Past: a New Economic History* (Englewood Cliffs, NJ: Prentice Hall, 1983) 112.

[16] North, Anderson, and Hill 121.

Public Education

The overall system of education in the US—emphasizing the education of farmers and agricultural research—is generally recognized as one of the most fundamental factors in its economic success.[17] The public school system has been described as one of "several areas of intervention that demonstrate the productive role of government," mostly because it provided "an important stimulus to the growth of human capital in the US."[18]

Despite its proven success, the contribution of public education to the early development of the American economy was quite modest in scale and scope. It certainly bore little resemblance to more recent attempts to cultivate high technology in sophisticated R&D laboratories and industrial parks. It was, instead, aimed simply at developing basic knowledge and skills in the population, which among other things made the American worker more adaptable than agricultural and industrial workers elsewhere. As Peter George puts it:

> Many of the skills associated with nineteenth-century machine technology had to be learned on the job, since they included a large proportion of "know-how" or uncodified skills. These were not readily transferable through formal education or print and, thus, their transmission was predicated on a labor force which was well prepared through its educational background to receive and retain technical information and was receptive to the immigration of skilled persons who could impart technical knowledge.[19]

---

[17] Peter George, *The Emergence of Industrial America: Strategic Factors in American Economic Growth Since 1870* (Albany, NY: State University of New York Press, 1982) 119-20. The principal legislation involved was the Morrill Acts of 1862 and 1890.

[18] North, Anderson, and Hill 96. They go on the state that "the land grant college made possible a wider spread of higher education than would have occurred without it."

[19] George 48.

In short, education had a lot to do with the unprecedented capacity and willingness of the American workforce to accept new work practices and modes of production.

In this respect, the education system facilitated the industrialization of the US by contributing generally to both labour mobility and the capacity of the entire society to play, even if reluctantly, a part in major transformations. The prevailing social and cultural predispositions of the country's population reduced their resistance to "new ways of doing things" and smoothed the introduction of different products, methods of production, and social organization.

Letting Losers Fail

Most important to the pace and spread of innovation, however, is that the American central government, no less than the political-economic culture that shaped it, was prepared to see inefficient enterprises go broke and disappear. In the American economy, losers were allowed to fail. One advantage of this outlook was that it encouraged a "trial and error" approach to industrial and social innovation, whereby many paths were taken coincidentally with many others, but only a few—the successful few—led anywhere. However, the ones that survived did so on the basis of demonstrated efficiency (or at least survivability).

The significant public benefit of this orientation to economic life was that it opened the way to the introduction of new products and techniques of production, which most Americans tended to see as sufficient justification for the costs borne by the owners and workers eclipsed by technological advances. In contrast with most other industrial societies, however, proven losers were not artificially propped up by a central bureaucratic state (typically with some political interest in their continued existence). In short, whereas most societies make the entrenchment of established status easier to maintain than breaking into markets as a "new entrant," the US demonstrated almost from its beginnings that it was more willing than most societies to allow established interests to be swept aside in favour of new developments.

It would be misleading—some might say ridiculous—to suggest that American regulators have never acted to prevent, or at least delay, the introduction of new technologies in favour of the economic and political interests built up around existing ones.[20] Still, it is important to recognize that the US has generally attempted to do this much less extensively than other industrial countries, including Japan, Canada, and France.[21] A striking recent illustration of the durability of this broad difference in responses to "the new" is the significantly slower rate at which the latter countries have adapted to technological changes in the telecommunications sector, where the US was the first in subjecting its long-established telephone carriers to competitive products, services, and firms.[22]

Corporate Law

As the nineteenth century progressed, pressures began to build toward new forms of business organization and corporate law. The large-scale production of many new goods and services, especially such massive undertakings as the continental railways, required huge infusions of new capital that promised to return a profit only in the very long term (if at all).[23] This forced entrepreneurs to seek ways of spreading the risk and extending the time horizon for the investments associated with these projects. One of the principal responses to this problem was to weld the idea of the corporation as a distinct institutional form to the idea of the limited liability of individual investors, or shareholders.

---

[20] Indeed, American scholars—using mostly American case histories—have published some of the best studies of "regulatory protection." A good example of this is the way that the trucking industry was hamstrung by federal regulation in its attempts to steal the ground transportation market from the railways.

[21] See Norris Clement, et al., *North American Economic Integration: Theory and Practice* (Northampton, MA: Edward Elgar, 1999) 120: "... the US constitution and its interpreters have favored the rights of innovators over those that were financially harmed by innovation."

[22] See Steven K. Vogel, *Freer Markets, More Rules: Regulatory Reform in Advanced Industrial Countries* (Ithaca, NY: Cornell University Press, 1996).

[23] Easterbrook 124.

Historically in Britain as well as in the US, the corporation was a form of organization that allowed a group of individuals to establish and operate an enterprise that was legally separate from the individuals who created it. This form of organization was originally reserved for agencies (such as orphanages or colleges) that were generally recognized to serve a public purpose, that is, to promote the ends of the community as a whole. Thus, such agencies were granted charters by the state involving "a carefully defined function for the enterprise and limited scope for its activities."[24] Gradually, however, the category of undertakings that were eligible for this special legal status was expanded to include turnpikes, banks, canals, and the early railroads. Eventually, this mode of organization became the model for any large-scale business enterprise.

The corporate form of organization was valuable to business because it helped greatly to solve a number of problems. Specifically, it

- created a separate legal entity, which simplified the acquisition of capital because it allowed for investment by many small shareholders;
- facilitated the management of large accumulations of capital because it separated ownership from management of the firm and promoted the rise of a professional managerial class;
- conferred limited financial risk upon shareholders, who were personally liable only to the extent of the capital which they had invested in the corporation as opposed to the debts that might be incurred by the firm itself; and
- retained the advantage of proprietorship and partnerships, in that it was free from interference by government, except through legislative changes to the charter or judicial interpretation of the charter.[25]

In effect, the corporate laws adopted by various states during the last 30 years of the nineteenth century laid the groundwork for the

---

[24] George 79.
[25] George 78

massive corporate giants that are household names today. Unlike family firms or partnerships, corporations are legally immortal. Because they do not die off as human beings do, their assets are not periodically broken up and separately distributed among their inheritors. Nevertheless, these a-humans enjoy most of the rights of all "legal persons." Laws of business incorporation thus sowed the seeds of corporate concentration in the American economy. However, they also provided the foundation for a transcontinental economy, at first across the length and breadth of the US itself and then throughout almost all of North America through investments by American companies in Canada and Mexico.

According to Easterbrook, the expansion, both industrially and geographically, of the US in the mid-nineteenth century is inextricably connected to the expanding role and increasing power of business corporations, a trend encouraged by a shift from state authorities to private firms and sanctioned by the courts. Especially following the end of the Civil War (1865), the process of industrialization was marked by a combination of free enterprise and belief in the benefits of economic development. As Easterbrook describes it, such values prompted state authorities to promote the fortunes of the private corporation to the point where they effectively escaped their continued control. "Legally," he writes, "the states retained the power to stem the tide of corporate advance, but laxity in the administration of state laws and fear of impeding industrial growth in their regions ruled out a united front again the pressures exerted by interstate industrial corporations."[26]

Additional corporate law, first adopted by the State of New Jersey in 1889, helped to accelerate this expansion even further.

---

[26] Easterbrook 127. For a detailed discussion of the evolution of corporate law in the US, see Jason Kaufman, "Origins of the Asymmetric Society: Freedom of Incorporation in the Early US and Canada," paper presented to a seminar sponsored by the Centre for American Studies, The University of Western Ontario, 4 April 2005, mimeo. This study also documents the extent to which the private business corporation was much slower to develop and spread in colonial Canada than in the colonial and post-colonial US.

Specifically, New Jersey "amended its general act of incorporation in order to permit holding companies; that is, the amendment permitted corporations chartered in New Jersey to hold stock in other corporations whether chartered in New Jersey or elsewhere."[27] The passage of this law then put pressures on other states to act in a complementary manner to permit companies within their states to be owned and operated as subsidiaries of firms chartered out-of-state. Thus the interstate company was born, and it began to operate on a multistate and interregional basis across the entire country. Many of these firms came to dominate the American market, either alone (as monopolists) or in conjunction with a few others (as oligopolists).

As Stephen Hymer once observed, this corporate concentration in the national market proved to be a powerful springboard for the international expansion of American firms as well, and the age of the "American multinational" soon followed.[28] This transformation was not, however, strictly a function of the large size or extraordinary profitability of the new form of business; it also included innovations in the management of firms. The managerial requirements of continental-scale enterprises, pioneered by the railroads, also produced innovations in the organization and management of the corporation that later became part of the international competitive advantage enjoyed by US companies.[29]

By the end of the nineteenth century, the American federal government undertook a broad and intrusive program of regulation aimed at reining in some of its most powerful and significant new corporations. This was especially true in major sectors of the American economy such as railway, petroleum, telephone, and pharmaceutical companies. Although the new regulatory regime may have served to protect consumers and workers from some of the worst abuses by these giant firms, it still did not amount to the strategic direction of businesses by the central government. Nor, with very few exceptions,

---

[27] George 81.
[28] Stephen Hymer, *The International Operations of International Firms: A Study of Direct Investment* (Cambridge, MA: MIT Press, 1976).
[29] See also North, Anderson, and Hill 106.

did the American government ever own businesses directly or employ them as instruments of national policy. The American style of regulatory protection of major firms was primarily aimed at maintaining the stability of particular markets, often in the interests of the dominant players themselves; it was rarely applied to impose a government plan on those markets. American law has also been generally more than usually effective at reducing the overall cost of doing business—generally referred to as transaction costs—through the reliable enforcement of contracts, which inspires the mutual confidence at both ends of business deals that their terms would be completely met.[30] In sum, American government policy was mostly enabling, rather than strategically interventionist.

CONCLUSION

From the beginning, the US was richly endowed with what it required to develop economically, and it did so as rapidly as the world has ever witnessed. As we have seen, this very growth impaired the ability of Canada and Mexico to do likewise, at least in the same manner. But there were also deeper, entrenched reasons why Canada could not have expected to show the same trajectory of economic development as the one we have just traced for the US. We will explore these other reasons in the next chapter.

---

[30] Clement, et al. 121.

chapter 4
THE EVOLUTION OF THE
NORTH AMERICAN ECONOMY II: CANADA

In comparison with the overview of American economic development presented in Chapter 3, the Canadian case diverges in three major ways. The first is the small size of the Canadian market, which is about one-tenth the size of the American domestic market. As a result, the second difference is that Canada for most of its history has relied heavily on exports to promote its economic growth. Moreover, those exports have typically consisted of natural resources or resource-based commodities, commonly referred to as "staples," which have not only provided the impetus for the expansion of employment and incomes, but also for the development of Canada's infrastructure, such as ports, canals, railroads, and networks of communication. Thirdly, because the size of the country is so great and the population so small and widely scattered, Canada's national systems of transportation and communications have tended to be very costly to create and operate, so that the national government has had either to provide massive subsidies to the major firms in these industries or to own them outright. In sum, where the American economy has been large, self-sustaining, and dominated by the private sector, the Canadian economy has been (relatively) small, export-dependent, and state-oriented.

EXPORT OF STAPLES

There has been a long and intense debate among Canadian political economists about the importance of staples in Canadian economic development. Some scholars have suggested that Canada was gripped for a long time in a "staples trap" of slow growth and low diversification, while others have claimed that staple exports, especially the export of prairie wheat to Britain, provided a springboard to manufacturing and advanced service industries. These contending arguments grew into distinct schools of thought, the former being associated with Harold Innis and the latter with W.A. Mackintosh.

No attempt will be made here to resolve this dispute. However, two points deserve attention. First, the US also went through a period when the export of agricultural products was an important part of its economy. However, compared with Canadians, Americans appear to have extracted greater benefit from such exports for the rest of its economy, especially the manufacturing sector. To quote one economic historian,

> As in the cases of the Canadian and Australian economies for much of their histories, discussions of the economic history of the United States in the eighteenth and early nineteenth centuries often take as a focal point the production for export markets of staple products ... The significant difference compared with the Canadian and Australian economies is that in the United States, regional concentration on staple production seemed to give rise to diversification around a staple base, whereas in Canada and Australia the process of diversification was less noticeable. In fact, many economic historians have argued that Canadian and Australian economic development was retarded by concentration on staples.[1]

In other words, comparatively speaking, Innis's view of Canada may have been more correct than Mackintosh's.

---

[1] George 1-2.

The second point also relates to Innis. For him, the primary significance of the development of Canadian staples for export was not their linkages with Canadian manufacturing industries but rather their impact on the country's transportation and communications systems.[2] From a nation-building perspective, the historical sequence of major staple exports following the era of the early cod fishery—furs, then square timber, then grains—had the virtue of unifying Canada along an east-west axis. National transportation systems carried resource exports in a west-to-east direction on the way to their ultimate European markets and then on the return trips took European goods and immigrants in an east-to-west direction. A major problem for Canada more recently has been that this early unifying pattern of export trade has declined throughout the twentieth century.

About all that is left of the original trans-Atlantic connection with Europe is a reduced grain trade, while the exploitation of the later staples—metals, petroleum, and forest products—has been heavily dependent on exports to the *American* market. It has hence contributed to a north-south, rather than an east-west flow of trade. This, if anything, has accentuated not the unity, but the regional fragmentation of the country by integrating parts of Canada with adjacent regions of the US while disassociating them (relatively speaking) from one another.

Meanwhile, the political-economic effects of these shifting trade patterns have been amplified by a massive reorientation of foreign investment over the past 80 years. Foreign investment, much of which had been directed into the exploitation of natural resources, shifted decisively from being predominantly British and in the form of loans, toward being predominantly American and in the form of capital stock.[3] As a result, the US has displaced Britain as Canada's primary

---

[2] See especially, Harold A. Innis, "Transportation as a Factor in Canadian Economic History," in Daniel Drache, ed., *Staples, Markets and Cultural Change: Selected Essays* (Montreal and Kingston: McGill-Queen's University Press, 1995) Ch. 7.

[3] See Kari Levitt, *Silent Surrender: The Multinational Corporation in Canada* (Toronto: Macmillan, 1970) Table 3, 66.

source of capital and technology, and American firms and investors have acquired ownership and continuing operational control of major firms in key sectors of the Canadian economy.

The export of staples, then, largely defined the fundamental orientation of Canada toward first Europe and later the US, primarily by determining the patterns of trade, investment, transportation, and communications associated with them. It also had much to do with the Canadian orientation toward government and what might be called "strategic uses of the state." This pattern of state intervention extends all the way back to the French regime and the earliest years of the fur trade, and it has been sustained ever since. It is therefore important to look more closely at the origins and consequences of this Canadian tradition, if only because it is a pattern that the new era of North American free trade is finally beginning to break.

THE FUR TRADE AND THE ORIGINS OF THE "TRANS-CANADIAN ECONOMY"

Easterbrook's account of the impact of the fur trade on the subsequent economic and political history of Canada is a textbook case of the "path dependency" discussed in the previous chapter. As argued there, the original make-up of institutional structures tends to have a long-lasting effect on their evolution, and the persistence of such structures is more probable than their transformation. For this reason, knowledge of the North American fur trade is vital to a full understanding of Canadian society, as well as of the relationship between Canadian and American society.

The main point, however, is not that the fur trade got Canada off to a "weaker" or "slower" economic start than the US, although that case can also be argued; it is, more importantly, that the fur trade placed Canada on an entirely different path of economic, social, and political development. This divergence, which lasted at least 200 years, was redirected into a trajectory of convergence with the US that was largely the result of the massive American

investments in Canada's resource industries in the early twentieth century and continued with the American takeover of its
manufacturing industries in the middle of that century. This new
Canadian trajectory can be predicted to converge even more
rapidly in an era of completely open trade and investment relations
across North America.

The Fur Trade

Easterbrook has provided an excellent overview of the differences between the Canadian and American political economies and how the
fur trade laid the foundation for Canada's side of those differences.
In particular, he summarizes effectively the long-term impact of the
nature and structure of the fur trade on the subsequent evolution of
Canada. In fact, following Easterbrook, this chapter argues that the
fur trade is usefully regarded as the first "trans-Canadian economy"
(TCE), in that it constitutes the template for subsequent versions of a
distinctly Canadian economy.

In the following passage Easterbrook describes the earliest origins
of the TCE as the foundation for a separate nation in the northern
half of North America:

> When exploration of the Gulf of St. Lawrence was undertaken by
> Cartier in the 1530s, a small and sporadic fur trade had emerged
> as an offshoot of the [Newfoundland] fisheries, and contact
> with migratory Indians versed in the techniques of trapping
> beaver opened the prospect of a new staples trade of continental
> proportions. The vast Laurentian Shield with its wealth of fur
> resources, river systems that appeared designed for expansion
> of the trade, and the expertise of the hunting Indians—these
> elements awaited only the appearance of a strong and effective
> demand for the product.[4]

---

[4] Easterbrook 52–53.

The requisite growth in demand arrived in the last half of the sixteenth century, when the wearing of felt hats (derived from beaver pelts) became a mark of high fashion in much of Europe. Shortly thereafter, in 1608, Quebec was established and soon became the centre for the control of the entire St. Lawrence area, most of the Great Lakes, and eventually the interior of all of North America.

Subsequent developments in the fur trade reveal even more about its essential character—Canada's congenital makeup, as it were. These, too, Easterbrook summarizes well:

> Dependence on a highly exhaustable staple the exploitation of which demanded rapid penetration of the interior in search of supplies, a process marked by an increasing burden of overhead costs in the face of wide fluctuations in prices and returns of trade, constituted a source of instability throughout the history of the trade ... Committed to a trade in which continued expansion was a condition of survival, there was no turning back from this drive into the continental interior.[5]

Thus, according to Easterbrook, monopoly, centralization, and state support and/or control are key characteristics of Canada's first industry. If this portrayal is accurate, if the fur trade was in fact the template for most of Canada's later economic development, then it is important to examine more precisely the key characteristics of "the first TCE." In keeping with the theory of path dependency, several such characteristics are still discernable in the economic and political realities of Canada today.[6]

---

[5] Easterbrook 53.

[6] It must be noted that the following analysis is framed around the fur trade centred on Montreal between the mid-seventeenth and the early eighteenth centuries. During most of its history, this system competed with the Hudson's Bay Company, which—as the name implies—also traded with native peoples across much of western Canada via the rivers draining into Hudson Bay. None of the following points about the fur trade as a template for the TCE pertain to the latter system, or to any aspect of the fur trade after 1821, when the two systems merged and shipments through Montreal virtually ceased in favour of other ports.

Two enduring characteristics stand out. The first is that the earliest TCE was not, in fact, fully national. After shifting the centre of the fur trade from Quebec City to Montreal, the merchants of that city undertook to exploit furs in the interior of almost the entire continent, creating a westward system of trade, transportation, defence, and communications. Utilizing the Ottawa and French Rivers, as well as the Great Lakes, it also branched south through the Ohio, Missouri, and Mississippi river systems, as well as west across the plains as far as the eastern slopes of the Rockies. The Atlantic region was not an integral part of this system, despite the fact that the port at Louisbourg (and later Halifax) helped defend it. The Pacific northwest and most of today's southern Ontario were also marginal to the fur trade, although some minor trade routes did include Lake Ontario and Lake Erie. Instead, Detroit acted as the hub of the trade involving the lower Great Lakes and the Ohio and Mississippi valleys. Thus, the first TCE failed to encompass all of Canada as we know it today, excluding such major regions as the Atlantic provinces, southern Ontario, and the west coast (except in later stages), while heavily involving northern Ontario, the prairie provinces, and the Northwest Territories.

Secondly, from its very inception, the fur trade was drawn into the interior of all of North America. During the French phase, the "commercial empire of the St. Lawrence" extended far into territories that later were to became part of the US. In essence, the creators of the first TCE constructed the first *continental* (as opposed to coastal) system of trade and communication (and, it might be added, did so long before the Americans were to do). One of the pivotal points in the history of Canada occurred when its economic leaders were forced by the success of the American War of Independence to abandon their commercial ambitions associated with their emerging continental economy in favour of the combined economic and political objectives of creating a separate Canadian economy. Donald Creighton, possibly the pre-eminent scholar of Canada's constitutional inception, depicted the historical linkages at work here in this way:

At first, during the French regime and the early days of British rule, the undivided west was sought as a whole; but after the Treaty of 1783 had drawn an unnatural and unhistorical boundary line across the middle of the continent, the Canadians were faced with a choice between two alternatives and two quite different kinds of western expansion. They could seek to gain either an international commercial empire on both sides of the new boundary or a commercial and political empire to the north of it.[7]

The economic and political leaders of British North America opted for Creighton's second choice, with the TCE centred on Montreal and with Canada becoming first a political unit by means of Confederation in 1867 and subsequently an economic unit beginning with the National Policy of 1878.

However, carving a national economic and political unit out of a continental economic one created ambiguities that have persisted throughout Canada's history, ambiguities between continent- *versus* nation-wide strategies for economic development as well as ambivalence within the Canadian economic and political elite concerning which choice was the surest way to prosper and survive. (Even Sir John A. Macdonald, who crafted the National Policy paradigm for the Canadian economy, wondered about the degree to which it might be compatible with "unrestricted reciprocity" in the year preceding the opposition Liberal adoption of that goal as a major plank in its 1891 national election.)[8] Following the Second World War, however, these ambiguities began to resolve themselves in the continental direction

---

[7] Donald Creighton, *Toward the Discovery of Canada* (Toronto: Macmillan, 1972) 160-61, as quoted in David R. Cameron, "Post-Modern Ontario and the Laurentian Thesis," in Douglas M. Brown and Janet Hiebert, eds., *Canada: the State of the Federation 1994* (Kingston, ON: Institute of Intergovernmental Relations, 1994) 128.

[8] According to J.L. Granatstein, the American response to an overture from Macdonald along such lines was disappointing, even scornful. Canadians were dismissed by the American Secretary of State as seeking to "wave the British flag" while enjoying the "remuneration of American markets" and attempting to be Americans and Canadians at the same time. See J.L. Granatstein, *Yankee Go Home? Canadians and Anti-Americanism* (Toronto: HarperCollins, 1996) 47-48.

as the centre of Canadian commerce and finance shifted decisively from Montreal to Toronto. Later, as David Cameron argues, "Post-war North American economic integration contributed to the step-by-step scrapping of the residual elements of the old National Policy and the dismantling of the policy paradigm."[9] Reflecting the original design of the genuinely continental commercial system stretching westward from Montreal, decades of American investment, combined later with trade liberalization, has allowed economics once more to prevail over politics. As a result, "the earlier potentiality of the commercial empire of the St. Lawrence to which Creighton alludes begins to assert itself—in reverse—in post-modern garb."[10]

Thus, the geography of the continent constituted a strong argument against the long-term sustainability of the TCE, as the built-in inefficiencies of the original fur trade also attest. Clearly, to be successful, trans-Canadian projects needed to be part of a *continentally integrated* system, something Canadians learned again in the late 1950s when they tried to build pipelines connecting Alberta's oil and natural gas reserves to Ontario's consumers. Three hundred and fifty years after the creation of the fur trade, the Canadian government created a network for the distribution of Alberta oil and natural gas that, in order to improve its overall economic efficiency, was designed to export roughly half its deliveries into parts of the US. It is tempting to conclude from this that every trans-Canadian system ever built might well have worked better as part of a more comprehensive continental system. As if to confirm this observation, the two Canadian railways that once formed the backbone of the national economy—the Canadian Pacific Railway (CPR) and the Canadian National Railway—have applied to the American Federal Transportation Agency for approval to merge with two American railways, each to become the Canadian portion of two continental rail systems. Not only that, but ten years ago, the CPR adopted as its new company logo an image consisting of a combination of the Canadian and American flags, a symbolic acknowledgement of the economic realities it was originally created to resist.

---

[9] Cameron 128.
[10] Cameron 128-29.

In any case, when after independence the Americans began their own assault on the interior of North America, they too had designs on all of it. It fell to Canadian authorities to work hard for the survival of their half of North America by constructing subsequent versions of the initial TCE (most notably, the CPR). However, as Easterbrook points out, none of these subsequent systems could escape the intrinsic limitations of the first: large distances, sparse traffic, high overheads, and highly variable revenues. In sum, at the close of the twentieth century, two bedrock realities of Canada's current political and economic existence showed traces of major features of the fur trade as a system of authority, commerce, and communication. First, the fact that the fur trade never truly encompassed all of what is now Canada is reflected in the fracturing of Canadian society into distinct and largely separate regional economies—roughly speaking, the Atlantic provinces; Quebec and eastern Ontario; Toronto and southwestern Ontario; northern Ontario; the prairie provinces, Nunavut, and the Northwest Territories; and British Columbia and the Yukon. Secondly, just as the fur trade, at its high point, encompassed much of the North American interior, most of these regional economies are more effectively integrated with adjacent regions of the US than with the rest of Canada. Moreover, even the partial unity achieved by various forms of the TCE is now eroding in the face of new north/south trade and investment flows.

Role of Government

As we have seen earlier in this chapter and in Chapter 3, both Easterbrook and Innis have explained how and why the fur trade demanded—and got—a heavy dose of intervention from the French state. However, after the (formal) French surrender to the British in 1763, this statist tradition need not have survived, even if the major features of the fur trade did. In fact, given that the British had allowed the Thirteen Colonies a fairly substantial degree of local autonomy (as we also saw in Chapter 3), one might have predicted the opposite. Despite this, according to Elizabeth Mancke, the exercise of British imperial authority over Canada was more heavily statist than it had been previously over the American colonies.[11] She further stresses that institutional factors are the key to understanding the differences in the role of the British state in both cases. In particular, she argues that all but one of the American colonies (Georgia) was established under British authority prior to 1688 (marking the Glorious Revolution in British constitutional history) while all of the Canadian colonies came under British rule after that date. There were at least two important and related consequences of this difference.

Most of the Thirteen Colonies had been created during the 1600s under some form of charter from a British monarch. Thus, they were largely self-governing with respect to their internal affairs and had at least some rudimentary form of representative government for the management of local affairs, including elected assemblies capable of holding their executives to account. In contrast to this, all of the British administrations in what was to become Canada "were unequivocally subordinate to Parliament, one of the central issues that led to political unrest and then revolution in the [American] colonies with seventeenth-century governmental antecedents."[12] Moreover, during the 1700s, the British state

> participated more actively in overseas governance and expansion, manifested in greater involvement in the governing of conquered colonies, the funding of colonial projects, such as the building of Halifax, the control of natural resources and the financing of exploration....[13]

---

[11] Elizabeth Mancke, "Early Modern Imperial Governance and the Origins of Canadian Political Culture," *Canadian Journal of Political Science* 32, 1 (March 1999): 12. The dates for the establishment of these colonies are: 1713 for Nova Scotia, 1791 for Canada, and 1849 for Vancouver Island/British Columbia.

[12] Mancke 12.

[13] Mancke 13. One of Mancke's other main observations of the differences between the Canadian and American colonies is that, with the exception of New York and New Jersey, all of the American colonies were developed by means of British settlement (typically under private charter), while all of the Canadian ones were acquired either by conquest or through commercial occupation. This suggests strongly that it was the American, not the Canadian, colonies that had the deeper opportunity to build positively on the foundations of British social and economic values.

Following the American War of Independence, the "Second British Empire" was designed to function as a centralized and strategically coordinated system of trade and security. The "Canadian colonies" were therefore more centrally governed and directly administered than the American colonies had been governed before the war. Most importantly, the Crown's subjects in the remainder of British North America generally supported this, given the fact that they had fled from the revolt and (ostensibly) favoured, rather than resented, British authority.

To quote Mancke on this point,

> What set the Loyalists apart from their American Patriot counterparts was not so much ideology, but a far greater acceptance of a stronger imperial state. In the years leading up to armed revolt and independence, prominent Loyalists had urged Patriots to adjust to the enlarged state presence in the internal affairs of the colonies, and to recognize the need for a more administratively and fiscally integrated empire.[14]

In sum, the statism that developed in British North America after the federation of the Thirteen Colonies amounted to the timely joining together on Canadian soil of two elements: (1) the creation of a newly designed, more centralist imperial project; and, (2) the presence of compliant subjects who chose or were obliged to live under its authority.

Thus, within Canada itself, the statism that marked the exercise of political authority in New France was carried over into the era of British imperial rule, despite the differences in the domestic structures of authority within the two colonizing countries. Britain and France were quite different politically but did not act all that differently as colonial powers, especially in the colonies that eventually became Canada. The degree of economic and political centralization inherent in (and inherited from) the fur trade centred on Montreal

---

[14] Mancke 17.

was complemented by the pattern of political authority that both the French and the British felt it necessary to establish in their newly acquired provinces of Canada and Nova Scotia.

SMALL MARKET, LARGE OVERHEADS, AND THE CANADIAN STATE

Canada's "genetic statism" became even more deeply entrenched as the new British colonial authority extended its control over essentially the same economic geography that had called for a centralized strategy of economic development under the French. There were some early indications of the continuing costs and problems that British government had to contend with. Records in the archives of the Canadian Post Office provide examples of this as they reach all the way back to the brief period when both the former New France and the Thirteen Colonies were governed together as parts of British North America, that is, from 1763 to the American War of Independence in 1776.

One document quotes from a report that Benjamin Franklin, then Deputy Postmaster-General of North America, sent to the Imperial Government in 1766:

> The posts generally travel along the sea coasts and only in a few cases do they go back into the country. Between Quebec and Montreal there is only one post per month. The inhabitants live so scattered and remote from each other in that vast country that the posts cannot be supported among them.[15]

Franklin appears to have grasped about communications in Canada what Innis later wrote about them, namely, that Canada's systems of transportation and communication were inescapably expensive and

---

[15] Anonymous, quoting Benjamin Franklin, "A History of the Mails," *Records of the Post Office* Vol. 3296 (Ottawa, ON: National Archives of Canada, n.d. [probably 1861]).

problematic.[16] For Innis, this inefficiency resulted from the "unused capacity" that was unavoidably present in all of the nation-wide systems that provide Canada's social and economic infrastructure.[17] He argued that Canada inevitably overbuilds its infrastructural systems because their minimally viable scale inevitably exceeds the capacity required by its small and scattered population and its relatively low level of economic activity. To put it another way, as a result of indivisibilities in the systems created to provide infrastructural services across such a vast country, the capacity of even a barely sustainable, all-Canadian system must exceed the Canadian demand for its services, resulting in either unacceptably high costs of service or substantial government support.

Moreover, the inefficiency of Canada's infrastructure was a factor in the tendency of Canadian users of communication and transportation services to bypass Canadian systems, that is, to route their traffic through lower-cost systems operating in the US. At any rate, the anonymous author of "A History of the Mails" recorded that, as late as 1851, the mails from Canada West (Ontario) to the United Kingdom, "instead of passing by way of Montreal were conveyed by the more direct route through the United States...."[18] It is evident from this that, in offering public services, Canadian authorities have traditionally had to find ways to meet the interconnected problems of overbuilding and bypass, whether with respect to traditional postal services, transportation services, contemporary courier and telephone services, or advanced modes of data transmission such as fibre optic cable.

---

[16] Thus, we can compare Franklin's observation to this statement, over 200 years later, by the then chairman of Bell Canada Enterprises, in answer to a question about the prospects for open, US-style competition in the Canadian telecommunications industry: "I think we have to be very careful in Canada. If we permit too much competition in telecommunications, the quality of service will deteriorate very quickly ... To say that they have allowed competition in the United States and it should be the same in Canada is being very unrealistic. They have a population ten times ours and they have a network. We don't have a network, we have a corridor...." See A. Jean de Grandpré, "Adjusting to Win," interview, *The Canadian Business Review* 16, 4 (Winter 1989): 11.

[17] See Harold Innis, "Unused Capacity as a Factor in Canadian Economic History," in Daniel Drache, ed., *Staples, Markets and Cultural Change: Selected Essays* (Montreal and Kingston: McGill-Queen's University Press, 1995) Ch. 8.

[18] Anonymous, note 9.

This task has never been a simple one. It is true that the economic problems complicating the creation of national systems of transportation and communication could be surmounted with either public ownership or massive government loans to the private entrepreneurs undertaking such developments, and they often have been. However, the economic problems did not end there; at least two other forms of support proved necessary. Depending on the system concerned, Canadian governments have also had to provide further subsidies for the ongoing operation of these systems (or to underwrite their losses, if they were government-owned). Beyond this, they have frequently had to establish a set of protective regulations to prevent them from being taken over by foreign interests or losing their markets to American-centred systems extending their operations into Canada. In this way, a Canadian government tradition of "regulatory protectionism" can be seen as the opposite side of the coin of the more commonly studied Canadian tradition of "defensive expansionism."[19]

Chapter 5 will argue that harmonization of Canadian and American policies under NAFTA is certain to impose more significant political adjustments upon Canada than upon the US. Although that argument is not relevant to the present discussion, the ground for it is. As we have just seen, the development of the Canadian economy has depended upon discriminatory national policies and regulations to ensure that it was established and maintained as a *national* (as opposed to continental) economy. In addition, majority foreign ownership of key service industries was forbidden, most notably, in transportation, communications, and banking.

Thus, to over-generalize slightly, Canada has traditionally relied on an array of legislative and regulatory instruments—government ownership, foreign-ownership restrictions, national subsidies, and regulatory barriers to entry—to pre-empt, forbid, or severely limit either foreign ownership of, or competition with, a significant number of Canadian industries. (The legislation typically specified "foreign" ownership or

---

[19] The definitive treatment of this theme is found in H.G.J. Aitken, "Defensive Expansionism: The State and Economic Growth in Canada," in W.T. Easterbrook and M.H. Watkins, eds., *Approaches to Canadian Economic History* (Toronto: McClelland and Stewart, 1967) 183-221.

competition, but the target was almost invariably American.) It is the essence of such policies that they discriminate in favour of national over foreign firms and investors, and all of them represent forms of discrimination that are contrary to the "national treatment" ethos embedded in NAFTA, which insists that national policies extend identical terms and conditions to nationals and foreigners alike.

In fact, a separate economic system north of the American one could not have existed—or could not have persisted for very long—if those in command of the Canadian economy during and after the British colonial era had not engaged massively in the kind of discriminatory and protective policies that are now ruled out by NAFTA. The tradition of such policies goes back a long way, given that the British takeover of Canada simply meant that the continental fur trading system developed under the French fell under British control. It remained the overarching ambition of the Montreal commercial class to monopolize the movement of goods between the North American interior and Europe, the only difference being that agricultural products began to overtake furs as the dominant export commodity. In short, the "commercial empire of the St. Lawrence" was to be, like the fur trade preceding it, a continental project.

However, the fur trade itself had shown that the success of this ambition was threatened by competition from rival, American-controlled trade and transportation systems. The earliest signs of this concern are to be found in British regulations that were introduced during the American War of Independence to restrict navigation on the Great Lakes to "the king's own vessels," and they remained in force until well after the cessation of hostilities. According to the governor of Canada, the extension of this prohibition after the war was aimed at the preservation of the fur trade centred on Montreal, his fear being that commercial shipping on the Great Lakes would facilitate the transportation of goods and furs through American lake ports.[20] This fear, moreover,

---

[20] While these regulations were abandoned in 1788, progress in commercial vessels remained slow until the end of the War of 1812-15, and lake shipping was dominated by military craft. See G.P. de T. Glazebrook, *A History of Transportation in Canada*, Foreword by H.A. Innis (Toronto: The Ryerson Press, 1938) 31-32. See also Harold A. Innis, *The Fur Trade in Canada: An Introduction to Canadian Economic History*, rev. ed. (Toronto: University of Toronto Press, 1956) 180-85.

foreshadowed the approaching era of canal-building in Canada, as well as the later move to construct a transcontinental railway.

The American construction of the Erie Canal and the Canadian construction of the Welland Canal were strategic moves in a fundamental rivalry between the cities of New York and Montreal to dominate the trade generated by the westward march of the North American frontier. As an early promoter of the Welland Canal put it, if a canal linking Lakes Ontario and Erie (to get past Niagara Falls) were built on Canadian soil, it would allow Canada to counteract "the American scheme" and "take down the whole produce from the Western country."[21] Later, the same logic applied to an even more ambitious project, the transcontinental railway. An economic "grand strategy" was under way in British North America, namely, the defensive expansion of Canadian systems in order to pre-empt American penetration of Canadian territory.

Unfortunately, the Canadian systems designed to do this were largely unnecessary in purely economic terms, given that the services they were constructed to provide could have been more efficiently provided by marginal extensions into Canada of systems operating in the US. Even despite the gradual eclipse of the fur trade, the definitive character of Canadian systems of transportation and communication had been set by it: the transcontinental building of railways, broadcasting networks, long-distance telephone networks, airlines, highways, communications satellites, and pipelines. While the promotion of these systems has been the hallmark of Canadian nation-building, one of their most consistent economic features has been the contestability of the Canadian market for their services.

In sum, the Canadian government has adopted various strategic uses of the central state to prevent the encroachment of more efficient American-centred systems on the markets of existing Canadian

---

[21] As quoted Glazebrook 85. For a superb recapitulation and reconceptualization of the early history of the state and transportation development in Canada, see Easterbrook 172-78 and 186-89.

systems. This is all the more understandable in view of the fact that, typically, the protected Canadian system was initially established as a deliberate attempt to pre-empt the intrusion into Canada of American-centred systems. Most frequently, when the government has faced a need to pre-empt American intrusion into Canadian markets not yet served by any Canadian network, it has adopted what is often called the "chosen instrument" approach to the problem of encroachment.

Most of the time, the instrument chosen has been a government-owned corporation, with the Canadian Broadcasting Corporation (CBC) and Trans-Canada Airlines (later renamed Air Canada) providing two prime examples. According to Marc Raboy, the idea for the CBC—a publicly owned, monopolistic, nation-wide radio network—came from a visit to the National Broadcasting Company in New York by members of the Royal Commission on Radio Broadcasting in 1928 when the commissioners learned that the American radio network planned to "cover" Canada as "part of the North American radio orbit."[22]

It is perhaps no coincidence that Graham Spry chose this occasion to support the creation of a national government-owned radio network by coining his famous observation that Canadians faced a choice "between the State and the United States."[23] Similar considerations, according to Garth Stevenson, motivated the government in the 1930s to establish air services across Canada:

> It was considered necessary to link the scattered regions of Canada together and to do so without reliance on the United States. Given the proximity of Canada's major cities to the border, and the fact that the shortest lines between southern Ontario and the major cities of western Canada run through U.S. territory, it would be easy for airlines in the United States to tap Canadian traffic....[24]

---

[22] See Marc Raboy, *Missed Opportunities: The Story of Canada's Broadcasting Policy* (Montreal and Kingston: McGill-Queen's University Press, 1990) 23.

[23] Quoted in Raboy 40. Spry, perhaps Canada's most vocal advocate of government-controlled national radio, was addressing the House of Commons Special Committee on Radio Broadcasting in 1932.

[24] See Garth Stevenson, *The Politics of Canada's Airlines from Diefenbaker to Mulroney* (Toronto: University of Toronto Press, 1987) 10-11.

On other occasions, and in different circumstances, the policy instrument has been a private corporation acting with significant support
from the federal government, of which the CPR and the TransCanada
PipeLine are perhaps the best examples. To expand briefly on the less
familiar pipeline case, in the mid-1950s, when the trans-Canada natural gas transmission system was still at a conceptual stage, American
natural gas pipeline systems were on the verge of expanding into
Ontario and Quebec. Government regulatory and financial support for TransCanada was required to ensure that American-based
pipeline companies did not capture these markets before a Canadian-
based system had the opportunity to do so.[25]

In sum, Canadian elites have (until recently) consistently
defied the economic analysis of Benjamin Franklin, despite constant
pressure from the economic and geographic factors he put his finger
on. They accomplished this through a sustained commitment to the
existence of an autonomous community on the northern half of the
North American continent. The provision and protection of Canadian-
controlled, Canada-wide networks of transportation and communication seemed such an integral part of this goal that allowing these
systems to fail was tantamount to the abandonment of the original British North American project, along with the commercial
opportunities it entailed. However, a new version of the "Franklin
challenge" has recently arrived in the form of a revolutionary
change in communications technology. As discussed in Chapter 9, it
is not clear that Canadian elites still possess the will or the capacity
to protect existing Canadian communications systems in these new
circumstances.

---

[25] For a detailed discussion of the circumstances surrounding the TransCanada
project, see H.G.J. Aitken, "The Midwestern Case: Canadian Gas and the Federal
Power Commission," *Canadian Journal of Economics and Political Science* 25, 2 (May
1959): 129-43. I have discussed the TransCanada case in the context of Canadian
economic nationalism in *Fuels and the National Policy* (Toronto: Butterworths,
1982) Chs. 4 and 8. It is generally known that the government of John A. Macdonald
extended massive support to Canada's first transcontinental railway (the Canadian
Pacific Railway) because of similar concerns that the American Northern Pacific
Railroad was threatening to penetrate the Canadian west.

CANADA'S EARLY INDUSTRIALIZATION

So far, this brief history of Canadian economic development has focused almost exclusively on resource-based industries and the transportation and communications infrastructure created to promote them. This emphasis is appropriate given that the development of large-scale manufacturing in Canada came relatively late and remained relatively weak compared with the US. However, Canada's industrialization cannot be entirely ignored, although investigation of it here will necessarily be restricted to three broad themes: (1) the extreme geographic concentration of Canada's industrial development; (2) the very heavy reliance of Canadian manufacturing industries on American capital, technology, and, to a lesser extent, markets; and (3) the role of national policies in bringing about these characteristics.

Canada's manufacturing economy is limited almost exclusively to southern and southwestern Ontario (one of the regions that the original TCE essentially omitted). Iain Wallace, a Canadian economic geographer, has noted that "Canada did not develop the regional-scale concentrations that dominated the industrial geography of Western Europe and the northeastern United States from the late nineteenth to the mid-twentieth centuries." In keeping with the staples-based tradition, he adds:

> Most resource-processing plants (smelters, pulp mills, petrochemical producers, etc.) ship their output to distant fabricators; and it is only in the Montreal region and in southern and southwestern Ontario (approximately from Oshawa to Windsor and from Niagara Falls to Barrie) that one finds large and long-established concentrations of diversified manufacturing. [26]

Moreover, southwestern Ontario is so close to the automotive industries in and around Detroit, Michigan, that its share of Canadian manufacturing is concentrated further in the automobile sector. In

---

[26] Iain Wallace, *A Geography of the Canadian Economy* (Don Mills, ON: Oxford University Press, 2002) 69-70.

the late 1980s, for example, "passenger autos & chassis," "motor vehicle parts excluding engines," and "trucks, truck tractors & chassis" ranked first, second, and fourth (respectively) among 20 of Canada's leading manufactured and resource-based exports, accounting for roughly 37 per cent of the total value of the top 20 categories.[27] (The bulk of the remaining categories were resource-based commodities such as softwood lumber, petroleum, and natural gas.)

Apart from this degree of regional and industrial concentration, early Canadian manufacturing also represented a high concentration of foreign, especially American, investment. One of the strongest and simplest explanations for this is that the tariff protection afforded Canadian manufacturing industries by the National Policy made American goods (in particular) more expensive in the Canadian market, leaving the provision of such goods largely to producers operating within Canada. Those producers, however, did not have to be Canadian-owned, and from the earliest days of the National Policy, but especially after the First World War, American firms learned how to substitute foreign investment in Canada for exports to Canada. In short, American manufacturing firms "hopped over the tariff wall" by establishing branch plants to sell directly in the Canadian market. As early as 1920, American investment stood at over 60 per cent of the total investment in such Canadian industries as paints, drugs, and chemicals; petroleum refining; and automobiles and auto accessories.[28]

More recent levels of American investment, and an analysis of the problems associated with foreign control of key Canadian industries, are provided in later sections of this chapter. However, it is important to understand the contribution that Canada's reliance on a strategy of "import substitution industrialization" (ISI) has made to its overall dependence upon the US for capital, technology, and (more recently) exports. As Glen Williams states, the ISI model

---

[27] Canada, *Summary of Canadian International Trade* (Ottawa, ON: Statistics Canada, December 1988). Percentages were calculated by the author.

[28] See Glen Williams, *Not for Export: Toward a Political Economy of Canada's Arrested Industrialization* (Toronto: McClelland and Stewart, 1983) 29, Table Two.

relies on a tariff structure as an instrument for domestic manufacturers to capture primarily consumer-oriented sectors of the
home market with a production process borrowed from foreign
industrialists. Its two major components, import replacement
and technological dependence, when fused, produce an industrial structure with little potential to grow beyond its domestic
horizons.[29]

Moreover, Williams suggests, there is a strong link between the adoption of an ISI strategy and the staples-based economy onto which it
was grafted: given its preoccupation with the export of resources
(including agricultural products) and the infrastructure to facilitate
them, "industrialization was placed basically in the position of being
an afterthought of capitalist expansion in Canada."[30]

One final point stressed by Williams brings us to the third theme
concerning Canada's process of industrialization, the role of national
policies. Again, the next section of this chapter has more to say about
this topic, but Williams's analysis helps to show how a favourable
view of American ownership of the Canadian economy, and closer
economic ties with the US more generally, almost became an official
part of Canada's public philosophy in the post-Second World War
period. Of course, that war and its aftermath saw an enormous expansion of both Canadian industrial capacity *and* foreign ownership:
between 1938 and 1968, the value of Canada's manufacturing output
rose by 600 per cent, while in the two decades after the war the book
value of foreign investment increased by 700 per cent. The problem
was—from the standpoint of the later public debate on foreign control
and as Williams points out—Canada's economic and political elite
generally believed that the latter *caused* the former.[31] The conviction
grew that Canada's continued economic expansion was contingent
on a favourable climate for foreign direct investment, a conviction
that not only fostered decades more of even higher levels of foreign

[29] Williams 13.
[30] Williams 32.
[31] Williams 103.

control, but also found its way eventually into the sections of the FTA guaranteeing the rights of investors.

CANADIAN ECONOMIC DEVELOPMENT FROM THE SECOND WORLD WAR TO THE FREE TRADE ERA

To this point, the story of the evolution of North American economic integration has stressed Canada's attempts to impede the process through various forms of state intervention. This section takes up an opposing theme: the government of Canada's welcome embrace of one of the key engines of such integration, the American-based multinational corporation (MNC).

As we have seen, Canada began to industrialize well before the Second World War. However, the Canadian and American demand for manufactured products during the war, and the rapid increase in incomes and consumer expenditures that followed it, gave an enormous boost to the country's manufacturing sector. The same factors stimulated an expansion of several of its resource-based industries as well. Thus, access to the American market and the availability of capital from American-controlled firms with an interest in Canada played a major role in the expansion of both sectors. The significance of this fact in the context of the economic dimension of the Canada-US relationship is that, on the whole for Canada, industrialization has meant Americanization. More than that, most of the Americanization that took place during the two decades following the Second World War was subsidized by tax breaks from the Canadian government.

In retrospect, this same period—that is, roughly the late 1940s to the late 1960s—can be viewed as the time of a crucial upsurge in the long-term process of the Americanization of the Canadian economy that stretches all the way back to the 1920s, a process involving both increased trade and investment dependence on a single economic partner. As mentioned in Chapter 2, shortly after the First World War, the US replaced Britain as both a major destination for Canadian exports and the major source of its foreign capital. Canada-US economic transactions during the war itself clearly provided the hinge of this transition. In 1913, investment from Britain represented 73 per cent of total foreign investment in Canada, while the US represented only 22 per cent. By 1926, Britain's share had dropped to 44 per cent and the American share had risen to 53 per cent. Over the same period, direct foreign investment grew significantly relative to portfolio investment, increasing from 20 per cent to 30 per cent of all foreign investment. By 1952, direct investment represented exactly half of all foreign investment, and American investment represented 77 per cent of total Canadian foreign investment.[32]

Meanwhile, a shift in the axis of Canada's foreign trade paralleled these capital flows. In 1901, trade with Britain represented (in round numbers) 41 per cent of Canada's total trade, while trade with the US represented 43 per cent.[33] By 1926, this slight margin in favour of the US had widened to a substantial gap, with Britain dropping to 27 per cent and the US rising to 50 per cent. By 1952, the numbers had continued on the same trend, with Britain falling further to 13 per cent and the US rising to 63 per cent. In terms of Canada's dependence on the US specifically for its exports, it stood at 26 per cent of total exports in 1901, 36 per cent in 1926, and 53 per cent in 1952. Since thus passing the 50 per cent mark a half-century ago, this concentration of exports in a single foreign market has marched steadily toward the current figure of over 80 per cent.

Crudely stated, Canada's economic independence of the US suffered a "double whammy" during the period following the end of the Second World War. In fact, it might be argued that free trade with the US had become almost inescapable by the mid-1980s because of Canadian policy failures during those years. The validity of that interpretation rests on the degree to which the commanding presence of foreign-controlled companies in so many of Canada's industrial

---

[32] Percentages calculated from data provided in Levitt 66, Table 3.
[33] Trade percentages were calculated by the author from data provided in M.C. Urquhart and K.A.H. Buckley, eds., *Historical Statistics of Canada* (Toronto: Macmillan, 1965) 181-83, Series F334-341, F342-347, and F348-356.

sectors has fundamentally undermined Canada's capacity to remain economically independent. Views on that question—the economic and political costs of relying so heavily on foreign investment for economic development—tend to divide along lines similar to the debate between nationalists and integrationists reviewed in Chapter 1. Economic nationalists were highly critical of the *political* impact of foreign investment on Canada, while the integrationists saw foreign investment as a politically neutral way of overcoming a chronic shortage of investment capital.

That debate will not be rehashed here. However, it is important to appreciate how the Canadian economy become so beholden to American corporations during the second half of the last century, the extent to which that happened, and how it may have helped to weaken structurally the Canadian economy to the point where the country had no choice but to accept a trade and investment deal with the US. We will now turn to answering these questions, leaving to Chapter 5 a discussion of the role which MNCs may have played politically in Canada's decision to adopt the FTA and NAFTA.

Government Policies and the Expansion of American Investment in Canada

David Wolfe argues that the main stimulus to the growth of American investment in Canada was the postwar tax policies of the government of Canada, although that was not the primary intent of those policies.[34] The main culprits were the government's absolute priority on maximum growth of the economy and the belief that the best way to achieve this goal was through public inducements to private investors. Wolfe traces the early history of accelerated depreciation rates along with a variety of other incentives to stimulate growth, all of

---

[34] David A. Wolfe, "Economic Growth and Foreign Investment: A Perspective on Canadian Economic Policy, 1945-1957," *Journal of Canadian Studies* 13, 1 (Spring, 1978): 3-20.

them focused on the balance sheets of private firms. Foreign investors were not the specific target of these policies, but in the immediate aftermath of the war, American investors were in a much better position than Canadian or other foreign ones to take full advantage of the incentives on offer.

Wolfe summarizes the connection between the government's taxation (and trade) policies of the postwar period and the expansion of foreign control of the Canadian economy as follows:

> The two key government policies of selling off wartime production facilities at reduced prices and of permitting accelerated depreciation allowances were both instrumental in encouraging a high degree of foreign participation in the growth of the Canadian economy. A large number of government plants were sold to foreign enterprises and the accelerated depreciation allowances, which provided one of the fastest rates of tax write-off in any western economy, were a strong incentive to foreign investors. However, the import control policy, instituted in 1947, represented the most direct attempt by the government to induce foreign manufacturers to locate in Canada. In the minds of the government's economic policy-makers the primary goal of the controls was "import substitution." The Emergency Exchange Conservation Act was designed to encourage the substitution of domestically manufactured products for imported consumer goods, frequently through the establishment of a branch plant in Canada by the foreign manufacturer.

He goes on to say that there can be no doubt that it was the explicit goal of the government to provide "an attractive inducement for encouraging increased industrial expansion and foreign investment in Canada." Growth was the objective, business investment was the means, and "the origin of the investment capital, whether from domestic or foreign sources, was clearly a subsidiary question, if it was raised at all." [35]

---

[35] Wolfe 7.

Wolfe proceeds to argue that capital cost allowances and deferred taxes provided a substantial portion of the "total expansion funds" of foreign-controlled enterprises in Canada. In so doing, he documents the role of the Canadian government in deepening the dependence of the country on the US. His analysis largely agrees with Maureen Molot's summation of the relationship between the economics and politics of foreign control:

> Economic growth in Canada since the Second World War has depended significantly on inflows of foreign investment, direct and portfolio, but these same capital flows have helped to shape an economy characterized by high levels of foreign ownership in some of its most dynamic sectors, and by regional balkanization and closer economic ties between some of its constituent parts and the U.S. than among them. As the Canadian economy has expanded, the structural constraints on the capacity of the national government to direct and regulate it have similarly grown.[36]

We will examine in more detail the structural impact of decades of foreign direct investment under the stimulus and guidance of Canadian economic policies later in this chapter. For the moment, however, it is important to review how extensive foreign control of the country's economy had become by the early 1970s, when the government began to pay attention to it.

The Extent of American Control of Canadian Industry

In 1970, the government of Canada commissioned a comprehensive study, commonly referred to as the Gray Report, of foreign-controlled

---

[36] Maureen A. Molot, "The Political Implications of North American Capital Flows," in John H. Pammet and Brian W. Tomlin, eds., *The Integration Question: Political Economy and Public Policy in Canada and North America* (Don Mills, ON: Addison-Wesley, 1984) 178, Ch. 19.

corporations in Canada.[37] The topic had been a source of controversy for almost two decades, and the debate reached a crescendo in the late 1960s. It seems likely that the government that ordered the study—the first administration of Prime Minister Pierre Trudeau, elected in 1968—felt that public concern over the issue had reached the point where it could become a source of political damage and thus saw an inquiry as the beginning of a tangible response to public pressure on the issue. Numerous other, more limited studies had been published over the previous 15 years, but most observers then and since consider the Gray Report to be the most comprehensive and detailed one available. It ran to over 500 pages and presented 59 tables of data on a sweeping range of subjects relating to the extent of foreign investment in Canadian industries and the performance of foreign-controlled firms.

At the aggregate level, the report showed that American capital invested in selected major Canadian industries had grown from $6.9 billion to $19.9 billion between 1954 and 1967, representing an increase in the share of American control of these industries from 24 to 28 per cent.[38] While some might look at these figures and wonder what all the fuss was about, the more telling story lay in the numbers showing the extent of American control of some key sectors of the Canadian economy. For example, as of 1967, American investors (usually companies headquartered in the US) controlled 45 per cent of all Canadian manufacturing, 60 per cent of petroleum and natural gas, and 56 per cent of mining and smelting.[39] In specific industries, the share of non-resident (American and other foreign) ownership of total assets ran even higher: 84 per cent of the tobacco industry, 99 per cent of rubber, 71 per cent of machinery, 86 per cent of transport equipment, 64 per cent of electrical products, 99 per cent of petroleum and coal products, 39 per cent of paper and allied products and 81 per cent of chemicals and chemical products.[40]

---

[37] Government of Canada, *Foreign Direct Investment in Canada* (Ottawa: Information Canada, 1972).
[38] Government of Canada 16, Table 2.
[39] Government of Canada 20, Table 4.
[40] Government of Canada 21, Table 5.

The Performance of Foreign-controlled Firms

More important than these raw numbers, however, were the effects that such high percentages of foreign control of businesses had on the functioning of the Canadian economy. Here, too, the Gray Report proved to be a valuable source of information. (One of the six parts of the report, comprising 13 of its 27 chapters, was devoted to "The Impact of Foreign Direct Investment.") Simply to review the subjects explored by individual chapters of Part Four of the report conveys the range of Canadians' concerns about the consequences of American ownership for their country. The report investigated all of the alleged problems associated with foreign-controlled subsidiaries operating in Canada: export performance, procurement policies and import practices, and transfer pricing and tax administration.

Beyond these questions concerning the economic performance of foreign-controlled firms, there were still broader issues, each receiving a chapter's worth of attention, relating to secondary effects on government and the wider economy and society: the balance of payments, monetary policy, the behaviour of Canadian-controlled firms, Canadian culture and society, political processes and public policy, the formation and conduct of Canadian foreign policy and relations, and the adequacy of economic information. Other chapters in Part Four examined further matters connected to foreign ownership, such as the use of government procurement, grants and loans, and tax policy; the impact of certain foreign laws and policies ("extraterritoriality"); and the relations between the host and home governments of foreign-controlled firms. As if this were not enough, still other parts of the report delved into such ramifications of foreign control as the level of spending on R&D in Canada by both foreign- and Canadian-controlled firms and the quality of business management in the country.

Given the extraordinarily wide range of these effects of foreign control, it is impossible here to summarize them or to assess the arguments concerning the balance of costs and benefits associated with

each. To highlight several key points, the Gray Report concluded that
the foreign control of Canadian firms:[41]

> ▪ has no negative, and possibly a positive effect on export per-
> formance. Parent firms and their other, non-Canadian affili-
> ates are frequently the buyers of the output of Canadian firms.
> Some multinationals assign worldwide product mandates to
> their Canadian subsidiaries, which improves their export op-
> portunities beyond those available to otherwise comparable
> Canadian firms.
> ▪ has a measurable detrimental effect on Canada's trade bal-
> ance by promoting imports. Canadian subsidiaries of foreign-
> controlled firms source a wide range of inputs from the foreign
> parent firm and/or its other, non-Canadian affiliates, often to
> the detriment of otherwise competitive Canadian suppliers of
> those same inputs.
> ▪ allows for the practice of transfer pricing, whereby the prices
> charged by the Canadian subsidiary for its exports to foreign
> affiliates, as well as the prices charged by foreign affiliates for
> imports by the Canadian firm, are set arbitrarily and often to
> the detriment of the (apparent) net earnings of the Canadian
> firm. This practice, which includes over-pricing for such im-
> ported inputs as components, R&D, licences, and managerial
> fees, has serious implications for Canadian tax receipts and tax
> policy, since the operations of the Canadian subsidiary can earn
> substantial profits for the parent corporation while showing no
> taxable profits within Canada.
> ▪ benefits the Canadian subsidiary, and indirectly the Canadian
> economy, by acting as conduits for industrial R&D, although
> this very availability may also act to suppress levels of R&D
> in Canada, both within and without the foreign-controlled
> segments of industry.

---

[41] See Government of Canada 417-28. The following list presents a selection and
paraphrasing of the report's own conclusions on the effects of foreign control. The
report itself contained no such point-by-point summary.

▶ benefits the Canadian subsidiary, and indirectly the Canadian economy, with the supply of foreign managers, or with the training of Canadian managers at the parent company or in foreign subsidiaries of the international firm. However, as with R&D, this can have a depressing effect on the local development of managers.

▶ promotes or prohibits actions by the subsidiary in conformity with American law, leading to potential conflict with Canadian law.

▶ promotes or prohibits action by the subsidiary in conformity with the expressed interests of the parent corporation, quite apart from the requirements of American law, complicating and frustrating enforcement of domestic laws. Taxation and competition legislation, in particular, can be adversely affected in this manner.

Apart from these specific conclusions concerning the impact of foreign control, the Gray Report drew a more general conclusion that foreign direct investment represented a set or package of economic factors and that this package of factors represented a mix of potential costs and benefits to host countries like Canada, depending on the policy environment established by government. The report therefore recommended that the government consider the establishment of a review agency to screen out types of foreign investments that might do Canada more harm than good and to set conditions upon the performance of firms created or taken over by foreign corporations.[42] Most critics of foreign control, however, felt that neither the report nor the government action that followed it went far enough in correcting the disadvantageous effects of MNCs operating in Canada.

---

[42] This was one of the most widely debated recommendations of the Gray Report and one which the government did implement with the creation of the Foreign Investment Review Agency (FIRA).

ECONOMIC POLICY FAILURES AND
THE PROBLEMS OF FOREIGN CONTROL

One critic in particular dismissed the idea of a foreign investment review agency as largely beside the point. Eric Kierans, one of the most
vocal and well-known Canadian economic nationalists of the 1970s,
felt that the problems foreign control created for the Canadian economy could not be eliminated or mitigated through policies aimed at
the foreign-controlled firms themselves, but rather required a wholesale change in Canadian economic policies generally. Kierans was the
owner of a small but successful manufacturing firm and a classic economic liberal at heart, someone who believed in free trade and open
capital markets. As President of the Montreal Stock Exchange in 1963,
he strongly opposed regulations placed on foreign investment by an
earlier champion of economic nationalism, Walter Gordon. However, in 1966, Kierans became highly critical of American investment
in Canada because, in his estimation, the US had begun to treat its
MNCs as instruments of American foreign policy.[43]

In that year, the American government had issued a new set of "guide-
lines" for American firms operating abroad, mostly designed to ensure
that they would bring more of the profits they earned abroad back home.
Kierans feared that American parent companies would make their business decisions and those of their foreign subsidiaries, including a large
number in Canada, according to the course set by the American government, rather than according to their own commercial interests and the
signals they were receiving from the Canadian and global marketplaces.
In this case, Kierans argued, American-owned firms in Canada would
begin to act like "Trojan horses," that is, like foreign intruders invited
in under false assumptions about their willingness and capacity to act
according to Canadian economic interests and national policies.

However, Kierans's primary complaint was not with the policies of the American government, but rather with those of his own.

---

[43] See John N. McDougall, *The Politics and Economics of Eric Kierans: A Man for All
    Canadas* (Montreal and Kingston: Queen's University Press, 1993), Ch. 8. The
    entire discussion of Kierans's policy critique is taken from this source.

During his years as a minister in the first government of Pierre Trudeau, he had become extremely dissatisfied with its economic policies. His main complaint was that Canadian taxation favoured "extractive" industries over manufacturing, promoted the interests of large-sized corporations over small and medium-sized businesses, and encouraged rather than impeded foreign takeovers of Canadian firms. He was also concerned that, broadly speaking, the Canadian tax system subsidized capital investment, mostly by already large corporations, at the expense of "social investment" and tax relief for individual Canadians. In his own words,

> Canadian experience in using the tax system to achieve swift growth has not been a happy one. The choice of factors of production has been distorted. Favouring capital favours not only those with capital, foreigners, but regions where capital normally locates, adding to concentration and inflation in high growth areas ... Social investment, if the taxes had been paid, could have been more productive and beneficial.[44]

Kierans was particularly opposed to Canadian finance ministers giving "gifts" to large corporations in the form of generous capital cost allowances. He noted that the use of this sort of fiscal instrument had a long history in Canada. For example, in 1955, the budget of Walter Harris ushered in the strongest investment boom in Canada's history to that point, by making "a permanent part of our law" special tax provisions for oil, mining, and oil and gas industries. While he was at it, Harris introduced the practice of permitting corporations to report depreciation to *shareholders* on the basis of actual wear and tear but to record depreciation to *tax authorities* on the basis of maximum tax advantage under regulations. As a result, profit as recorded on the books of corporations began to diverge sharply from income reported for income tax purposes.

These policies were all extensions of the postwar Liberal approach to Canadian economic development addressed by Wolfe earlier in

---

[44] Quoted in McDougall, *Politics and Economics of Eric Kierans* 165-66.

this chapter. Kierans's main theme, however, was the way in which both high unemployment and foreign ownership were the product of these misguided approaches to Canada's economic problems:

> Some [Canadian economists] have again called for investment stimulants or incentives. I am completely opposed to them as providing a solution to Canada's long-term chronic unemployment problems. I also believe that they have contributed more than any other single policy to the concentration of American ownership that now exists in Canada. In other words, it is not what the Americans have done to us but what we have done to ourselves.[45]

Kierans drove home his point by means of a set of tables that were designed to reveal just how deep a hole Canadian governments had been digging themselves into for the past 25 years. The first of these tables compared the book profit of corporations (as reported to shareholders) with their taxable income for the years 1965-68, which revealed that taxable income represented 60 per cent of book profits in 1968 and that the comparable percentages for the other three years ranged between 56 and 59 per cent. A second table depicted the distortive effects of such practices, particularly among industrial groups, by comparing book profit before taxes and taxable income, by selected industries, aggregated over the years 1965-68. It showed that, among seven different industries, taxable income as a percentage of book profit ranged from a high of 90 per cent for "Retail Trade" to a low of 5.7 per cent for "Mineral Fuels." "Manufacturing" was at 63 per cent; "Metal mining" was at 13 per cent.

To sum up, Kierans—along with numerous other critics such as University of Toronto political economist Mel Watkins and New Democratic Party (NDP) leader David Lewis—felt that Canadian economic policies were encouraging corporate concentration, promoting the takeover of Canadian firms by American MNCs, and subsidizing through the tax system the exploitation of Canadian natural

---

[45] Quoted in McDougall, *Politics and Economics of Eric Kierans* 159-60.

resources for export to the US. It is not necessary to prove that these critics were right and that all Canadian governments between 1945 and 1984 were wrong in order to establish the validity of two critical points about American control of the Canadian economy. First, if it is in fact proper to talk about an "American takeover" of Canada, the role of Canadian government policies in permitting, if not promoting that process must be acknowledged. As Kierans emphasized, Americans did nothing to Canadians, Canadians did it to themselves.

Second, successive Canadian governments did not lead Canadians blindly down this path. The central issues were actively debated for at least a decade and—as notably in the case of the NDP—figured prominently during the 1972 national election. That election returned the Trudeau Liberals to power, but as a minority government. The Foreign Investment Review Agency (FIRA), along with the so-called Third Option (see below), was the result. However, within two years, Trudeau sought and achieved a majority mandate. By 1975, his finance minister, John Turner, brought in a major budget initiative that decisively placed the Liberals back on the trajectory that Wolfe and Kierans had found so detrimental to the prospects for an independent Canadian economy.

THE "THIRD OPTION" versus DEEPER INTEGRATION WITH THE US

The point has just been made that the Canadian government's heavy reliance on foreign investment in the quest for economic growth did not pass without significant public debate and even played a vital role in at least one national election. To that extent, it can be said that Canadians generally were conscious of their growing dependence on the US as a source of capital and as a trading partner, and many were becoming anxious about it. Beyond this, however, for a brief period the Liberal government itself made a conscious and deliberate attempt to reverse the tide of Americanization of the Canadian economy. It seems more than a coincidence that they did this in 1973: following the 1972 election, they were a minority government dependent on support from the NDP and its leader, David Lewis. However, some observers believe the "Nixon Economic Package" of 1971—in which the American president flexed his country's economic muscle against its major trading partners in order to reform the international financial system and improve the sliding American balance of payments deficit—gave a jolt to Liberal complacency as well. Nevertheless, it is significant that at that time and in those circumstances, the government explicitly chose "another way" than deepening dependence upon the US. This choice, short-lived though it was, deserves some attention.

The "Third Option" represents the high-water mark of concern by the Liberal government over Canada's economic vulnerability to conditions and policies in the US. At issue was the degree of integration Canada wished to have with its southern neighbour, economically, culturally, and politically. The alternative courses of action were spelled out in a major task force on the issue: Should the Canadian government keep relations more or less as they stood (Option 1); move deliberately toward closer integration with the US (Option 2); or "pursue a comprehensive, long-term strategy to develop and strengthen the Canadian economy and other aspects of its national life and in the process to reduce the present Canadian vulnerability" (Option 3)?[46] One of the key components of this strategy was the intention to divert a substantial portion of Canada's trade away from the US and toward Europe, Japan, and parts of the Third World.

Within a few short years, the trade diversification element of the Third Option was a complete failure. However, it ushered in a wider range of economic nationalist policies over the next decade: the Export Development Corporation, the Canada Development Corporation, FIRA (as recommended in the Gray Report), Petro-Canada, and—as the last gasp of Canadian statism—the National Energy Program of 1980 (discussed in the next chapter). Practically all of these initiatives were to fall victim within another ten years to the philosophy and economic policy constraints associated with trade liberalization, and after more than a decade of experience with the new

---

[46] See Mitchell Sharp, *Which Reminds Me ... A Memoir* (Toronto: University of Toronto Press, 1994) 184.

free trade paradigm, this brief spike of Liberal concern over a loss of autonomy seems more like a quaint diversion than an undertaking worthy of detailed attention.

Mitchell Sharp, the lead architect in the construction of the Third Option, provides a valuable case study of the fitful ambivalence of successive Liberal ministers toward the economic dominance of the US throughout the decades under review in this chapter. Sharp was a senior civil servant in the departments of Finance and Trade and Commerce in the 1940s and 1950s, worked in private business from 1958-63, and between then and 1974 was in turn Minister of Trade and Commerce, Minister of Finance, and Secretary of State for External Affairs. It was in the last of these roles that he oversaw the development of the Third Option strategy. In his memoir, Sharp admits that he had intended the Third Option, in part, "as a pre-ferred alternative to the more extreme kinds of nationalistic mea-sures that were being advocated in some quarters at the time." In fact, he laments the fact that, "the Third Option came to be invoked enthusiastically by the government and by others to support poli-cies that were far more nationalistic than my paper had proposed, a consequence that I deplored."[47]

In hindsight, it is interesting that Sharp links his discussion about the internal Liberal politics surrounding the Third Option to the idea of continental free trade. He points out that no government minister or official favoured the second option of closer integration with the US or of the negotiation of a free trade agreement with that coun-try. He then comments that some who participated in discussions of the three options, "notably Donald Macdonald and Simon Reisman," changed their views on the free trade issue in the 1980s, which he did not. His opposition to the FTA, he adds, was not based on econom-ics. To the contrary, he had always been an advocate of freer trade who had, moreover "spent a large part of [his] political life fighting the economic nationalist and protectionists within and outside the Liberal Party." He also records that he strongly supported consecutive

---

[47] Sharp 186.

rounds of tariff reductions in the GATT. The FTA, however, was another matter, especially since it accorded better treatment to trade with the US than to trade with Europe and Japan, a departure from more judicious Liberal policies of the past. Prior to this, he reassures us,

> we had done what we could to resist the overwhelming influence of the United States in our economy, our culture, and our politics. By entering into an exclusive free-trade agreement designed to integrate the economies of our two countries, we were not only abandoning our resistance, we were deliberately inviting ourselves to be overwhelmed.[48]

As this section has tried to show, it is at least doubtful that Canadian governments between the end of the Second World War and the early 1970s can justly be said to have done as much as possible to reinforce and extend Canada's economic, cultural, and political autonomy. To the contrary, some would even say that the FTA did not represent the beginning of continental integration at all, but rather the capping off—"formalization" may be a better word—of a prolonged drift toward integration with the US that was to a marked extent a product of the postwar economic strategy of the Liberal governments of the era. (With the exception of Joe Clark's months-long interregnum in 1979-80, there was only one Progressive Conservative government between 1945 and 1984—that of John G. Diefenbaker—and most observers considered him a nationalist, or at least an anti-continentalist.) The tide beneath this drift has been the extensive foreign ownership of Canada's largest and most profitable corporations and the relations between them, their American parents, and Canada's own largest firms, a tide which the Liberal policies of Sharp's era made no serious attempt to stem.

---

[48] Sharp 185.

chapter 5
THE ORIGINS AND NATURE OF
NORTH AMERICAN FREE TRADE AGREEMENTS

By now, there are not only numerous and varied accounts of how "free trade" came to North America, there are also many that detail the contents of both the FTA and NAFTA. Added to these are a growing number of assessments of what these agreements are doing to the economic and other aspects of the relationships between Canada, the US, and Mexico. In this chapter, we will look at: (1) the overall background to North American free trade in its global and continental aspects; (2) the motives of the Canadian, American, and Mexican governments in making these agreements; (3) the contents of NAFTA; and (4) a general assessment of the consequences of North American free trade, including a brief summary of the conflicting interpretations of what it all means.

CONDITIONS PROMOTING FREE TRADE
AGREEMENTS IN NORTH AMERICA

As people become more accustomed to living in the present century, North American free trade begins to look more and more like an historical product of the late twentieth century, rather than a current or ongoing development. After all, for most Canadian and American young adults, the signing of the first FTA occurred shortly after they were born. The world appears to have changed very dramatically over the years since Canada-US free trade was first seriously contemplated in the mid-1980s. For example, not only did the Soviet Union still exist, but it was seen as the West's mortal enemy—American President Ronald Reagan's "evil empire"—and globalization had scarcely been heard of. It may be useful, therefore, to draw a picture of the conditions in North America and the world that set the stage for the process that culminated in the ratification of NAFTA on January 1, 1994.

In fact, the last 30 years have been an emotional roller coaster for most Canadians and Americans old enough to have been aware of the changes that occurred during them. Most of the 1970s and 1980s were tense and trying times, given such events as the fall of Saigon and the humiliating American withdrawal from Vietnam, the overthrow of the Shah of Iran and the energy crisis of 1979, the rise of the sovereigntist movement in Quebec, the repatriation of the Canadian Constitution, and the escalation of Soviet-American tensions in the early 1980s. Then the end of the Cold War set off a decade of unprecedented "triumphalism" politically and "irrational exuberance" economically, especially in American business, political, and intellectual circles. Finally 9/11 arrived like a SWAT-team at a graduation party. The psychological aftermath to that event resembles to some extent—though for different reasons—the deep anxieties in the US of the early 1980s.[1] As yet another recent twist, terrorism's blow to the American psyche has produced an assertive demonstration of American military superiority in the form of two foreign invasions in two years, making it difficult to remember (or for young people to imagine) that only 20 years earlier Americans also feared for their future—or at least for their continued greatness. This earlier fear, though, is important to understand, for it was a crucial factor in the movement toward North American free trade.

---

[1] See G. Bruce Doern and Brian Tomlin, *Faith and Fear: The Free Trade Story* (Don Mills, ON: Stoddart, 1991) 15. According to these authors, in the second half of 1980, "the U.S. economy quietly entered a downward spiral into an economic collapse on a scale not experienced since the Great Depression of the 1930s."

Twenty years ago, America's pre-eminent place in the world seemed threatened from several directions at once. Some of the key developments that led directly or indirectly to talk of North American economic cooperation and partnership were:

> ▸ the Soviet Union's invasion of Afghanistan in 1979 and the apparent inability of the US to do anything about it, except bluster;
> ▸ the Islamic revolution in Iran (a neighbour of Afghanistan) during the same year, the consequent four-fold increase in crude oil prices, and increasing anxiety about the stability and security of the Middle East, the world's largest oil-exporting region;
> ▸ the challenges to American economic leadership from the European Community and Japan, combined with growing frustration on the part of the American government in promoting its multilateral free trade agenda through the Uruguay Round of the GATT;
> ▸ a deterioration of normally amicable relations between the US and its two closest neighbours and major trading partners, Canada and Mexico, across an expanding range of difficult economic and social issues.

The contributions these factors made to the movement toward continental free trade are diverse, but the common element among them is the desire of the US to consolidate its home base in the face of the challenges confronting it from an increasingly uncertain world. If Middle East oil supplies were denied to the US, then Mexican and Canadian oil supplies must be opened up. If independently minded European and Asian trading and investment partners were going to insist on economic protectionism, then a contrary and demonstrative move toward the liberalization of markets must begin among the countries of North America. If American overseas interests were at greater risk from Third World revolution and Second World militarism, at least the US's own borders and regional relationships could be made more secure and predictable. And even if Canada and Mexico had little to contribute directly to the military strength that the US could align against the Soviet Union, its major superpower rival, continental free trade could at least reinforce the strength and dynamism of the American economy, the foundation on which American global might had rested throughout the Cold War.

OBJECTIVES OF NAFTA'S MEMBERS

These background factors produced a set of more specific bilateral issues that combined to generate interest in a formal trade and investment pact among the three national governments of North America. We will review these specific areas of interest for each country in turn.

The US

Since most of the background factors listed above focus on the position of the US, that country's more specific motives for pursuing North American free trade will be only briefly summarized here.

Energy

The history of American interest in continental free trade reaches back to the administration of Democratic President Jimmy Carter (1977-81) who, along with a number of Democratic senators, began to talk vaguely about the possibility of a North American energy market. This speculation was carried a small step forward at a 1979 meeting of the National Governors Association, which issued a call for increased energy cooperation with several Canadian provinces. Moves in this direction gained even more momentum when a number of Democratic and Republican presidential candidates seeking nominations for the 1980 presidential elections floated similar ideas. Most notably, Ronald Reagan, who later became the Republican presidential nominee and then president, called for the creation of a "North American Accord" on energy between the US and its two neighbours.[2]

This momentum toward a continental energy market received a major setback in late 1980, when Canadian Prime Minister Pierre Trudeau, who had recently been returned to office after the premature termination of the government of Progressive Conservative Prime Minister Joe Clark, introduced the National Energy Program (NEP). This initiative was a Canadian response to the same oil price shocks that had motivated so many American politicians to seek continental free trade in energy, but it represented a move by Canada in exactly the opposite direction. It provided a blueprint for massive government intervention into the pricing and marketing of Canadian oil and natural gas (diverting supplies away from the American market in favour of eastern Canada and charging more for exports than for domestic consumption) and set out new regulations to curtail the role of foreign-owned oil companies in the Canadian petroleum industry. Not surprisingly, the program produced a storm of American diplomatic and economic pressures to dismantle it completely.

By 1982, as world oil prices returned to more traditional levels, Canada began to wind down the NEP, and politicians on both sides of the border began to explore ways to stabilize the terms and conditions under which Canada exported oil and gas to the US. From the American perspective, such stabilization required secure access to Canada's energy production and an end to discrimination against American firms in Canada's policies affecting the petroleum industry. In essence, the US saw a free trade agreement with Canada as a way of preventing a future revival of the NEP, and it was prepared to engage in a broad trade-off with Canada in energy matters in order to assure this. In essence, the US promised not to obstruct access to the American energy market for Canadian exporters—something it had done periodically in the past—while the Canadian government

---

[2] Donald Barry, "The Road to NAFTA" in Donald Barry, ed., *Toward a North American Community?* (Boulder, CO: Westview Press, 1995) 4-5.

promised secure access to Canadian supplies and equal treatment for American oil companies under Canadian law.

Removal of Tariffs and Non-tariff Barriers (NTBs)

In addition to obtaining reliable energy supplies, the US wanted unrestricted access to larger markets for all of its goods and services. Canada and Mexico played two main roles in relation to this objective. First, and more important, free trade with Canada and Mexico would permit the American economy to become truly continental in scope. The market open to American goods, services, technology, and investment would significantly expand, and American firms could become just that much larger and more efficient by selling into this wider, unobstructed market. Second, American policy-makers saw North American free trade as a way to overcome the lack of genuine progress toward global market liberalization in recent rounds of trade negotiations at the GATT.[3] If free trade was not to be achieved multilaterally, then it might better be pursued bilaterally (or trilaterally) with partners who—unlike the Europeans, Japanese, and some nations of the Third World—were in no doubt about accepting American pre-eminence and had no dream of challenging that pre-eminence.

As a final and related bonus, the US hoped to obtain leverage against its larger, less cooperative partners in Europe and Asia through a shift in emphasis away from multilateral trade negotiations to a possible series of deals with its continental, and possibly hemispheric, trading partners. This tactic, sometimes referred to as "the domino factor," indicated that the American interest in its North American trade agenda was partly based on a desire to promote its multilateral agenda. In short, successful bilateral trade deals were partly meant to produce more rapid movement at the GATT.

---

3 Doern and Tomlin 19.

Market Access

Yet another global economic priority by which the US attempted to shift away from multilateral to continental negotiations was the broad area of "market access." The problem of market access involves what are sometimes referred to as "behind the border" (as opposed to "at the border") obstacles to trade and investment. Market access tends to be more about the "rights of establishment" of foreign investors than about simple trade in goods; it is about the terms and conditions under which producers from one country can create subsidiary companies in other countries and use them to produce goods for sale in the host economy or for export back to the home country or to the rest of the world. As we shall see in the next chapter, the ability of American MNCs to expand their operations in the markets of other countries has been a 50-year ambition of the US, and many of the issues that became stalled in later rounds of GATT negotiations were largely about the rights of establishment for American firms.

Broadly speaking, the American government's priorities with respect to a continental trade and investment pact were very different from those of the Canadian and Mexican governments. Indeed, the Americans saw it largely as an investment charter, while the Canadians and Mexicans saw it as a set of new trade rules and, in effect, a licence to export to the US.[4] Thus, the widespread tendency to refer

---

[4] This difference in emphasis concerning trade agreements was evident from the earliest "preliminary soundings" of the possible contents of a Canada-US deal, which were conducted during a day-long sail on Chesapeake Bay in late July 1985, as described in Doern and Tomlin 29: The lead American negotiator "emphasized that the Americans would want a big deal, one that would address the key U.S. issues of investment, services and intellectual property." Meanwhile, Canada's lead negotiator "made clear the overriding Canadian interest in achieving secure access to the U.S. market, and the threat to security posed by the anti-dumping and countervailing duty provisions of U.S. trade-remedy law." However, as one of Canada's former trade ministers, Roy MacLaren, recently pointed out, American trade remedy laws were unaffected by the FTA, despite their removal being a primary objective of the Canadian government's decision to negotiate the agreement. As he describes it, "we capitulated on that fundamental question on being warned that the US Congress would never forgo what it regards as its constitutional right to regulate commerce." See "The three amigos have work to do," *Globe and Mail*, 30 May 2005: A13.

to both the FTA and NAFTA as "free trade agreements" creates a misleading impression of the fundamental nature of the deals. The deals were not about (or not *merely* about) the creation of a new regime governing the trade of goods on the same terms for all parties. Rather, they were about a larger, more fundamental trade-off between Canadian and Mexican access to the American market for goods, on the one hand, and American access to the Canadian and Mexican market for investors, on the other.

This, of course, is not to deny that both the investment and trade provisions in the deals were the same for all parties, but it is to say that the deals were not entirely reciprocal, when measured against the primary interests and stakes of the three parties. As we shall see in more detail in the next section, the Canadians in particular wanted "protection from protection" in American trade policies. The Americans were prepared to embrace this objective only at the price of the end of discrimination against its firms in Mexican and Canadian laws and policies, an immediate and regional version of a long-term and global objective of American economic foreign policy for over four decades.

Canada

Many of Canada's reasons for embracing continental free trade can be attributed to the same background factors introduced earlier in this chapter, although in some instances the precise form of their influence is less direct for Canada than for the US. For example, the energy shocks of 1979 did not influence Canada to favour continental solutions. As we have just seen, it did the opposite. However, the strong American reaction against Canada's early retreat into economic nationalism under the Liberal government, combined with strong provincial pressures from western oil and gas producing provinces, moved the succeeding Progressive Conservative government of Brian Mulroney to consider acceptance of the kind of continental arrangements suggested by the Americans. Thus, in a roundabout way, the global energy picture brought about a Canadian commitment to free trade in energy in North America.

Some of the factors, however, were more immediate and direct, and we will now look at the most important ones in turn.

Regional Economic Competition and Integration

Like the US, Canada was increasingly concerned about its competitiveness in the international economy and felt growing unease because multilateral trade negotiations were not moving very rapidly or comprehensively toward open access to world markets. If anything, the international marketplace seemed to be consolidating around regional economic blocs. This was happening formally among the members of the European Community, which was deliberately liberalizing markets internally but effectively raising barriers to countries outside it, and less formally in the Asia Pacific region, where Japan remained highly protective and was promoting various exclusive investment and trade relations with a variety of newly industrializing Asian countries.

As noted earlier, these developments began to feed anxieties that Canada might soon find itself the only member of the G7[5] without unrestricted access to a market of over 100 million people. If markets across the world were in fact opening up, then Canada might not have anything much to worry about; however, disappointments with the GATT suggested that movement was actually in the opposite direction. In the "real world" of more-or-less closed trading blocs, Canada could not afford to remain without a major partner. In the early 1970s, under the short-lived initiative termed the "Third Option" (discussed in Chapter 4), the Canadian government had considered that Western Europe might play such a role. By the early 1980s, however, the US appeared to be the only alternative. In sum, with the world's economic regions displaying (rather inconsistently) simultaneous signs of import protectionism and export aggressiveness, Canada seemed hardly in

---

[5] The G7 is a group of leading industrialized countries—Japan, Germany, France, Britain, Canada, and the US—that meet in order to discuss and forge international economic cooperation.

a position to "hunker down" all by itself and chose instead to attach itself to the American market as a permanent economic haven in an increasingly turbulent trading world.

Improved Business Efficiency

In the minds of many business, academic, and government observers, more competition for Canadian firms from imported products and services complemented the objective of more open and reliable access to the American market for the country's exports.[6] Sometimes simplistically referred to as the "cold shower" (or "efficiency") strategy, it reasoned that the only way to increase the productivity and competitiveness of Canadian firms was to wean them away from their existing dependence on a protected position in the Canadian market.[7] At one extreme, this led some prominent Canadian economists to suggest that a case could be made for a unilateral reduction in Canadian trade barriers, forcing Canadian firms to become "leaner and meaner" in the face of unreciprocated reductions in Canadian trade barriers.[8] In view of this, they argued, the case for bilateral reductions to such barriers in a deal with the Americans was incontrovertible.

This argument, whether entirely consistent with the preceding one about the increasing regionalization of the world economy or not, boiled down to the case that, for Canada, the status quo was untenable and unsustainable. The days of a reasonably independent national economy had passed; Canada as a stand-alone component of a genuinely open international economy was a chimera; and the

---

[6] It was largely on such grounds that the Royal Commission on the Economic Union and Development Prospects for Canada (the Macdonald Commission), declared in a report released on 5 September 1985 that a free trade agreement with the US was Canada's only viable option for the 1980s and beyond. Broadly speaking, the Commission saw free trade as an instrument of industrial restructuring rather than simply of expanding exports, that is, as *industrial policy* rather than simply trade policy. In adopting this stance, they were in step with a highly influential study by Richard G. Harris and David Cox, *Trade, Industrial Policy and Canadian Manufacturing* (Toronto: Ontario Economic Council, 1984).

[7] Doern and Tomlin 33-34.

[8] See the conclusions and policy recommendations in Harris and Cox 146-47.

only remaining option was for Canada to become part of a free trade association in a world economy that was balanced in an uneasy equilibrium between protective and competitive elements.

Rationalization of Business Operations

One of the primary sources of pressure toward the liberalization of markets in the last decades of the twentieth century was the emergence of what might be called "the new multinational corporation (MNC)." The changing form of the multinational firm produced a different attitude toward the border on the part of American-owned subsidiaries operating in Canada but run by head offices in the US. In the past, Canadian subsidiaries of American firms were virtually clones of their parent companies; their Canadian plants replicated (though often on a smaller scale) those in the US itself. As noted in Chapter 4, during an era of high Canadian tariffs, most American-owned manufacturing firms located in Canada acted as substitutes for exports from the US into the Canadian market. American firms invested in Canadian subsidiaries as a way to jump over Canada's tariff wall and avoid the duties which gave a price advantage to Canadian producers in the Canadian market. This induced what was known as "the miniature replica effect" whereby American-owned firms were set up in Canada to replicate the kind of manufacturing facilities that they had going in the US.[9]

This era began to pass in the 1980s and has by now been eclipsed in a large proportion of industrial sectors. New forms of multinational

---

[9] There are numerous studies of the presence of American corporations in Canada. Many of the most influential were published in the late 1960s and early 1970s. Perhaps the most influential and controversial of those written from a critical perspective is Kari Levitt's *Silent Surrender* (cited earlier). A contemporary, less critical overview of the economic performance of multinationals in Canada is A.E. Safarian, *The Performance of Foreign-Owned Firms in Canada* (Montreal: Private Planning Association of Canada, 1969). In addition, as we saw in Chapter 4, a comprehensive overview of the potential economic and political impact of foreign ownership was provided by the 523-page "Gray Report," published in 1972 (see Government of Canada).

business operations have replaced the formerly dominant model of the MNC as a constellation of national clones of the parent firm. The new model is that of a super-rationalized global production system, still managed from world headquarters in the parent country, but with different elements of the firm's global production processes (often referred to as "supply chains") distributed widely across numerous countries to maximize the benefit from the various types of competitive advantage available in different parts of the world.[10] This means that now any given country (or region within a country) may be the preferred location for the production of only one (or a limited number) of the components of the firm's final product (or products).

According to this new model for the MNC, it is possible that only one location in the world may actually assemble, box, and ship the firm's finished product for sale in all other countries, whereas other locations in dozens of countries may be responsible for the various components and services that go into it. This places an enormous premium on the fast and efficient movement of goods and services of all kinds across national boundaries and argues strongly against tariffs and all other national policies and regulations that obstruct or add costs to the import and export of goods, services, and personnel between countries. It also makes it important for MNCs to be able to operate under similar—preferably identical—policy environments; a wide diversity of national business climates severely complicates the efficient, centralized management of these finely tuned multinational operations.

Such cross-border exchanges of goods and services between different branches of the same corporation are commonly referred to as "intra-firm transfers" (and in the aggregate constitute "intra-firm trade"). Such transfers among the different branches of North American firms are extremely prominent in Canada-US trade relations, and by some estimates now constitute in excess of 60 per cent of annual

---

[10] David Held, Anthony McGrew, David Goldblatt, and Jonathan Perraton, "Corporate Power and Global Production Networks," in D. Held et al., *Global Transformations: Politics, Economics and Culture* (Stanford, CA: Stanford University Press, 1999) Ch. 5, especially 260-62 and 276-78. See also John H. Dunning, *Alliance Capitalism and Global Business* (London: Routledge, 1997) 100.

Canada-US trade. (Similar transfers have been estimated to account for nearly 50 per cent of global trade.) This is one of the reasons that American-owned firms became so interested in freer trade between the two countries—an "open border" in fact—in the last decades of the twentieth century. Perhaps it is not so surprising, given this, that foreign-based companies form a substantial portion of the member-ship of the Business Council of National Issues (BCNI), one of the most active private associations promoting the cause of free trade during the 1988 election in Canada.[11] Foreign-controlled companies also play a prominent role in the decision-making of their respective industrial trade associations, which are frequently consulted during negotiations between the Canadian and American governments.

The Canadian automobile industry represents a significant case study of most of the main points just made about the importance of foreign-controlled companies to the progress of Canada-US integra-tion. This is true in at least five different ways. First, the substantial American ownership of the industry that prevailed throughout most of the last century was originally a product of "tariff jumping," that is, of American automobile producers substituting the production of their cars in Canada for exports of cars to Canada. In addition, during the 1920s and 1930s this effect was strengthened by an attempt to take advantage of the British policy of imperial preference, which in effect made a free trade zone out of the British Empire; thus, American cars made in Canadian plants could be sold duty free in Britain and other parts of its empire, such as Australia, New Zealand, South Africa, and the West Indies.[12]

---

[11] Doern and Tomlin 19-20, show that, from 1982 on, the Canadian business community pressed the federal government to negotiate secure access to the American market and that the BCNI, along with the Canadian Manufacturers' Association, was at the forefront of this business campaign. Broader consultations with Canadian business during the course of the free trade negotiations was institutionalized in the form of Sectoral Advisory Committees on International Trade (see Bashevkin 108 and 128.) For a detailed discussion of the composition and activities of the BCNI, see David Langille, "The Business Council on National Issues and the Canadian State," *Studies in Political Economy* 24 (Autumn 1987): 41-85.

[12] Thompson and Randall 110.

Second, especially following the adoption of the Auto Pact in 1965, automobile production was highly integrated across the border. The Auto Pact allowed each country to manufacture approximately the same percentage of automobile production as it purchased in any given year. However, the mix of models sold on either side of the border was not identical, so Canadian plants began to specialize in the assembly of particular models that were sold predominantly in the American market, meaning that key components such as (typically) engines and transmissions were shipped from American to Canadian plants.[13]

Third, because of this process of internal rationalization of the North American-based segment of the industry (which became even more intense with the advent of free trade), a premium came to be placed on the "just-in-time" delivery system for the shipment of automobile components. This made, fourth, the smooth functioning of the border a vital interest for the automotive sector.[14] Fifth, and finally, the automobile industry is very active politically in promotion of its economic and policy interests. It has, moreover, had considerable success in its lobbying activities to acquire direct financial assistance from both the federal and provincial governments; moreover, auto companies play a prominent role in several key business associations.[15] In all these ways, the sector provides an excellent example of the manner in which economic integration becomes a force for political integration, particularly in the form of policy harmonization and government accommodation of cross-border interests.

---

[13] Thompson and Randall 232.

[14] James Laxer, *The Border: Canada, the U.S. and Dispatches from the 49th Parallel* (Toronto: Doubleday Canada, 2003) 303-04. See also Robert Pastor, *Toward a North American Community: Lessons from the Old World for the New* (Washington, DC: Institute for International Economics, 2001) 72.

[15] J.L. Granatstein specifically mentions General Motors as a leading firm in the Canadian Alliance for Trade and Job Opportunities, a major association of business in support of free trade during the 1988 election. See Granatstein, *Yankee Go Home* 268. The 2005 webpage for the Canadian Council of Chief Executives shows the Ford Motor Company of Canada as one of its members; the 2001 site showed both Ford and General Motors as members. See <http://www.ceocouncil.ca/en/about/members.php#g>.

Party Politics and Electoral Calculations

A few years before the FTA was signed, but right in the middle of the debate about whether or not it was a good thing to do, Canadian economist William Watson presented readers of the influential journal *Canadian Public Policy* with a carefully argued analysis of why the Canadian government was energetically seeking a free trade agreement with the US at precisely that time rather than earlier, or later, or not at all.[16] He reviewed in detail three possible answers to this question. A close look at his assessments of the relative strengths and weakness of these three explanations provides a useful and coherent framework for a balanced determination of what were, after all, the key considerations.

1. Economic costs and benefits. The first answer Watson considered was that the net benefit of free trade with the Americans—that is, the potential gains minus the potential losses—had improved beyond what they had ever been before. However, he could find little convincing evidence that this was so, either logically or empirically. A lot of movement toward free trade had already taken place prior to the mid-1980s, largely as a consequence of tariff reductions and other steps toward trade liberalization under the GATT during the 1960s and 1970s. (By 1987, the average incidence of American tariffs against Canadian goods was only 0.9 per cent, down from 1.8 per cent in 1976.)[17] So there was not that much more to be gained from the remaining steps toward free trade compared, say, with the situation in the mid-1960s. Meanwhile, the costs of free trade had remained about the same. Watson concluded that there had been no recent increase in net benefits from free trade with the Americans.

---

[16] William G. Watson, "Canada-U.S. Free Trade: Why Now?" *Canadian Public Policy* 13, 3 (September, 1987): 337-49.

[17] See John Walley (with Colleen Hamilton and Roderick Hill), *Canadian Trade Policies and the World Economy* (Toronto: University of Toronto Press, 1985) 24, Table 1-7.

It is worth noting, however, that Watson did mention one benefit of a free trade deal with the Americans that may have gained in significance, namely, stemming the tide of increasing protectionism in the American Congress. Congressional trade actions against the US's leading trading partners (especially Japan, but including Canada) had been increasing significantly through the early 1980s. In Canada's case, this general congressional anxiety over rising levels of American imports was amplified by a drop in the value of the Canadian dollar relative to the American dollar (which was making imports from Canada less costly for American buyers). As a result, creating a free trade regime governed by set of formal rules rather than the prevailing political winds in Washington began to appear more desirable than ever before. In fact, Canadian exporters were beginning to count on even greater export sales in the American market and were correspondingly less willing to take chances with a possible sudden loss of access to that owing to actions by Congress against foreign suppliers, commonly referred to as "trade remedy legislation." We will discuss this possibility in more detail later in this section.

2. Rational choice. Watson's second possible answer was based on "rational choice" theory, an approach to political explanations based on the assumed individual self-interest of various actors in relation to an issue such as free trade. For example, a prime minister would be expected to gear his or her actions to maximizing the government's chances of re-election. Here, Watson did not detect a sufficient shift in public opinion toward free trade to give the Mulroney government any more incentive to promise it than previous governments had had. However, with enough money to fuel the campaign, public opinion can often be turned around during the course of an election. Thus, Mulroney could have calculated that electoral gains would arise as a consequence of a significant shift in the attitude of Canada's business community away from support for the "National Policy" style of protection of their home markets and toward an endorsement of free trade, because this in turn might lead them to boost their financial support for a party committed to free trade. Finally, he also saw free trade winning the votes of both Quebec nationalists, who favoured it as a way of diminishing the importance of economic ties to

Canada, and peripheral regions such as the western provinces, which traditionally had supported freer trade because of their dependence on resource exports rather than manufacturing. Moreover, Quebec and the west had done the most to elect his government in the first place.

While he thinks them worth considering, Watson doubts that these electoral factors add up to a convincing case in favour of free trade as an election grabber. However, he misreads another electoral factor that deserves closer attention. He points out that it is typical in modern democracies like Canada for both governing and opposition parties to crowd the middle of the political spectrum, because that is where the majority of the voters are on most issues. The distribution of public attitudes toward most political questions tends to resemble the "bell curve" typical of the distribution of many human attributes (such as student performance on exams). As a result, parties contending for power essentially make an appeal to "the median voter," who holds opinions, attitudes, and interests found at the peak of a normal distribution of them, that is, the point where half the voters stand to the left of it and half to the right. It is true, though, that a political party can also consolidate its support from voters on one side of the issue by moving to the right or the left of this central position on the electoral spectrum. However, that same move away from the centre of the spectrum leaves the larger group of voters near its middle—not to mention all the voters far on the other side of it—open to an appeal from the other party.

Watson's application of this model to Canada's free trade debate led him to conclude that it was political suicide for Prime Minister Mulroney to strike a clear and unambiguous position on free trade based on electoral calculations, since the bulk of Canadians occupied a more moderate or centrist view of the issue. He failed to note, however, that median-voter analysis conventionally assumes a two-party electoral system like that of the US, where national elections, with few exceptions, are contested exclusively between the Democratic and Republican parties (and where a large number of rational choice theorists ply their wares). The fact is, however, that when an election is contested by three or more political parties—such as the Progressive Conservative, Liberal, and NDP parties in Canada in 1988—a move away from the centre can consolidate a party's position to the right or the left of the spectrum, while leaving the other parties fighting over the rest of it, thus dividing the opposition vote. The party making this move will end up with less than a majority of all votes, but the largest single share of the vote. This, it can be argued, is what happened in the Canadian "free trade election," and there is little reason to assume that Prime Minister Mulroney was not aware of the potential of the free trade issue to divide opposing voters between the Liberals and the NDP. (As it turned out, the Progressive Conservatives received only 43 per cent of the vote, but the Liberals and NDP divided up the rest, leaving the Progressive Conservatives—and the free trade option—with a significant majority of seats in the House of Commons.)

3. Political ideology. Watson's third candidate for an explanation of the government's adoption of free trade was ideological: the government wanted free trade for Canada because it believed it was the best thing to do. Mulroney was a conservative and therefore favoured free trade because it involved—apart from its effects on trade and investment—a larger role for markets and a smaller role for governments, thus representing a "shift to the right" in Canadian politics. It is important to remember that a similar shift had already occurred in Britain under Margaret Thatcher and in the US under Ronald Reagan, politicians Mulroney clearly admired.

In the end, however, Watson did not find ideological conviction a very convincing explanation for the adoption of free trade, suggesting that the Mulroney Progressive Conservatives had, to the contrary, shown themselves to be "more corporatist than laissez-faire, more Japanese than American" during their first term of office. He did allow that the government had shown signs of being "business-oriented," though this did not necessarily mean it was "market oriented."[18] He also conceded that the government may have been open to the influence of the country's economists from both the financial and academic communities, who were almost unanimously behind the free trade option. (Remember that free trade had just been endorsed by the Macdonald Commission

---

[18] Watson 345.

in which academic economists had also played a very substantial role.) In the end, seeing no more compelling explanation, Watson concluded that the free trade initiative came about most probably because Mulroney and the Progressive Conservatives "simply stumbled into it, more or less unwittingly."[19]

Apart from this somewhat anticlimactic assessment, Watson tentatively floats two other possible factors: the growing strength of American protectionism and the political parties' desire to solidify the strength of their core constituencies. In hindsight, the first of these factors seems to have played the central role. One of the biggest changes in Canada relevant to the free trade decision was the shift in the attitude of the Canadian business community.[20] The Canadian Manufacturers Association (CMA) had traditionally been a strong supporter of Canada's nationalist economic policies and of the protective tariff structure that was a key part of those policies. This shift receives a dramatic portrayal from J.L. Granatstein, who likens the campaign of the CMA (and other business organizations) in favour of free trade during the 1988 election to that of the Canadian Home Market Association *against* free trade in the 1911 election. In both cases, the Canadian business elite went to great lengths, disseminating both cash and propaganda, to ensure the electoral victory of the party—conservative, in both cases, to add even greater irony—that represented their position on the issue.[21]

These business pressures, combined with Canada's three party system that divided electoral opposition to free trade and Prime Minister Mulroney's apparent personal determination to reverse the previous acrimony in the Canada-US relationship, provide the more purely political conditions for his free trade initiative. His interest in consolidating his political support in Quebec and the west reinforced this ambition, since both these regions had an interest in superior relations with the US as

---

[19] Watson 346.

[20] This interpretation is supported by the systematic review of possible influences on the free-trade initiative presented by Sylvia Bashevkin in "The Adoption of Canada-US Free Trade," in S.B. Bashevkin, *True Patriot Love: The Politics of Canadian Nationalism* (Toronto: Oxford University Press, 1991) Ch. 5, 104-35.

[21] Granatstein, *Yankee Go Home* 59 and 267-72. One striking difference between the two elections in Granatstein's account is the prominent role of MNCs in the pro-free-trade campaign; he singles out IBM, General Motors, Dow Chemicals, and Shell Oil.

well as the general reduction in central-state intervention that the
free trade environment would promote.[22]

Mexico

For reasons outlined in Chapter 1, this study cannot spend a great
deal of space examining American relations with Mexico. However,
on some topics—including continental free trade—comparisons
between Canada and Mexico can be instructive, both by allowing comparative analysis of the US's relationship with each of the
other two and also by identifying ways in which Mexico affects the
Canada-US relationship.

The historical point has already been made that Mexico, like
Canada, has frequently relied on a range of interventionist policies in order to cope with the pressures upon it emanating from
the US. However, as oil prices declined after a spike in late 1970s, a
spike that had brought a surge of high income to Mexico through its
oil and gas exports to the US, Mexico's financial situation rapidly
deteriorated, ending in a major debt crisis in the mid-1980s. As a
consequence, the Mexican government began a long-term program of "de-nationalization" by opening up the Mexican economy
to foreign investors, privatizing many of its state-owned firms,
and generally liberalizing its economic policies.[23] Increasingly, the
prospect of free trade with the US came to the forefront of these
initiatives, especially after the FTA came into force in 1989. By 1994,
Mexico successfully negotiated NAFTA with Canada and the US.

It is interesting, therefore, to reflect on the fact that both Canada
and Mexico—two countries that most Canadians are used to regarding as very different in composition, history, and economic development—had closely similar experiences during the last two decades

[22] Doern and Tomlin 32.
[23] Gil R. Winham and Heather A. Grant, "NAFTA: an Overview," in Barry, ed., *Toward
a North American Community* 16-37.

of the twentieth century. For example, the US came to value both trading partners more highly in the 1980s, primarily as potentially secure sources of energy during a time of heightened instability in the world petroleum market. Both entered a period of financial difficulties at approximately the same time, and both eventually turned to privatization, trade liberalization, and increased foreign investment as part of the solution to those difficulties.

Further, this new direction in economic policy represented for both Canada and Mexico the gradual dismantling of a long historical attachment to a statist approach to economic development, which amounted to a conscious shift in strategy from keeping distant to convergence. The parallels here are striking, given the fundamental differences between Canadian and Mexican society. Most observers would have said, and may still tend to say, that Canada was years if not decades ahead of Mexico in terms of economic development and status; yet only five short years separated the timing of the same move by both countries toward formalization of their economic relationship with the US. One wonders whether or not Canada and Mexico—both sharing a continent and already heavily integrated economically with the world's most powerful country—ended up doing much the same thing at almost exactly the same time simply because neither had any viable alternative.

Having said this, it is worth noting the fact that, for Americans, NAFTA is about Mexico more than it is about Canada. American scholars have tended to pay less attention to the impact of the FTA/NAFTA on their country's relationship with Canada and more on their relationship with Mexico.[24] This American bias toward Mexico in the politics of NAFTA is largely driven by two factors. First, the

---

[24] This assessment is mostly based on the present author's experience of American sources, especially anthologies and journal articles consulted during the preparation of this book. To quantify the latter category of sources, however, I did a Proquest search, respectively, of peer-reviewed articles on "the United States, Canada, and NAFTA" and "The United States, Mexico, and NAFTA" for the years 1994-2000. The first search yielded 59 entries, the second 98.

primary opposition toward free trade in the US came from organized labour. Major American trade unions, such as the Teamsters
and the United Auto Workers, have consistently voiced concerns
about the relocation of American production to Mexico to take advantage of the latter's lower wage rates. This concern was less pronounced in connection with free trade with Canada, because in that
case the wage-rate differential was less pronounced. Second, many
Americans are very concerned about illegal Mexican immigration
(which was estimated to total 2.7 million people in 1996 and to be
rising at over 160,000 per year between 1982 and 1992).[25] Consequently, much of the American interest in free trade with Mexico
has been its potential to promote better social and economic conditions there as a substitute for legal and illegal emigration to the US,
a factor that again has no significant parallel with the Canadian
case. Finally, NAFTA contains an implicit assumption of symmetry between the Canada-US and the Mexico-US relationships, since
they all have equal standing as signatories. However, the objective
circumstances surrounding the two relationships are very different.
Canada (along with the US itself) is a member of the G7, the club of
the world's most advanced economies. Mexico is generally regarded
as a Third World country. Logically—and, prior to NAFTA, historically—this large difference between the US's two partners justified a
correspondingly different type of relationship with each. However,
the dynamics of NAFTA tend to demand "equal treatment" by the US
of the other members of the pact.

As recent difficulties over the regulation of the two international
boundaries has illustrated, this logic of symmetrical treatment by
the US of its partners in the agreement has a significant potential
to complicate Canada-US relations because policies designed to meet
American problems with Mexico tend, whether intentionally or not,
to sideswipe Canada. One can expect examples of this to proliferate.
In fact, as the twenty-first century progresses, Canadians may find

---

[25] Condon and Sinha 67-68. Drache (98-99) reports that between September 2000
and November 2001, over 300,000 illegal immigrants were apprehended at the US-
Mexican border.

themselves in the grip of collective shock as they discover that they can no longer take their special status in the eyes of the American government for granted. This prospect is likely to be amplified by the fact that Mexico is gaining on Canada in the world ranking of international economies as measured by aggregate annual GDP (although, of course, their per capita GDP is still far behind.)[26] Meanwhile, both Mexico and China are also overtaking Canada as the largest source of imports into the US.

TERMS AND CONDITIONS OF THE FTA AND NAFTA

NAFTA is a large and complex document, and can be said to touch on practically every aspect of Canada-US relations (although as we shall see, there are some sectors of all three economies that are expressly omitted from its terms). However, for convenience, numerous commentators have summarized NAFTA's provisions for the benefit of non-specialist audiences. One of the most helpful of such summaries is that of three Canadian economists, Richard G. Lipsey, Daniel Schwanen, and Ronald J. Wonnacott, who claim that "in a nutshell" the agreement:

- eliminates all tariffs on trade in goods among the three countries within ten years;
- greatly liberalizes trade in services as well as access to government procurement contracts among the three signatories;
- provides substantial protection from investors against discriminatory practices in partner countries, as well as ensuring protection for intellectual property;
- recognizes the right of each country to adopt any health, safety, environmental, or other standards it requires on its territory;

---

[26] *Globe and Mail*, 1 June 2000: B15. See also World Bank, *Total GDP 2004* at <http://www.worldbank.org/data/databytopic/GDP.pdf>, which places Canada in ninth place with a GDP of US$979.7 billion and Mexico in twelfth place with a GDP of US$676.4.

- builds on the experience of the FTA to improve many aspects of that agreement, including clarifying rules of origin; and
- establishes a set of institutions for resolving trade and investment-related disputes that is largely based on the FTA model.[27]

Winham and Grant summed up NAFTA's contents by bunching and summarizing its provisions under 11 separate headings, which give a strong indication of the massive scope and complexity of the Agreement: Tariff and Non-Tariff Barriers; the Auto Industry; Agriculture; Textiles and Apparel; Energy; Services; Financial Services; Government Procurement; Investment; Intellectual Property; Dispute Settlement; and Side Agreements on Labour and the Environment.[28] Without going into each of these areas in detail, it is possible to provide a more rounded appreciation of NAFTA's contents by suggesting, instead, what *functions* NAFTA is designed to perform or, in other words, what objectives the agreement was designed to accomplish.

In setting out NAFTA's different functions, it may be helpful to conceive of the agreement as a building, perhaps an office tower (possibly housing the headquarters of a new Institute for the Joint Management of the North American Economy). On different floors are the offices concerned with each major function performed under the terms of NAFTA. It is possible to imagine five such floors and to set out briefly what is done on each.

Floor 1: Free Trade in Goods and Services

What goes on on this floor is reasonably straightforward and is closest to what most people mean by the phrase "free trade." NAFTA creates what is essentially a comprehensive free trade association by which, after 2004, tariffs on practically all categories of goods disappeared.

---

[27] Richard G. Lipsey, Daniel Schwanen, and Ronald J. Wonnacott, "The NAFTA in Outline," in R.G. Lipsey, D. Schwanen, and R.J. Wonnacott, *NAFTA: What's In, What's Out, What's Next* (Toronto: C.D. Howe Institute, 1994) Ch. 3, 26-27. I have abbreviated some of these clauses.

[28] Winham and Grant 19-25.

However, despite the fact that just about everybody speaks as though "free trade" is the sole objective of the entire agreement and despite the fact that free trade is the *only* function actually to appear in its title, it can be argued that the achievement of free trade, while certainly fundamental, is at best *one* of the significant functions assigned to the agreement.

Moreover, a very substantial portion of what goes on under the free trade provisions of NAFTA is caught up with one particular on-going problem, namely, that of enforcing "rules of origin." Rules of origin essentially define what is, and what is not, a "North American good." They are necessary because the free trade of goods in North America is meant to apply exclusively to goods produced by the member countries. Anyone who reads the entire text of NAFTA is bound to be struck by the large amount of space it devotes to the seemingly straightforward problem of establishing whether or not a good is, in fact, made in North America.

Thus, a very large part of the space on the first floor of our office building has been assigned the job of assessing the origin of goods in North American trade or, as one source puts it, of identifying "goods that are substantially produced within the free trade area and thereby entitled to move duty free across borders between member countries—that is, across the area's internal borders...."[29] If NAFTA had been established as a customs union, rather than merely a free trade area, it could dispense with this burdensome task. Rules of origin are not needed in customs unions because members share a common tariff against non-members. Since Canada, the US, and Mexico created only a free trade area, they are allowed to retain separate tariffs against the rest of the world. This means that, without rules-of-origin restrictions, non-member countries would be in a position to export goods to the member country with the lowest external tariff—say, Mexico—and then have the goods trans-shipped duty free to Canada and the US. To prevent this, NAFTA members must establish ways of

---

[29] Lipsey, Schwanen, and Wonnacott 27.

defining and interpreting rules of origin and maintain an elaborate system of customs agents and other forms of border control.

For reasons too complex to be reviewed here, the problem of rules of origin was especially vexing in relation to automobiles (including auto parts) and textiles and footwear, where significant domestic and international pressures exist to open North America to much cheaper overseas imports. It seems likely that, over time, pressures will build to reduce the complexities (and inefficiencies) surrounding the issue of rules of origin by upgrading NAFTA to a customs union. In fact, as noted in the Preface, this possibility was recently examined in detail in one of the "Border Papers" published by the C.D. Howe Institute.[30] It is worth noting that this step, among other things, would require the harmonization of Canadian, American, and Mexican tariffs against goods from the rest of the world.

Floor 2: Market Access

Most of what needs to be said about the market access floor of the NAFTA office building has already been introduced in earlier discussions of national treatment and the demands from MNCs for a level playing field with respect to the implementation of national policies. These provisions of NAFTA are aimed to eliminate national restrictions on the ability of foreign investors to set up shop in each member country. In short, market access is about reducing the friction between different market systems.

One of the most obvious ways in which NAFTA has opened national markets is by reducing the scope of policies designed by previous Canadian and Mexican governments to review, set conditions upon, or even block takeovers of particular national firms by foreign companies. Foreign takeovers under $150 million dollars are no longer subject to foreign investment review legislation (a far cry from the old FIRA screening limit of $5 million). More significantly, *no*

---

[30] See Introduction, fn. 8.

foreign investments, whether original investments or acquisitions of existing national firms, can be subjected to the kinds of performance requirements that used to be quite common in Canada and Mexico, such as reaching a certain level of export performance or giving precedence to locally produced goods or services.[31]

One important new feature of NAFTA in relation to international trade and investment law is the introduction of a binding international arbitration mechanism to resolve disputes between investors and governments (Chapter 11). Essentially, foreign firms seeking to invest in a given member country can sue the government of that country if the firm can make the case that a particular national law or regulation is denying it an economic benefit—read: opportunity to make a profit—it might otherwise enjoy through its proposed investment or takeover.

Government procurement is yet another special form of market access that warrants specific attention. These provisions are not necessarily about rights of establishment, but a large portion of government purchases these days are of services. The export of services frequently involves investments in the purchasing country. The telecommunications and construction industries are good examples of this. National government contracts for services over US$50,000, for construction over US$6.5 million, and for goods over US$25,000 must be open to bidders from any of the NAFTA countries on exactly the same terms and conditions—an important practical application of the underlying principle of national treatment.

Financial and transportation services have also been liberalized under NAFTA, but not comprehensively. Rights of establishment in these sectors have been improved, but there remain important limitations on foreign ownership in, for example, Canada's branch-banking system, air passenger services, and culture-related industries such as publishing and broadcasting. Nevertheless, with these exemptions set aside, it seems safe to say that NAFTA

---

[31] Lipsey, Schwanen, and Wonnacott 161.

has substantially delivered what Prime Minister Brian Mulroney pledged to a large number of American investors shortly after his election: "Canada is open for business again."[32]

Floor 3: Trade Dispute Resolution

Earlier in this chapter, it was pointed out that one of Canada's primary objectives in seeking free trade with the US was to obtain legal recourse from American protectionist trade legislation and congressional intervention. For many years, one of the best kept secrets about NAFTA was that on this front—Canada's *quid pro quo* for many of the market access provisions pursued so actively on the American side—very little was achieved. (More recently, several set-backs on the softwood lumber file have made most Canadians dramatically aware of the fact and have even caused some of its staunchest defenders at the time to second-guess themselves.) There are, indeed, dispute resolution mechanisms under NAFTA, but their mandate is not sufficient to protect Canadian (or Mexican) exporters against the arbitrary application of American trade remedies, especially with respect to "unfair subsidy" and "anti-dumping" accusations. In particular, the trade remedy panels constituted by NAFTA do not involve any review of the fairness or appropriateness of American trade measures, only the fairness of the application of existing American law. As we saw earlier in this chapter (see note 4), an exemption from American trade remedy laws was one of Canada's primary objectives in the first free trade negotiations, and most commentators agree that this goal was, at best, only partially realized.

Thus, while the FTA and NAFTA incorporated dispute resolution mechanisms ostensibly to reduce the negative impact of such decisions on the free flow of goods across the border, "the reason that

[32] Jamie Murphy, "Hanging Out the Welcome Sign" *Time*, 24 December 1984; <http://www.time.com/time/archive/preview/0,10987,951396,00.html>. Mulroney was speaking before the Economic Club of New York.

such mechanisms need to exist under NAFTA at all is that parties to the agreement *retain the full use of their antidumping and countervailing duty laws against one another.*"[33] If anything, under the NAFTA version of dispute resolution, it is even less possible for such panels to override the decisions of national agencies than it was under the original FTA. Essentially, then, the elaborate dispute resolution mechanisms operating under NAFTA may help to ensure fairness in the application of each country's own trade laws; they do not constitute, and have no capacity to develop, a North American system of trade regulation that might prevent such disputes from occurring in the first place. In fact, in December 1993, a parallel accord among the three countries was struck to negotiate such a dumping and subsidies code; more than a decade later, it has still failed to produce any tangible results.

Floor 4: Policy Harmonization

There are a variety of institutional arrangements under NAFTA designed to bring about the harmonization and standardization of a number of national policies and regulations with the capacity to hinder the free movement of goods and capital across national borders. These arrangements, which can be thought of as the "fourth floor" of the NAFTA edifice, are described in the next chapter on the capacity of the agreement to promote supranational decision-making in the North American context. For now, it is worth noting that they include a high degree of private-sector participation, especially by business associations seeking the maximum reduction in differences in national economic policies.[34]

---

[33] Lipsey, Schwanen, and Wonnacott 141.

[34] See, for example, Alan M. Rugman, John Kirton, and Julie A. Soloway, "Canadian Corporate Strategy in a North American Region," *The American Review of Canadian Studies* (Summer 1997): 199-219.

Floor 5: Labour and Environmental Cooperation

NAFTA also created a pair of commissions concerned with environmental and labour practices in all three countries that could affect
the operation and outcome of the new free trade regime. It did this
by way of two side agreements negotiated in order to allow President
Bill Clinton to win enough Democratic support in Congress to get
the deal approved. Again, because these aspects of NAFTA involve
institutional developments, they will be left to Chapter 6. However,
it is worth noting in passing that, especially with respect to environmental issues, the policy and bargaining processes surrounding
these new North American agencies are attracting a lot of attention and activity on the part of non-governmental organizations
(NGOs). Moreover, unlike the harmonization working groups, this
NGO participation extends well beyond the business sector to include a variety of environmental and other organizations. Some observers are beginning to see in this emerging form of activism a new
dimension of North American civil society, or what one observer
has termed "private diplomacy."[35] This theme will be revisited in the
next chapter.

THE CONSEQUENCES OF NORTH AMERICAN FREE TRADE

It seems likely that, for most readers, the detailed activities conducted
on the various floors of the agreement, as outlined above, will appear
less important than some broad conclusions about the overall impact
they have had on significant dimensions of the Canada-US economic
relationship. Since this question could be the subject of an entire book,
we will focus briefly here on one such dimension: energy. This seems

---

[35] Julian Castro-Rae, "Toward Single North American Polity? The Effects of NAFTA
on Mexican and Canadian Domestic Policies," in C.C. Paraskovopoulos, R.
Greenspun, and G.E. Eaton, eds., *Economic Integration in the Americas* (Cheltenham:
Edward Elgar, 1996) 88-102.

appropriate for three reasons. First, as we have seen, access to Canada's energy resources was from the start one of the key factors motivating American decision-makers to seek a free trade association with Canada. Second, on the Canadian side, it was one of the sections of the agreement that attracted the most intense and sustained opposition during the debate over its ratification. Third, it is the one aspect of the agreement that clearly illustrates the central trade-off in the agreement between the American priority on rights of investors, on the one hand, and the Canadian priority on reliable access to the American market for goods (or, in this case, commodities) on the other.

During the pre-free trade era, there was considerably less international trade in oil and natural gas than otherwise might have been expected, and this gap between trade potential and actual trade was at least in part a consequence of the kinds of national policy restrictions permitted under the reigning international trade regime. That is, while there was substantial international trade in oil throughout most of the twentieth century, national oil and natural gas markets were heavily regulated.

The most common instruments of such national market regulation were:

- quantitative trade restrictions (import/export quotas),
- discriminatory price structures,
- restrictions on foreign ownership, and
- investment and regulation of infrastructural development.

Space permits only the briefest review of how the new North American free trade regime has constrained the use of nearly all of these approaches to the control and shaping of national energy markets. Broadly speaking, under the current regime of market liberalization, the first three of these four national policy instruments are explicitly ruled out for oil and gas. In addition, Chapter 11 of NAFTA gives foreign investors in all resource sectors the right to legal action against any future national policies and regulations that might have the effect of denying them the opportunity to realize a financial return on previous or prospective investments. More specifically, to begin with quotas and preferential prices, it may be simplest to say that North American free trade completely ruled out another NEP. That is to say, trade agreements forbid two of the key pillars of that program: the diversion of Canadian energy supplies from existing American markets in favour of expanded Canadian markets and the imposition of higher prices on remaining exports than the price charged to domestic consumers. [36]

Similarly, the kinds of preference that the NEP extended to Canadian-owned firms over foreign-owned firms in the exploration and development of "Canada Lands" (territory under federal jurisdiction) would today be in violation of several NAFTA provisions in its investment chapter. Generically, these fall under the "national treatment" principle, which specifies that, in the wording of one section of that chapter, "[e]ach Party shall accord to investors of another Party treatment no less favorable than that it accords, in like circumstances, to its own investors with respect to the establishment, acquisition, expansion, management, conduct, operation, and sale or other disposition of investments."[37] In other words, the NEP's provision of special tax, subsidy, regulatory, and other advantages to oil and gas companies with more than 50 per cent Canadian ownership—as an incentive both to encourage those firms to engage in particular kinds of performance and to encourage the "repatriation" of existing firms operating under federal jurisdiction—are now out of the question.

If the energy industry thus provides a clear illustration of the strength of the market access provisions of the FTA/NAFTA that mattered most to the American negotiators, the softwood lumber industry provides an equally clear illustration of the weakness of the protections against American trade remedy laws that mattered most to the Canadian negotiators who faced them. On the one hand, the industry illustrates exactly the kind of congressional trade

---

[36] NAFTA, Articles 603, 604, and 605.
[37] NAFTA, Article 1102.1. The next article (1102.2) uses identical language with respect to investments of the other parties.

harassment that the Canadian government sought to avoid by means of joining a free trade agreement with the Americans in the first place. On the other hand, the long-running dispute also illustrates how unreliable and complicated the protections afforded by NAFTA are.

According to Gordon Ritchie, who was a key Canadian representative during the original free trade negotiations, the American industry claims that Canadian lumber enjoys an unfair price advantage from provincial resource management policies and so has imposed punitive duties on Canadian exports, a claim that he describes as only a pretext. The real problem is the inefficient and undercapitalized state of the American producers, whose true objective is to fix the level of Canadian penetration of the American market to less than one-third.[38] Because of an ongoing controversy surrounding this issue at the time that the FTA was being negotiated, both sides preferred to keep the sector outside those negotiations. Since the adoption of free trade, Canada has attempted—as yet, with no tangible success—to use free trade mechanisms to force the US to remove restrictions on Canadian shipments of lumber into the country. Recently, the US industry is becoming even more aggressive, threatening to challenge the very constitutionality of the idea that Americans can ever be subjected through adverse NAFTA dispute resolution panel decisions to rulings in which foreign judges take part.

Partly at stake in the current impasse—in what Ritchie describes as a move that is "indisputably" in direct contravention of NAFTA and amounts to nothing less than a unilateral abrogation of the central provisions of the free trade agreement—is over $4 billion dollars accumulated over the past four years in the form of countervailing duties, which the Americans now insist will not be paid back to the Canadian industry unless it accepts American terms. In other words, in a flagrant version of near-coercive policy harmonization, the Canadian industry cannot sell to the US unless its forests are managed the same way in Canada as they are in the US. As Daniel Drache sums this matter up, "the US Commerce Department wants to reserve

---

[38] Gordon Ritchie, "Who's Afraid of NAFTA's Bite?" *Globe and Mail*, 15 February 2005: A21.

the right to determine whether or not Canada's forest-rich provinces have fully complied with its standards."[39]

In closing, however, and in the service of balance, it is important to recognize that, in relation to both energy and non-energy provisions of the agreement, various "reservations" to the existing agreement that each national government stipulated as a condition of signing it were almost as important as the provisions that were adopted.[40] For instance, (taken by sector) the financial, transportation, and tele-communications industries stand out as important components of the continental economy whose liberalization fell far short of both the substance and spirit of most of the "goods" provisions in the treaty. Some provisions relating to agricultural goods also fell short.

More generally, it is widely recognized that NAFTA remains deficient in relation to the mobility of labour generally and of investment in some key sectors. It also remains murky in the politically contentious field of intellectual property rights. Despite the praise which the NAFTA negotiators widely received for surpassing the provisions of either the GATT or the WTO relating to such matters, the fact remains that anyone committed to "comprehensive free trade" on the continent is unlikely to be satisfied until these outstanding issues are drawn fully within the scope of the existing agreement.

---

[39] Daniel Drache, *Borders Matter: Homeland Security and the Search for North America* (Halifax, NS: Fernwood, 2004) 109.

[40] Alan M. Rugman and Michael Gestrin, "NAFTA's Treatment of Foreign Investment," in Alan M. Rugman, ed., *Foreign Investment and NAFTA* (Columbia, SC: University of South Carolina Press, 1994) Ch. 3. A detailed list of each country's reservations is presented in that chapter's Appendices 1-3, 67-78.

chapter 6
POLITICAL INTEGRATION
IN EUROPE AND NORTH AMERICA

The last three chapters have traced the evolution of the Canadian and American economies from their beginnings to the point where, with the FTA in 1989 and NAFTA in 1994, the two countries formally committed themselves to a process of economic integration. This chapter will evaluate the extent to which this process is likely to promote political integration as well. We have already seen that there is a body of political theory concerned with relations between "disjoined partners," defined as two or more countries that are highly integrated in economic, social, and cultural terms, but remain politically separate. The issue there was how and why the smaller countries in such partnerships avoid absorption or assimilation by the larger partner. The theories we will now look at address a different question: How does economic, social, and cultural integration promote a *reduction* in political autonomy, that is—very broadly—how do economic and other non-political forms of interaction and interdependence bring about political integration?

In some respects, the perspective presented in this chapter is in tension with the perspectives presented in Chapter 1. Canada and the US do represent an excellent example of "disjoined partners," or at least they have done so to date. However, theories of political integration suggest that this might not remain the case forever, since they essentially argue that economic and other non-political forms of integration will, over time, result in political integration. This "Grand

Hypothesis" of integration theory will be examined here in some detail primarily to evaluate the possibility that the US and Canada (and possibly Mexico) are destined to become a single country.

In making this evaluation, the theory of international political integration plays a central role since it was largely developed to explain roughly 50 years of progress toward political unification in Western Europe. It is true that some observers argue that the ultimate goal of a "United States of Europe" has not played a major, or even necessary, part in the degree of political integration that the EU has achieved so far. However, it seems impossible to deny that the prospect of the political unity of Western Europe has consistently inspired at least some political leaders in Europe to press for higher levels of integration of all kinds. Two book titles from the 1960s—*The Uniting of Europe* and *Beyond the Nation-state*—attest to this.[1]

ECONOMIC AND POLITICAL INTEGRATION

It is important at the outset to have clear definitions of various key concepts that inform the process of integration. Among the most fundamental is the notion of interdependence. As discussed in Chapter 1, countries are considered to be interdependent when they come to rely on one another for some goods or services that they value and would prefer not to give up. So, international interdependence and integration grow out of exchanges, transactions, and communication between countries that believe them to be beneficial. Theory has it that, under the right conditions, high levels of such interdependence promote economic and political integration. As outlined by Robert Jones, integration in general means "the coming together of separate units to form a whole."[2] In the present context, then, *economic integration* amounts to forming a new,

[1] Ernst B. Haas, *The Uniting of Europe: Political, Social, and Economic Forces, 1950-1957* (Stanford, CA: Stanford University Press, 1968); Ernst B. Haas, *Beyond the Nation-state: Functionalism and International Organization* (Stanford, CA: Stanford University Press, 1964).
[2] Robert A. Jones, *The Politics and Economics of the European Union* (Brookfield, VT: Edward Elgar, 1996) 32.

single economy (or market) out of formerly separate and distinct national economies. Similarly, *political* integration means the creation of a new, single country out of two or more separate countries.

By this simple definition, *international integration*—economic or political—is rare. The EU represents the most advanced case of formal economic integration the world has seen so far, but few observers would argue that the progress of European economic integration is complete. There is not yet a single European economy. Many vestiges of the previous national economies remain, including national currencies for countries (like Britain) that have not adopted the Euro, despite the fact that many of the barriers to the free movement of goods, services, capital, and people among the member states had been removed or severely curtailed. International political integration is even rarer and further from realization in Europe or anywhere else.

To date, nearly all of the available studies of political integration have to do with individual nation-building, such as the role of Prussia in the unification of Germany in the nineteenth century or the coming together of federal states such as the US and Canada, rather than the combining of different countries into new and bigger ones.[3] In contrast, most of the twentieth century witnessed far more examples of political *disintegration* than integration, as the process of decolonization broke up the former European empires, and the collapse of communism led to the fragmentation of Eastern and Southern Europe and much of Central Asia. Meanwhile, over the same period, a large number of attempts at regional federations in such locations as the West Indies, Central America, and East Africa went nowhere and soon fell apart.

---

[3] Nevertheless, some theorists argue that past instances of national *federation*—such as the formation of the United States of America, Germany, Italy, and Canada— represent important cases of economic and political integration. They certainly are critical cases for understanding the relationship between the two forms of integration, but there is some doubt about their suitability as models for the voluntary coming together of sovereign states with diverse languages, histories, and cultures.

International political integration is difficult for governments to accomplish because it represents a loss of national sovereignty. As we saw in Chapter 1, the notion of national sovereignty is highly complex, but for the purposes of this chapter it may be defined simply as "supreme decision-making authority." Again, Jones provides a good working definition:

> Sovereignty has two principal aspects: firstly an *internal* aspect, meaning supremacy, or authoritative decision-making power, within a state (for example we speak of parliament, the supreme law-making body within the UK). Secondly, an *external* aspect, meaning the independence of states in international affairs.[4]

So defined, it may seem obvious that sovereignty is automatically canceled, or at least severely compromised, by interdependence, but this is true only in a practical, not a formal or legal sense. In law, sovereignty is an absolute quality; a political entity either has it or does not have it. As the associated notion of supremacy implies, a state cannot be "more or less" sovereign or sovereign in some areas but not in others. Sovereignty, then, is a different notion from independence, which countries can experience to varying degrees and can exercise more in some areas than in others. Thus, states may be sovereign and equal in law (sometimes labeled sovereignty *de jure*) but lack independence of action in practice (sovereignty *de facto*).

Even more subtle distinctions are necessary with respect to the status of countries, such as most of the countries of Western Europe, that have transferred much of their decision-making authority to the EU. As Jones points out, the EU is regarded as a *supranational* organization and many of its institutions are regarded as *supranational authorities* precisely because they exercise authority over (and "above") the states that created them. As he further points out, agencies such as the European Commission, the European Parliament, and the European Court of Justice are deemed to be supranational bodies

---

4 Jones 34.

because "they perform functions on behalf of the Union as a whole and do not represent the interests of the individual governments of member states."[5] However, it is less confusing overall to say that, even when they join supranational organizations (which are exceedingly rare, in any case, apart from the example of the EU), states do not so much "give up" their sovereignty as "exercise" it in choosing to become members.[6]

However, it is central to the argument presented in this book that international political integration should not be identified exclusively with the supranational form that has been adopted in Europe. In fact, a key point about the relationship between economic and political integration is that the reduction or elimination of barriers to the movement of economic factors is largely independent of any particular international institutional arrangements. Specifically, moves toward international economic liberalization do not require the creation of common decision-making structures, certainly not ones with the scale and scope of those found in the EU. Theoretically, economic integration could be fully accomplished through mutual but independently enacted adjustments to national policies that need not involve significant transfers of authority from national to international levels of authority.

Thus, the prospects for "deep integration" within trade associations depend far more critically on the national policies adopted (or abandoned) by each of their members than on the creation of common

---

[5] Jones 35.
[6] Some observers draw a parallel between states signing treaties or joining international organizations and individuals making promises. To pledge to do something does place a limit on one's freedom to choose in the future: one will act or not act as one has promised to do or refrain from doing, rather than risk losing one's reputation for reliability and honesty. Nevertheless, making the promise in the first place is an expression, not a limitation, of one's individual autonomy. Similarly, for a state to sign a treaty, even one that includes a transfer of decision-making authority to an international agency, is in fact an expression of the sovereign powers of the state.

institutions among them.[7] That is to say, deep integration, which is generally deemed to be an intensification of *economic integration*, is essentially about reducing *political* differences between countries, that is, reducing differences between national policies, regulations, and standards that restrict the ease and efficiency with which goods, capital, and people move between national jurisdictions. The substitution of common supranational policies for existing national policies is certainly one way of removing these differences, but it is not the only way.

Despite this, the identification of political integration with institutionalization is generally taken for granted. For most of the history of international economy since the Second World War, economic integration has been almost completely identified with trade liberalization and been seen essentially as the reduction or removal of national tariffs on the importation of goods (i.e., shallow integration). The single major exception to this was found in the commitment of members of the European Community (now the EU) to the goal of

---

[7] Some readers may find it useful to pause over some of the terminology involved here. The politics of international economic integration is essentially about reducing the ways in which—and the extent to which—government policies impede the international movement of the factors of production. Government policies can block or encumber such flows *at the border* by prohibiting the entry of some or all such factors into national markets, or they may inhibit such flows *behind the border* by discriminating against foreign producers or investors in the application of national policies and regulations.

The distinction between impediments "at" and "behind" national borders roughly corresponds to a further distinction between *shallow* (more purely economic) and *deep* (more expressly political) integration. Governments engage in shallow integration when they agree to lift restrictions at their borders through commonly accepted changes to national trade policy, most typically by removing tariffs or quotas against one another's goods. Additionally (or alternatively) governments engage in deep integration when they afford each other's citizens "national" (that is, non-discriminatory) treatment in behind-the-border measures, such as the application of standards or performance requirements. Beyond this, governments may deepen integration even further by agreeing to reduce or eliminate differences in national policies, economic or any other, that impinge on the ability of each country's producers to sell in the other's markets. See Robert O. Keohane and Stanley Hoffmann, "Conclusions: Community Politics and Institutional Change," in William Wallace, ed., *The Dynamics of European Integration* (London: Pinter Publishers for the Royal Institute of International Affairs, 1990) 299, note 38.

deeper integration, a goal they pursued (for some special reasons to be reviewed later in this chapter) through the creation of a customs union, a common market, and eventually a full economic union. The objective of removing trade- and investment-distorting differences in national policies was advanced by replacing or overriding them with European-wide policies enacted through newly established supranational institutions. In other words, in the Western European experience, the political integration that accompanied deep integration has been practically synonymous with the creation of common policies by means of central state-like institutions.

The conventional understanding of the relationship between economic and political integration has been heavily influenced by this tendency to associate deep integration strongly (if not exclusively) with the institutional form that it has taken in Western Europe. However, this tendency is compounded by a related failure to give explicit recognition to the extensive domestic impact of any form of integration, however arrived at. The pervasiveness of such impact is undeniable, even where a commitment to supranational institutions plays no part in moves toward market liberalization. For instance, it was precisely the need for extensive changes in domestic policies that effectively derailed the later stages of the Uruguay Round of negotiations under the GATT, as the so-called trade agenda increasingly involved such matters as services and intellectual property rights that collided with the determination of most national governments to preserve deep-seated differences in their national business environments.

Apart from the historical association of political integration with institution formation in Western Europe, confusion over the relationship between economic and political integration is not helped by the failure of most theories of international integration to identify very clearly what the *outcome* of the integration process is supposed to be, either economically or politically; that is, these theories fail to specify with any precision what the "dependent variable" in the relationship between economic and political variables is hypothesized to be. Typically, both political and economic integration are modelled essentially as processes, but without identifying the determinable ends (or outcomes) of such processes.

Most economists would probably agree that "factor-price equaliza-tion" provides one good measure of economic integration: markets have become fully integrated when the returns to land, labour, and capital (respectively) have become uniform.[8] Unfortunately, there is no widely accepted measure of the end-point of political integration comparable to the economic concept of factor-price equalization. A measure of political integration that parallels it to some extent might be termed "subject-value equalization" (or possibly "citizen-value equalization"). While perhaps lacking in elegance and familiarity, the notion of subject value equalization is at least capable of reasonably objective measurement: political integration has taken place when the nationals of all member states are treated in the same manner by all governments. Significant progress toward political integration can thus be defined as the absence of discrimination on the basis of nationality in the implementation of government policies, as well as the elimination of differences in national policies. In other words, political integration has been fully realized when *government policies no longer favour members of their own society above members of other societies* or when *government policies on all trade- and investment-related matters are the same.*

In some respects, of course, the notion of subject-value equalization is only a more explicit political extension of the notion of "national treatment" that has become a central feature of trade associations, including the GATT (now the WTO). The key to the principle of na-tional treatment is that, while each country is permitted to maintain "its own" laws and policies, those policies must be applied in the same manner to all economic actors—domestic or foreign-based—operating within its jurisdiction. As the cliché goes, national treatment "levels the playing field" for all competitors within each country.

---

[8] Richard Cooper defines factor-price equalization as "uniform wages (except for differences in skills, etc.), common interest rates on comparable financial assets, and equal profits on comparable investments." He also identifies it as one of three useful definitions of economic integration, along with an end to discriminatory national policies and the achievement of optimum economic cooperation. See Richard N. Cooper, *The Economics of Interdependence: Economic Policy in the Atlantic Community* (New York: McGraw-Hill, 1968) 10.

However, recent trade negotiations are more concerned than in the past with creating "the same playing field" across all countries, a development that extends policy integration beyond the principle of national treatment and further into the realm of subject-value equalization. National governments are increasingly coming together to reduce the differences in their policy and regulatory regimes, to the point where all economic actors everywhere will be subject to the same, or at least less different, laws. Their objective is to reduce significantly the "system friction" in the global economy that is created by diverse national economic, social, environmental, and cultural policies.[9]

In the current dynamics of market liberalization, system friction is intended to succumb to the harmonization and standardization of all trade- and investment-related national policies. The ultimate end of such a process is equal standing before the law of all subjects in all countries, a condition here defined as political integration. As such, the world as a whole is unlikely to witness the achievement of significant political integration for a long time, if ever. However, its realization at a regional level, probably in Western Europe and at least plausibly in North America, may not be far off. The fact that the two regions have embarked on their journeys toward that destination at different times of departure and by different conveyances does not mean that they might not end up in the same place at roughly the same time.

INSTITUTIONAL VARIATION IN THE INTEGRATION PROCESS

With this in mind, it is important to establish a few other distinctions to sort out different kinds of cooperative arrangements that nation-states create in order to improve the mutual benefits available from their various exchange relationships. Such arrangements,

---

[9]   See, for example, Lipsey, Schwanen, and Wonnacott 7-8. The phrase is attributed to Sylvia Ostry.

which almost always involve the creation of some form of IGO, can be either functional, neo-functional, intergovernmental, or federal in nature, depending on the balance they strike between collective decision-making authority and individual state autonomy. In other words, the different kinds of cooperative arrangements that national governments make can be sorted according to the degree of supra-nationalism they embody. Again, Jones will be taken as our guide to these distinctions.

Functionalism

Functionalism is the term used to designate minimal transfers of state authority to IGOs. Agencies such as the World Health Organization, the Food and Agricultural Organization, the International Telecom-munications Union, and the International Civil Aviation Authority are examples of IGOs that deal with narrowly defined, technical areas of responsibility and do so under conditions of unanimity among their members. These agencies do enormously useful work on behalf of all member states in some vitally important areas of regulation, scientific research, and delivery of services. The fact that most of them are, nev-ertheless, scarcely household names says a lot about the nature of the practical, everyday tasks they perform. Just as most people at the level of their local communities do not know (or very much care) exactly who is responsible for maintaining their roads or making their buses run on time, neither do they know at an international level who man-ages the international distribution of revenues from long-distance telephone calls, runs the Internet, or makes sure that 200 flights don't all arrive at Heathrow Airport at 5:00 p.m. on a given Tuesday.

Nevertheless, functional IGOs—of which there are now over 300—represent a victory of "technical determination" over "national self-determination." That is, they amount to a pledge by all member governments to be bound by decisions based upon the knowledge of experts in the technical requirements of the task (function), as op-posed to narrow calculations of national advantage. For this reason, functional agencies tend to operate in a "depoliticized" manner and therefore represent an insignificant transfer of national decision-making capacity. Indeed, they could almost be seen as an international extension (and fusion) of national bureaucracies, rather than a submission to international political rule.

Neo-functionalism

Neo-functionalism is the formula for international cooperation that has been most extensively adopted in Western Europe. It places more emphasis than does functionalism on centralized and politicized decision-making agencies acting on behalf of the members of a regional economic organization. Another principal difference lies in this emphasis on regional, as opposed to global, cooperation. A further contrast is the combination of a whole range of tasks under a single decision-making and administrative structure as opposed to the narrow and self-contained tasks assigned to a multiplicity of functional agencies. Indeed, one of the key processes of neo-functional integration is *spillover*, that is, the tendency for successful cooperation in one area of responsibility (such as transportation) to spread to others (such as energy), thus promoting or demanding an accumulation of different functions and jurisdictions under one central agency. Accordingly, the major political institutions of the European Community can be said to parallel quite closely the cabinet, bureaucracy, legislature, and judiciary of a typical nation-state. In that sense they do represent the creation (or at least the gestation) of a new nation-state, the "United States of Europe." No other regional association has progressed this far in the direction of genuine supranationalism.

Intergovernmentalism

Intergovernmentalism is based on the recognition that, even in Western Europe, important issues are still decided by states acting out of a commitment to their individual national interests, rather than the needs and priorities of the integrating region as a whole. Thus, major steps in the integration process, such as the Single European Act of the mid-1980s or the more recent European Monetary Union, can only take place with each member's formal consent, usually after a long process of international bargaining at "summits" involving the heads of all the governments concerned. In short, intergovernmentalism is a form of international negotiation. It is not even unique to regional economic associations, but can also work at a global level, such as at the WTO.

Federalism

Federalism is the kind of economic and political integration arrived at by some of the world's most successful countries, such as the US, Germany, Australia, and Canada. It represents the creation of a powerful central government out of formerly separate political units, but leaves the smaller constituent units with constitutionally defined governing powers. As Jones points out, there are several good reasons not to expect the members of the present EU ever to become a federation by this definition, that is, to become a United States of Europe resembling the present United States of America. However, there can be no doubt, either, that this has long been the ambition of Europe's most committed integrationists. The key point in the present context, however, is not to predict the future of the EU, but rather to establish the point that the federal model, unlike all the others, does represent the formal transfer of sovereignty to a new central government created by the constituent units, which thereby cease to be nation-states in their own right. In this sense, the federal model is theoretically, if not practically, significant. Since it represents the ultimate form of political integration, the complete formation of a "new whole," it provides a conceptual benchmark against which the lesser modes of sovereignty-transfer can be measured.

Before applying integration theory to the prospects for a "United States of North America," however, it is necessary to establish a number of key analytic distinctions in relation to political integration in general. One is to set out the four levels of *economic* integration or, as it is sometimes referred to, *market liberalization*. This differentiation is important, because most theories of political integration posit that political ties become closer as higher levels of economic integration are achieved. Following that will be a breakdown of five dimensions of political integration, along with some brief comments on the relationships among them. Finally, we will consider a brief comparison of economic and political integration in Europe and North America.

THE FOUR LEVELS OF MARKET LIBERALIZATION

Most text books on trade liberalization and the formation of free trade associations set out a sequence of "degrees," "levels," or "phases" of economic integration.[10] These levels are distinguished in order to mark progress toward the complete integration of national markets into a new, fully integrated single market (something that, as already noted, has not yet been fully achieved internationally, even in Europe). They range from the most modest degree of a *free trade area* to the highest and culminating level of an *economic union*. It is conventionally understood that each succeeding level incorporates all the features already established at the previous one and adds further elements until full economic integration is reached. Market liberalization, then, proceeds from lower to higher degrees, as follows:

1. Free Trade Area: eliminates tariffs and other barriers to trade in goods between two or more national economies. Member countries continue to maintain their own tariffs against countries outside the group, which means that their restrictions against non-members may differ from those of other members.
2. Customs Union: adds a common external tariff to an FTA. Members must establish a cooperative mechanism to negotiate the levels of the new common tariffs on their imports and to coordinate trade relations and negotiations with non-members, since all such policies must become identical.

---

[10] For a recent example, see Clement, et al. 48-49.

3. Common Market: progresses beyond a customs union to achieve the elimination of all internal barriers, including non-tariff barriers, to the movement of goods, services, capital, and people. Members must coordinate tax policies and regulatory standards to achieve compatible (though not necessarily identical) policy environments for business in each country.

4. Economic Union: further liberalizes a common market by creating common economic and social policies such as a single currency, uniform taxation policies, and common regulations. Government spending and taxation levels are decided in common, and a wide range of distributive policies are centrally determined.

THE FIVE DIMENSIONS OF INTERNATIONAL POLITICAL INTEGRATION (IPI)

As useful as they are, the categories of market liberalization say nothing about the political processes and institutions that need to go with it. This is where theories of political integration come in. Political integration theorists also speak about "levels" or "dimensions" of integration, but their focus is not so much on the removal of barriers to trade and investment (or whatever else) as it is on the creation of the institutions necessary to promote and sustain the freedom of those movements.

There is less agreement among political integration theorists than there is among trade theorists about how the levels of political integration ought to be categorized and labeled, and there is even less agreement among them concerning the interrelationships that exist between any given pair or set of levels. However, most theories of political integration break the process down into a minimum of five distinct dimensions, summarized as follows:

1. coercive power
2. joint decision-making

3. functional administration
4. social communications
5. public attitudes and values.

1. Coercive Power

The dimension of coercive power may be defined as the dimension of "final" or "ultimate" sovereignty. The renowned sociologist Max Weber defined national sovereignty in political (as opposed to purely legal) terms as a monopoly of the legitimate use of violence within a given society. In other words, sovereignty is an attribute of whoever possesses and deploys the official—that is, the non-subversive and non-criminal—use of physical force.[11] Like sovereignty itself, moreover, coercive power involves its application in two domains: the external, which entails the use of military forces to maintain national security against outside enemies; and the internal, which entails the use of police forces to preserve law and order against criminals and/or insurgents.

The implication of these definitions is that, if Canada and the US were to integrate completely at the level of coercive power, they would pool their national sovereignty and cease to remain independent countries. As in Western Europe, the countries of North America have remained a considerable distance away from pooling their sovereignty for the purposes of external defence and internal public safety. However, in recent times, some significant progress in this direction has occurred in both regions. The Maastricht Treaty contains provisions for common foreign and security policies for the 25 members

---

[11] In this context, coercion may be defined as the threat or use of violence—up to and including the taking of life—against a person or group of persons in order to make them do what they would otherwise prefer not to do. It may thus be used against other countries—as in external coercion, or "war"—or against individuals and/or groups within the society—as in internal security, or "criminal enforcement and political repression."

of the EU, although they still show signs of stubborn self-interest on many key foreign policy issues and stand far short of a unified European military. Similarly, since 9/11, Canada and the US have sought higher degrees of "interoperability" in their armed forces and have created a Military Planning Group within NORAD charged with the responsibility of coordinating national responses to natural or terrorist-inflicted disasters on either side of the border.

2. Joint Decision-making

The most marked of all the differences between the EU and North America with respect to international political integration (IPI) is the degree to which they have *institutionalized* the process, that is, the extent to which individual countries in the two settings have merged their governing capacities by creating joint agencies for the conduct of their mutual affairs. Over the course of almost 50 years, the Europeans have established a number of major decision-making bodies with powers over all of the members of the EU, including a host of regulatory agencies and directorates. Not only have these institutions proliferated in number and expanded in scope in recent decades, they have also made significant gains in genuine power over matters formerly under the exclusive jurisdiction of the respective national governments. In a phrase, the EU exhibits a genuine (though far from complete) transfer of decision-making autonomy to the supranational regional level.

For present purposes, it is unnecessary to detail the precise powers and processes according to which this supranational authority is exercised in Europe. The main point is that nothing remotely approaching it has been accomplished, or even attempted, in North America. The best known exception to this is the International Joint Commission established between Canada and the US in 1909, but the functional mandate of that organization is the extremely narrow one of cooperating in the management of the lakes and rivers along the international boundary. Beyond this, one might point to a degree of practical equivalence between the

European Council of Ministers and meetings that are held periodically between Canadian and American cabinet ministers in resolving issues of joint concern. Canada-US relations are, after all, binational in character (though they may begin to be increasingly trilateral with the signing of NAFTA) and are therefore relatively uncomplicated procedurally, compared to the 25-nation consultations required for the EU. This in itself reduces the need for more formal and detailed procedures for international consultation and negotiation.

3. Functional Administration

There are, indeed, a plethora of bureaucratic departments and agencies governing Europe, as many individual and corporate citizens of the EU have come to regret. In contrast, there is not even one joint department serving all of North America in any issue area, although the Commissions for Labour and the Environment created by side-agreements to NAFTA may be taken by some to be exceptions. There is practically no North American parallel to various branches of the European Commission that run major trans-European programs such as the Common Agricultural Policy (CAP). The closest possible candidate is the informal consultation that commonly takes place between various officials of the Canadian and American governments. But there is no "North American Department of Anything" or any common administrative program that even faintly resembles the CAP. In fact, when American President Ronald Reagan floated such an idea for energy—a North American Energy Accord with Canada and Mexico— both his intended partners ran away from the idea like children who knocked at the wrong door on Hallowe'en.

Even the extent of interbureaucratic cooperation and consultation between Canada and the US is difficult to measure with any confidence. For 25 years, occasional studies of the Canada-US relationship have referred to a variety of instances of this phenomenon, but thorough case-studies have yet to supplement the anecdotal evidence of the process. A recent overview of the Canada-US relationship pointed out the "host of bi-lateral agreements ... designed to structure and manage various aspects of the ties between the two countries" and argued that "given the complexity of the relationship and the number of issues continuously on the table, it is virtually impossible ... for issue linkage to occur," but did not document the manner in which these relations are conducted.[12] This lack of detailed evidence probably has to do with the fact that most such informal consultations occur over the telephone—or more recently the Internet—and leave little, if any, paper trail. It also appears routine that officials of the two countries take a large number of trips between their national capitals and frequently appear at the same international conferences, whether sponsored by government departments themselves or by private trade associations, policy research organizations, or universities. However, systematic measurement and analysis of this is difficult, and to my knowledge has not even been attempted.

4. Social Communications

The social communications dimension of IPI is really nothing more or less than the sum of the mutual interactions comprising international interdependence, that is, the sum total of all the movements of goods, capital, people, and information between two or more countries. Given their vastness, the volumes of such transactions taking

---

[12] Fen Osler Hampson and Maureen Appel Molot, "Does the 49th Parallel Matter Any More?" in M.A. Molot and F.O. Hampson, eds., *Vanishing Borders: Canada Among Nations, 2002* (Don Mills, ON: Oxford University Press, 2000) 3 and 5. The last point is not to fault these authors for failing to provide sources, but rather to add weight to the conclusion that such studies do not exist. More recently, John Higginbotham and Jeff Heynen have reviewed and categorized 15 different types of "bilateral processes" that help form the functional linkages between the two countries, ranging from prime ministerial and presidential visits and summits through various joint programs, working groups task forces, and exchanges of personnel. See John Higginbotham and Jeff Heynen, "Managing Through Networks: The State of Canada-US Relations," in David Carment, Fen Osler Hampson, and Norman Hillmer, eds., *Canada Among Nations 2004: Setting Priorities Straight* (Montreal and Kingston: McGill-Queen's University Press, 2005) 130-31.

place between Canada and the US will not, therefore, be fully itemized in this section. However, a general comparison between the European and North American experience along this dimension is important to the clarification of integration theory. North American progress in this direction is not only very large, but is so exceptionally large that it raises a question about the conspicuous lack of anything like commensurate progress along the institutional and political dimensions of IPI, a fact that seems to violate standard versions of integration theory, especially its neo-functional version. As already discussed, the core hypothesis of the theory of IPI is that intensifying relations of exchange and communications between people in two or more communities will produce, in time, some significant changes in the political relations between those communities. By a strict definition of political integration, the predicted change in political relations between such communities is movement toward their eventual fusion into a new, more comprehensive, and coherent political community, that is, a new or expanded nation-state.

Many consider the members of the EU to be on this predicted trajectory. In apparent confirmation of the theory of IPI, the increasingly close economic and social relations among Western European nations in the aftermath of the Second World War set in motion a train of commercial and political transformations that went through a sequence of phases over almost 50 years: the European Coal and Steel Community in 1952, the creation of the European Common Market under the Treaty of Rome in 1957, the Single European Act of 1986, and the creation of the EU under the Maastricht Treaty of 1992. From the very beginning of this process, and certainly no less today, part of the rationale for these major economic and political measures has been their contribution to the eventual creation of a United States of Europe, a new superstate in place of the numerous, formerly sovereign states of Europe. Many observers see the present movement toward a comprehensive European currency as yet another step in this direction.

No serious observer would contend that the evolutionary path of European integration represents a perfect fit between history and theory. In any case, the process remains incomplete, particularly since a common foreign policy for the members of the current EU remains highly problematic. Nevertheless, the European experience is the most powerful case to date of the fundamental idea that an increasingly deeply shared economic space will someday be capped by a common political space. The fundamental problem with integration theory, however, is that it seems to be disconfirmed by another major case in point: North America. It is precisely along the dimension of socio-economic transactions that North America surpasses all other instances of IPI, and yet, as already noted, North America is at best classified as a weak case of IPI with respect to the dimensions of joint decision-making and administration. To boot, there is a total absence, at least in the Canadian and Mexican cases, of any express enthusiasm for the eventual creation of a United States of North America embracing the three members of NAFTA.

The reason for the failure of this level of interactions in North America to produce the shifts in political alignments predicted by the IPI model is not (and for many observers, never has been) all that mysterious. As we saw in the discussion of "disjoined partners" in the previous chapter, two of the North American partners, Canada and Mexico, simply do not want, and to some extent fear that very prospect, while the third partner is largely indifferent to it. In short, North American political integration is extremely weak along the dimension of public attitudes and political opinion.

5. Public Attitudes and Values

This dimension represents the extent to which political integration is supported by the populations of the countries engaged in the process. There is little to choose between North America and Western Europe here: in both regions only a bare majority of the people, at best, can be said to endorse movement in the direction of closer political ties. This fact was more than confirmed, at least in relation to the people of France, who rejected by roughly 54 to 46 per cent a referendum on a new constitution for the EU.

Public opinion polls in Europe show either no growth or a slight decline in the numbers of Europeans in EU member countries who profess a stronger "European" than national identity. Moreover, whenever agreements promoing European unity have been put to national electorates, they have passed by the narrowest of margins. The proportion of the population in most European countries favouring closer integration tends to represent a slight minority.[13] Respecting (or fearing) their electorates, the British and some other European governments have stopped short of membership in the European Monetary Union, suggesting that the transfer of sovereignty threshold is still high for many European national populations.

Meanwhile, popular support for "doing away with borders" between Canada, Mexico, and the US is, respectively, at 24, 25, and 46 per cent of their national populations.[14] Such surveys scarcely tell the whole story, but the recent movement across Europe, North America, and parts of Asia Pacific toward more closely integrated free trade associations does not enjoy widespread popular support. "Loss of sovereignty" is usually cited as the deepest, albeit imprecise, reason for this lack of popularity outside as well as inside Europe.

Without going into further detail on the numbers and measures associated with this dimension, it is possible to summarize them: political integration in both Western Europe and North America is prone to what has been called a "democratic deficit." Simply stated, the economic and political elites of the countries involved are taking their citizens faster and further down the road to integration than they want to be taken. In this, the politics of trade liberalization under both NAFTA and the Single European Act seem prone to the same antagonisms between elites and broader publics as those that have marked recent protests against the Multilateral Agreement on Investment of the late 1990s and the more recent "battles" against the WTO in

---

[13] See Charles Haas, *Comparative Politics: Domestic Responses to Global Challenges*, 2nd ed. (St. Paul, MN: West Publishing, 1997) 187-88: "The European people will probably play a decisive role in determining the next phase in the EU's evolution, but probably more as a brake on rather than as a spur to further integration. While Europe is quite popular with ... post materialists ... there is probably more opposition to giving the EU further powers today." Haas adds that "Europe" is one of the most divisive political issues in most countries in the region.

[14] Ronald F. Inglehart, Neil Nevitte, and Miguel Basañez, *The North American Trajectory: Cultural, Economic and Political Ties among the United States, Canada and Mexico* (Hawthorne, NY: Aldine de Gruyter, 1996) 145, Figure 6.4.

Seattle, London, and Washington—although clearly neither NAFTA or the Single European Act have been the subject of violent protest or even much highly visible opposition.

RELATIONS AMONG DIMENSIONS

The most important observation to make about the interconnections among the five dimensions of integration is that there is absolutely no evidence that progress toward integration occurs along each dimension at the same rate or even in the same direction. As the discussion of each dimension has already suggested, equally significant movement toward integration on the socio-economic dimension can occur in two different regions—the EU and NAFTA—with no effect on decision-making institutions in one region but considerable effects in the other. Similarly, significant progress toward integration could be occurring on the decision-making, functional administration, and socio-economic dimensions in both regions, while it has no effect on coercive power (or formal transfer of sovereignty) in either region, despite neutral or even negative progress toward integration on the dimensions of attitudes and values.

Nevertheless, this overall discussion of the relationship between economic and political integration would remain incomplete without attempting a rough correlation between the degrees or stages of market liberalization and the dimensions of political integration. Broadly speaking, there is only a loose association between the "higher" stages of market liberalization and more advanced dimensions of political integration. In other words, it is fairly clear that free trade areas, and possibly even customs unions, can operate at extremely low levels of institutionalization and joint decision-making. It is not clear, however, that either a common market or an economic union either requires, or inevitably brings about, advanced degrees of institutional supranationalism. As we have seen at several points earlier in this chapter, the North American case clearly shows that market liberalization can advance very far without a commitment to supranational forms of political integration, and it is still not clear exactly how much further the Europeans

will go in that direction. It seems time, then, to draw some overall conclusions about the relationships at work (or not at work) in this area.

The "Integration Hypothesis"

Figure 6.1 highlights the fact that the Canada-US relationship
represents a crucial case-study in political integration by showing
the broad comparison between the European and North American
variations of the "Grand Hypothesis" of IPI, which is that increased
socio-economic interaction and interdependence lead to political
integration. That is, the European variation on this hypothesis proceeds down the left axis of the diagram and the North American
down the right. So framed, this schema can be used to depict how the
integration process in North America helps to clarify thinking about
the dependent variable in political integration theory.

Figure 6.1: Relationship between Economic and Political Integration

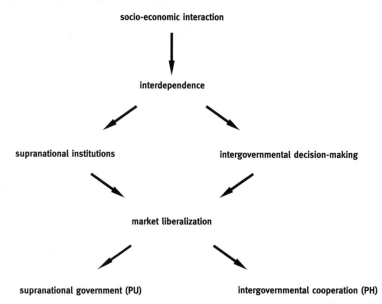

Note: The arrows stand for the phrase "leads to," and PU and PH stand for "political
unification" and "policy harmonization," respectively.

Most of the international scholarship concerning political integration over the past 30 years has shared two general characteristics: empirically it has been focused predominantly on Western Europe, and theoretically it has posited political unification as the ultimate end of social and economic integration. As argued in this chapter, however, the Canada-US relationship exhibits higher levels of almost all forms of socio-economic interaction than are found between the countries of Western Europe, and yet it has yielded practically nothing in the way of new central institutions to govern the relationship. This is inconsistent with most of the claims of neo-functional integration theory.

This paradox disappears if we adopt a "communications" as opposed to a "neo-functional" approach to the study of North American political integration, which means that (following Karl Deutsch) we define the dependent variable in the process of IPI in terms of the mutual responsiveness of the governments of the integrating countries rather than in terms of the formal institutionalization of their interactions. Specifically, the hypothesis is that, as socio-economic integration between the US and Canada has intensified, there has been a reduction in the degree to which the laws and regulations of the two countries discriminate against the other's goods, capital, persons, and firms. Stated differently, governments in the two countries have become more "receptive" (or responsive) to the other's nationals. Thus, the dependent variable in the North American portion of the model of political integration is the harmonization (or convergence) of national policy outputs, rather than the creation of formal arrangements for joint decision-making. Both, however, stand as forms of IPI.

THE "INSTITUTIONAL DEFICIENCY" OF
NORTH AMERICAN POLITICAL INTEGRATION[15]

Despite the prospect just noted that the processes of political integration in Europe and North America may be headed toward the

---

[15] The quoted phrase is taken from Kirston Appendini and Sven Bislev, eds., *Economic Integration in NAFTA and the EU: Deficient Institutionality* (New York: St. Martin's Press, 1999).

same destination, it is important not to understate the profound differences that exist in the respective means they have adopted to get there. There are, first of all, countless differences in the circumstances under which the process of economic liberalization got under way in Western Europe 50 years ago compared with those under which, more recently, it was undertaken in North America. However, it may be useful to review what the most significant differences are and, more importantly, to establish how they may have placed an enduring stamp on the two processes.

The most obvious contrast between the two cases of integration is that, from the start, the Europeans were self-consciously seeking political unity as well as economic integration, because of the historical and geopolitical conditions that prevailed in Europe after 1945. Another significant difference is that, even among the "original six,"[16] the European process was marked by a larger number of more equal national actors. It will be helpful to review a few of the details concerning each of these differences.

Historical and Geopolitical Factors

It is generally agreed that the EU represents the high-water mark of both economic and political integration over the past 50 years. The problem lies in accepting this correlation of economic integration with political integration as evidence of causation, not least because it is not even clear which direction the arrow of causality should be pointing. Sorting out the economic chicken from the political egg of European integration would be very like (to shamelessly pursue a related metaphor) unscrambling an omelet.

However, it seems difficult to dispute the interpretation that the unusually high degree of supranationalism in the European system—defined as the creation of powerful central institutions for the purposes of deciding and administering common policies for all members—is

---

[16] The original six signatories to the Treaties of Rome were France, the Netherlands, Belgium, Luxemburg, Italy, and the Federal Republic of Germany.

largely attributable to the political, rather than the strictly economic objectives of the founding states. The primary motives for the integration of Western Europe can be summarized as peace, power, and prosperity: peace between erstwhile major combatants, France and Germany; power both to defend against aggression from the (then) Soviet Union and to counter the pre-eminence of the US; and prosperity to meet the postwar demands of a devastated population. Most observers take as given that European integration differs significantly from North American integration, partly because of the former's explicit commitment to supranationalism, but also because of the consciously political origins of that commitment. Less frequently recognized, however, is the primary consequence (or corollary) of that fundamental difference, namely, that in Western Europe, unlike North America, the process of trade liberalization has been associated with the (re)creation, rather than the contraction of state power.

The sovereign power of European states, most notably France and (West) Germany, to take up arms against one another could not be reliably contained simply by diminishing the power and scope of the member governments to manage and otherwise intervene in their own domestic societies. To ensure peace between them, those sovereign powers needed to be overridden by the gradual creation of a "super-sovereign," one with the capacity to run all of the members' common affairs and eventually their societies. The fact that this ultimate objective has been (as yet) only partially and imperfectly realized does not diminish the effect that the historical origins of the integration process in Europe has had on the balance between state and markets that has prevailed there throughout. The process of integration in Western Europe is about pooling state authority, not eroding it.

In the meantime, the governments of the countries of North America have set out more modestly to achieve only one of the three European goals for integration—prosperity—and the institutional component of their steps in that direction has been correspondingly more modest. It is likely to remain that way. Nobody expects Canada and/or Mexico to go to war against the US, and, oddly enough, this means that the *formal* sovereignty of all three members of NAFTA is untouched by their commitment to economic integration. The "peace" and "power" objectives were either a foregone conclusion or beside the point in the North American context, given the inevitable deference of Canada and Mexico to the overweening power of the US.[17] One can at least speculate, therefore, that the three-item rationale for integration motivating political elites in Western Europe is responsible for their long-standing commitment to the achievement of supergovernment there, whereas the single-item agenda—or, rather, the absence of the peace and power agendas—of elites in North America is responsible for their lack of a comparable commitment to institution-building.

However, the fact that the North American commitment to economic integration, for all of the foregoing reasons, has not been accompanied by the creation of a supergovernment does not at all imply that it will not involve significant degrees of political integration. As this discussion will demonstrate in greater detail below, NAFTA has set in motion a number of joint decision-making processes with considerable potential to bring about common economic policies and standardized treatment of investors across the three parties to the agreement. In doing so, NAFTA represents for the US the achievement in its own neighbourhood of an agenda it originally set for the entire international economy in the aftermath of the Second World War: the convergence of national economic policies and greater accessibility of foreign markets to American-based firms.

Decision-theory Factors

The prospects for supranational decision-making in North America seem meager enough, given the discussion presented above. Moreover, the likelihood of its emergence is reduced further by the

---

[17] In a different context, the power dimension may not have been totally absent in relation to NAFTA: some have argued that one of the American motives in seeking continental free trade was to hedge against the consolidation of the world economy into European and Asian blocs. It is similarly argued that NAFTA was a shot across the bow of the members of the other regional blocs, warning them to pursue more seriously the agenda for deeper economic integration through the GATT/WTO (sometimes referred to as the "domino effect").

difficulty of designing the rules according to which such institutions might operate, particularly given the small number of unequal partners involved in the integration of North America. Once again, special circumstances can be seen to favour the "political integration as institutionalization" model for Europe, but only for Europe.

The number of actors in an organization and the degree of equality (or symmetry) among them are important characteristics of IGOs because they affect the manner in which each member weighs the costs and benefits of membership. For each party to the formation of any organization, the net benefit from joining it is the sum of the gains that forming the group is expected to promote minus the anticipated costs of belonging to it, such as the transaction costs involved in creating and running it, as well as the disadvantages that may flow from any unwanted decisions it may make. Thus, even where the creation of central authorities with particular supranational powers may seem to promise benefits, the perceived costs of designing, operating, and, not least, acting in conformity with such authorities may be reckoned too high, and the expected extra gains from trade or the elimination of negative externalities seem too modest by comparison.

Finally, even if a purely transactions-cost analysis proves positive, particular problems of institutional design may still render the creation and ongoing operation of joint decision-making institutions difficult or even impossible. The literature on international organizations does not pay much attention to the problems of institutional design in general or to decision rules in particular. This overall lack is equally true, to date, of studies of NAFTA. Peter Smith, however, has drawn several conclusions about the prospects for joint decision-making in NAFTA (and possible enlargements of it) using a combination of broadly theoretical perspectives and comparisons with the EU.[18] Writing just before NAFTA went into effect, he foresaw, first, that the three-party agreement would implicitly or explicitly entail

---

[18] Peter H. Smith, "Decision Rules and Governance," in P.H. Smith, ed., *The Challenge of Integration: Europe and the Americas* (New Brunswick, FL: University of Miami, North-South Center, 1993) Ch. 14.

unanimity among the members; second, that, for this reason, the decision-making machinery within it would be cumbersome and slow; and, third, that it would be subject to institutional paralysis.[19]

Smith recognized further that the considerable disparity in size among NAFTA members would reinforce their determination to hold on to the unanimity principle. By the same logic, he cited the absence of a "hegemon" in Western Europe as an important factor in promoting a spirit of give and take in negotiations within the (then) European Community. As he contended, it is "this condition of relative parity—or, better said, lack of acute disparity—that has enabled the Community to establish its system of decision-making by qualified majority."[20]

As Smith pointed out, there is no such prospect for North America, or even for the Western Hemisphere. The power of the US relative to all its neighbours is so overwhelming that

> it is difficult to conjure up any form of qualified majority rule for decision-making within the Americas. The United States would naturally resist any scheme that would allow it to be outvoted, and Latin Americans (and Canadians) are likely to resist any scheme that would assure U.S. domination.[21]

INSTITUTIONALIZATION AND HARMONIZATION UNDER NAFTA

Both history and theory, therefore, suggest strongly that national governments on this side of the Atlantic are not very likely to take a path of political integration similar to that of the EU. While both

---

[19] Smith 376-77. Smith sets out the logic that led to this conclusion as follows: "The range of decision rules bears a direct relationship to the number of parties involved. Almost by definition, bilateral arrangements entail the principle of unanimity: both parties possess a veto. Trilateral agreements present the theoretical possibility of majority rule, but without any system of qualification. The risk of losing out in a two-to-one vote leads parties to prefer unanimity (or to refrain from joining in the first place)."

[20] Smith 379.

[21] Smith 381.

experiences represent a blend of the "political integration as political unification" and the "political integration as policy harmonization" models, the former clearly dominates in Europe and the latter prevails in North America. However, NAFTA does create joint decision-making institutions, in fact, quite a number of them. However, while the capacity of these institutions to supersede national governments appears minor, NAFTA's provisions relating to policy harmonization, involving such matters as national treatment, rights of establishment, government procurement, and international arbitration, are substantial.

A general review of the institutions created by NAFTA will serve to document its relative balance in favour of the integration-as-harmonization model.

Institutional Provisions in NAFTA

At first, the North American Free Trade Commission (created directly under Article 2001) appeared to be the most prominent institution associated with NAFTA. The Commission on Labor Cooperation and the Commission on Environmental Cooperation (created, respectively, by two Supplementary Agreements) were also conspicuous because they were intensely debated during ratification by the American Senate. Since the early years of the NAFTA regime, however, the Environmental Commission has been the only one of the three to maintain a reasonably high profile, as measured by the degree of academic attention and interest group activity it has attracted. Also of interest to Americans, but less so to Canadians because they are not a party to them, are the Border Environmental Cooperation Commission and the North American Development Bank, both of which are primarily concerned with joint US-Mexican environmental projects.[22]

---

[22] See Frederick M. Abbott, *Law and Policy of Regional Integration: The NAFTA and Western Hemispheric Integration in the World Trade Organization System* (Dordrecht, NL: Martinus Nijhoff Publishers, 1995) 28-30.

These NAFTA commissions are not invested with supranational authority comparable to the chief agencies of the EU. The Free Trade Commission (FTC) is composed of cabinet-level representatives and was assigned the role of overseeing the implementation of the agreement, as well as supervising its dispute resolution processes. These roles are implemented on the basis of consensus (i.e., unanimous agreement) among the parties to it.[23] In any case, apart from routine administration by its secretariat, which operates strictly under mandates delegated by consensus among the parties, the FTC is practically dormant. It does not appear to have published or posted an annual report since 1999.

Arguably one activity of the FTC that does merit attention is the oversight and general direction it gives the secretariat's management and coordination of NAFTA's widening constellation of committees and working groups.[24] As of 1997, according to Sidney Weintraub, there were 24 committees and working groups under NAFTA, and "in each case their duties correspond to a particular clause in the agreement."[25] More specifically, NAFTA creates (among others) committees on Trade in Goods, Agricultural Trade, Standards-Related Measures, Small Business, and Financial Services. There are also working groups bearing titles such as Rules of Origin; Agricultural Subsidies; Meat and Poultry Inspection; Dairy, Fruit, Vegetable and Egg Inspection; Trade and Competition; Procurement; Services and Investment; Import Surges; and Subsidies/Countervailing Duties and Anti-Dumping. Finally, the agreement contains articles creating the Land Transportation Standards and Telecommunications Standards Subcommittees.

---

[23] Abbott 28.

[24] See Joseph A. McKinney, *Created from NAFTA: The Structure, Function, and Significance of the Treaty's Related Institutions* (Armonk, NY: M.E. Sharpe, 2000) 26-27: "In addition to their annual meetings, the Free Trade Commission has established other mechanisms for fostering communication and for overseeing the work program of the various NAFTA committees and working groups. At their meeting on 29 April 1998, the Free Trade Commission members directed their deputy ministers to meet regularly twice a year, 'to provide high-level, ongoing oversight of the NAFTA work program' ... Furthermore, NAFTA coordinators (chosen from within each of the respective ministries) ... confer monthly by telephone to discuss the progress of the various committees and working groups and to help keep their work organized."

[25] Sidney Weintraub, *NAFTA at Three: A Progress Report* (Washington, DC: Center for Strategic and International Studies, 1997) 71.

According to de Vanssay and Mahant, despite the presence of the FTC and the operations of some of its delegated agencies, NAFTA's institutional structure is "decentralized and apparently uncoordinated" compared with the quasi-federal institutional structure of the EU. Over all, they conclude that "NAFTA's institutional structure is far behind that of the European Union in terms of supranationality, if not in complexity."[26] In fact, the functional specificity of the responsibilities delegated by NAFTA is, in itself, a measure of this lack of supranationality; the assignment of narrow, essentially technical tasks is generally acknowledged to be a hallmark of IGOs designed to promote cooperation without impinging on the sovereign powers of member governments.

Despite the lack of supranational powers attached to these various agencies, however, their potential contribution to the harmonization of national policies—and, therefore, their contribution to North American political integration by that definition—should not be dismissed out of hand. Indeed, a recent article has described NAFTA "as an ongoing framework under which deeper and even broader economic and policy integration will occur."[27] According to this study, NAFTA's elaborate set of "new intergovernmental bodies"—meaning its commissions, committees, and working groups—are a key element in a wider dynamic of community formation, that is, "the emergence of a sense of North American community, beginning with an acceptance of a significant and irreversible interdependence and common future among those in the three countries—at the governmental, corporate, NGO, and individual levels."[28] When the mandate for each

---

[26] Xavier de Vanssay and Edelgard Mahant, "Three's Company and Fifteen's a Union: The Comparative Political Economy of NAFTA and the European Union—Integration or Liberalization?," in Till Geiger and Dennis Kennedy, eds., *Regional Trade Blocs, Multilateralism, and the GATT: Complementary Paths to Free Trade?* (London; New York: Pinter, 1996) 138.

[27] Rugman, Kirton, and Soloway 200.

[28] Rugman, Kirton, and Soloway 204. In the conclusions to their analysis (215), the authors succinctly characterize the FTA/NAFTA as "a quasi-political regime to complement the integrated economic and business systems of Canada and the United States."

committee or working group is tied back to its corresponding clause in the agreement, one can see that the standardization of national approaches is often an important part of that mandate. The NAFTA provisions with respect to "Standards-Related Measures" (Chapter 9, Article 913) are a case in point. According to Chapter 9, each party pledges nondiscriminatory treatment in the application of any such measures it adopts.[29] However, Article 913 also establishes a Committee on Standards-Related Measures with a mandate, among other things, to facilitate the process by which the parties make these measures compatible. It is also mandated to "consider non-governmental developments in standards-related measures."

Similarly, part of the terms of reference for the Working Group on Trade and Competition Policy is "to make recommendations on relevant issues concerning the relationship between competition laws and policies and trade in the free trade area" (Chapter 15, Article 1504). Among the tasks consigned to this working group are a review of "differences in mergers and vertical-restraint regimes," as well as possible participation with the private sector in a roundtable on trade and competition.

Further work on the actual operations of these agencies will be necessary before anyone can legitimately draw firm conclusions about their impact on Canada-US trade and investment relations. Yet, even this bare sampling of the institutional provisions contained in the agreement indicates their potential to promote, at the very least, mutual recognition of the parties' standards and practices and possibly harmonization of those standards and practices. Moreover, there are similarly strong indications, both in the language of relevant provisions of the agreement and in academic studies of the performance of NAFTA's committees and working groups,

---

[29] The section reads, in part, as follows: "Each Party shall, in respect of its standards-related measures, accord to goods and service providers of another Party: (a) national treatment in accordance with Article 301 (Market Access) or Article 1202 (Cross-Border Trade in Services); and (b) treatment no less favorable than that it accords to like goods, or in like circumstances to service providers, of any other country."

that business corporations are highly active players in the process of policy harmonization.[30]

Indeed, the "political integration as policy harmonization" model dovetails perfectly with the role of MNCs in the process of policy standardization. International firms have an interest in preserving the sovereign power of states to maintain property rights and to enforce international contracts. At the same time, such firms have no wish to see those sovereign powers invested in a global superstate, and therefore they have no strong desire to see existing nation-states disappear. However, they do hope to ensure that the continuing multiplicity of sovereign states does not also guarantee the survival of a patchwork of trade- and investment-related policies at the national level that both complicates their global management of assets, production, and marketing and inflates their transaction costs. Thus, to join actively in the negotiations among governments to reduce differences in national policies, whether through universal trade organizations such as the WTO or through regional organizations such as NAFTA, is the preferred remedy for the costs and complexities that system friction causes them.

This conclusion is consistent with the past 55 years of American leadership of the international economy. Sylvia Ostry has ably and convincingly demonstrated that a primary objective of American

---

[30] The author has not been able to find many academic treatments of business participation in NAFTA decision-making. Rugman, Kirton, and Soloway (212-15) develop a brief case study of business-government relations under the auspices of NAFTA in the chemicals sector. Indirect evidence that such activity is both present and significant is available in Stephen Blank and Jerry Haar, *Making NAFTA Work: U.S. Firms and the New North American Business Environment* (University of Miami: North-South Center Press, 1999). This study presents an excellent account of the close interconnections between North American business rationalization and deepening continental integration. The authors conclude (84) that "pressures on U.S. firms to integrate across North America will continue and even intensify," and they therefore "speak with confidence of a dynamic, rapidly evolving and deepening North American economy." Finally, Susan K. Sell has shown how American firms actively lobbied for favourable treatment of intellectual property rights under the WTO (modeled on provisions they had already achieved under NAFTA) in "Structures, Agents and Institutions: Private Corporate Power and the Globalization of Intellectual Property Rights," in R.A. Higgott, G.R.D. Underhill, and A. Bieler, eds., *Non-State Actors and Authority in the Global System* (New York: Routledge, 2000) Ch. 5.

economic foreign policy-makers since the end of the Second World War (apart from the reduction of foreign tariffs) has been to make the domestic economic policy environment in other countries more open to competition from American MNCs—what we today refer to broadly as "rights of establishment."[31] Indeed, one of the principal reasons for the US's failure to achieve international acceptance of a prospective International Trade Organization (ITO) after the Second World War was its inability to get its principal postwar economic partners to agree to measures designed to reduce the differences in national economic systems and to improve the contestability of foreign markets by American-based producers of goods and services.

Even more telling, the American administration's ITO initiative was ultimately aborted by its own Congress, and the weaker GATT was all that the US and its international negotiating partners could bring into being. Ostry contends that behind this congressional opposition, apart from some academic and ideological perfectionism, was the protectionism—or, perhaps more fairly, the counter-protectionism—of powerful American business lobbies. At its heart, she argues, "was a rejection of the idea that there can be many variants of market systems, with different institutional arrangements including different mixes of government and business roles. And where such differences existed, they were, in the view of American business, probably unfairly protectionist."[32]

In the present context, it is worth remembering that, back then, the US's preferred means of advancing this agenda was—as it has remained recently with the last round of the GATT negotiations and with the recent creation of the WTO—emphatically *not* to bring nations together under a world government, but merely to make national economic policies everywhere more closely conform with its own. From this perspective, NAFTA represents the realization of the US's postwar global economic agenda through the achievement of its "own" regional trade association.

---

[31] Sylvia Ostry, *The Post-Cold War Trading System: Who's on First?* (Chicago, IL: University of Chicago Press, 1997) 233.
[32] Ostry 65.

chapter 7
NORTH AMERICAN REGIONALISM

This chapter has two purposes: first, to document the increasing re-gionalization of Canada's political, economic, social, and cultural space; and, second, to assess a corresponding increase in the impor-tance of cross-border regional relationships in the overall Canada-US relationship. These two purposes are woven through the fabric of the chapter's four principal themes: (1) the relationship between conti-nental integration and Canadian disintegration; (2) the increasing prominence of several "city-regions" in the Canadian economy; (3) the development of "micro-integration" in several such city-regions spanning the Canada-US border; and (4) the tension in cross-border management between the desire to free up the border in order to maximize the economic benefits of border flows and the need to minimize the risk from terrorist and other illegal activity that an open border presents.

To draw attention to regions and regionalism in Canada is noth-ing new to Canadian political economy. In many ways, Canada has always been, and has always been regarded as, a "country of regions." However, the issues and studies addressed here are new, or at least bring new economic, social, and political perspectives to more fa-miliar understandings. Most of the earlier discussions of Canadian regionalism have stressed Canada's economic dependence upon the export of primary resources such as fish, furs, wood products, met-als, and oil and natural gas, since most of these resources tend to be concentrated in some parts of the country and are completely absent in others. Moreover, as world prices for these commodities have risen and fallen at different times and varying rates, individual regions of Canada have experienced, in effect, localized business cycles, so that any given set of national macro-economic policies has frequently had highly varied impacts across different regions of the country.

More recent perspectives on Canadian regionalism have generally been framed to capture the direct and indirect effects of continental and global free trade on the political, economic, and social structures of the country. The expansion of world markets generally promotes international specialization in the production of goods and services; accordingly, larger markets for Canadian goods encourage even greater regional differentiation of the Canadian economy. Meanwhile, the rise to pre-eminence of neo-conservative political and economic ideas has tended to shrink the role of the central government relative to that of provinces and municipalities. Against this background, it is perhaps no surprise that the themes presented here are emerging as the most significant characteristics of "Canada's new regionalism" or, indeed, of North American regionalism.

Before examining how these themes and developments bear on the Canada-US relationship, and particularly on two cases of economic regionalism in Canada, it may be useful to review in greater detail the developments that are contributing to North American regionalism and the growth of cross-border integration.

BACKGROUND FACTORS

There are three major background conditions to increasing regionalism in North America: the great diversity of the North American continent, the adoption of free trade, and a global trend toward economic regionalism and the accompanying decline of the nation-state and national economies.

North American Regional Diversity:
"Nations" along the Border

Over 20 years ago, Joel Garreau published an intriguing book that adopted an unusual perspective on the social, economic, and cultural make-up of North America. He called it *The Nine Nations of North America*, suggesting that the US, for example, did not consist of a single country with a uniform culture (in the broadest sense of that term), but rather of several different regional cultures, each with a distinct combination of economic conditions, social customs, lifestyles, and political priorities.[1] He gave these regions slightly peculiar labels—"Ecotopia" for the west coast, the "Empty quarter" for the Rocky Mountain corridor, and the "Foundry" for the Great Lakes region, for example—and then devoted a separate, detailed chapter to the distinguishing characteristics of each of his nine nations.

Garreau's presentation is a bit quirky in places, and the whole book is much more journalistic than academic, but it is nevertheless an interesting and engaging "take" on the presence of regional economies and subcultures on the continent. What is important for us to note is that five of the nations Garreau describes—Ecotopia, the Empty Quarter, the Breadbasket, the Foundry, and New England—straddle the Canada-US border and thus encompass a combination of Canadian provinces and adjacent American states. The Breadbasket, for example, includes parts of the prairie provinces with all or part of American border states such as North Dakota, Idaho, and Wisconsin, while New England combines Canada's Atlantic provinces with the northeastern US. (In Garreau's schema, Quebec, as some of the province's separatists were no doubt pleased to note, was a "nation" of its own.)

Again, Garreau does not so much account for as merely describe the distinguishing characteristics that define each of his regions. Nevertheless, his version of North America usefully serves to introduce an emerging reality that is finding an increasingly concrete expression

---

[1] Joel Garreau, *The Nine Nations of North America* (Boston, MA: Houghton-Mifflin, 1981).

in Canadian politics and Canada-US relations: Canada's provinces and regions interact more intensely with, and have more in common with, adjacent states in the US than they do with other parts of Canada. In short, cross-border integration is proceeding apace with national disintegration. This development is reinforced by several other factors (discussed below), such as the tendency of free trade to promote north-south instead of east-west linkages to the detriment of the centralizing capacities of the federal government. For the moment, however, it is sufficient to sketch the special character of each of Canada's five principal regions. (The North, except possibly for the Yukon and Alaska, does not fit into the cross-border framework under consideration here.)

A west-to-east tour of North America's borderland regions begins with the Pacific Northwest, the more northerly portion of Garreau's west-coast Ecotopia. This is a socio-cultural and economic region linking British Columbia with the states of Washington and Oregon, and specializing in such areas as fishing and fish-processing, forest products, eco-tourism, and links with Asia Pacific. A short distance to the east is the northern portion of Garreau's Empty Quarter, including the interior of British Columbia, the Rocky Mountains and "oil patch" of Alberta, and the mountain states of Montana, Idaho, and Wyoming. It also includes strong links between Calgary and the cities of the American southwest that are involved with the oil and gas industry.

Further to the east is the Breadbasket, comprising the Canadian prairies and the American plains and supporting a culture dominated by the production of grains and other agricultural products. Passing over the largely barren Canadian Shield, the next cross-border region is the Great Lakes Basin, encompassing southern Ontario and the states of Michigan, Ohio, Pennsylvania, and New York. This is Garreau's Foundry (although the recessions of the 1980s and 1990s caused some observers to term the area "the rust belt"). The Foundry is marked predominantly by heavy and light industry, most notably the automobile industry and related parts and service industries. Next is Quebec, on the Canadian side, which has no American (or Canadian) counterpart, owing to the uniquely French character of the province. However, economically it does have strong economic ties with New York and New England based largely on its massive exports of hydro-electric power. This linkage is supplemented by general economic ties between the cities of Montreal, Boston, and New York, as well as family ties stemming from Quebec migration to the northeastern states, particularly during the late nineteenth and early twentieth centuries. To that extent, in some respects Quebec deserves to be included as a functioning part of the Northeast of North America.

Our imagined tour of North American cross-border regions terminates at Garreau's New England, comprising the Atlantic provinces and the northern states of the American Atlantic seaboard. Their interactions are shaped by similar maritime economies and long-standing commercial ties between Halifax and Boston, which have historical roots in the fact that a large portion of the population of Nova Scotia (and to a lesser extent, New Brunswick) is descended from United Empire Loyalists and later immigrants from the US. More recently, oil and natural gas exports from Canada's off-shore deposits have assumed greater significance in the regional relationship relative to the declining fishing industry.

Free Trade Agreements

The economic geography of the cross-border regions of Canada and the US is not, of course, a recent development. The west-coast salmon industry, the trade relations centred on the St. Lawrence and Great Lakes Basin, and the forest industry in the northeast of the North American continent, in particular, have fostered distinct cross-border cultures that reach back a century or more.[2] However, the FTA and NAFTA have overlaid these long-standing linkages with two other

---

[2] Victor Konrad, "Borderlines and Borderlands in the Geography of Canada-United States Relations," in Stephen J. Randall and Herman W. Konrad, eds., *NAFTA in Transition* (Calgary, AB: University of Calgary Press, 1995) Ch. 11.

developments that are accelerating the trend toward stronger cross-border linkages and weaker transnational ones. First (as documented later in this chapter), they have enormously augmented north-south flows of goods and services to the point where every province of Canada with the exception of Prince Edward Island now exports more to the rest of the world (principally the US) than to the rest of Canada. Second, the agreements, along with the neo-conservative philosophy that inspired and consolidated the free trade option for Canada, have reduced the role of the federal government relative to its historical scale and scope and have done so in favour of provincial governments.[3]

To elaborate briefly on the second of these points, NAFTA either prohibits or strongly discourages the kinds of national policies and policy instruments that the Canadian central government used to rely upon to counter the pull of the American economy and to promote all sorts of trans-Canadian transactions. The best single example of this (and perhaps the most telling one in the light of recent significant increases in the price of oil, natural gas, and electricity) is that NAFTA rules out any prospect of the re-imposition of the NEP of 1980. As we saw in Chapter 5, NAFTA forbids the Canadian government either to restrict exports from Canada's petroleum producing provinces to the US in favour of expanded deliveries to central Canadian markets or to charge Americans more than Canadians for their energy.

Apart from dramatic interventions by the federal government similar to the NEP, there is some doubt whether Canada's "social safety net" is itself safe from erosion by the market forces opened up by free trade. As Thomas Courchene has remarked, it is at least doubtful that Canada can maintain an east-west social-transfer system on top of a north-south trading system.[4] The intricacies of that argument will not be reviewed until later, but its core is that free trade tips

---

3   See, for example, Clarkson, esp. Chs. 5 and 14.
4   Thomas J. Courchene and C.R. Telmer, *From Heartland to North American Region-State: The Social, Fiscal and Federal Evolution of Ontario* (Toronto: University of Toronto Press, 1998) 295.

the balance of power away from the federal government and toward provincial governments. As the government of Quebec, in particular, has complained loudly for over 30 years, much of national social policy—including medicare, the centrepiece of federal involvement in the lives of all Canadians everywhere—formally falls under provincial jurisdiction, and only the "abuse" of the federal spending power has allowed for the creation of the national social policies on which Canadians have come to rely. Courchene feels that, as the country regionalizes economically, powerful provinces such as Ontario, Alberta, and British Columbia will begin to assume Quebec's assertive stance against federal dominance in many of these fields (albeit for different reasons).

One does not have to dig very deeply to uncover signs of movement in the direction indicated by Courchene. Explorations by the governments of Alberta and Ontario into the extended privatization of health care are one such sign; another is speculation about the advantages of a "provincial income tax." In addition to such potential erosions of federal primacy in fields of domestic policy, there is also a trend toward increasing provincial activity in foreign relations, whether in the form of economic missions abroad, lobbying in Washington, or more active cooperation and consultation with the governments of adjacent American states.

The Global Trend toward Economic Regionalism

Finally, in relation to nearly all these developments, Canada is not alone. There is a world-wide trend toward the decentralization of political power from national to subnational governments and the regionalization of national economies. Part of this devolution of economic and political power, according to some, is that the key players in the world economy of the twenty-first century are no longer nation-states, but city-centred regions. In fact, the term "glocalization"—with a "c," not a "b"—has been given to this process, fusing the "global" and the "local" and squeezing out the national.

This pressure on the traditional role and power of the nation-state simultaneously from above and below is ably encapsulated in a recent, authoritative overview of globalization:

> In the post-sovereign condition that has arisen with contemporary accelerated globalization, states are players in a complex public sector that also includes multiple substate and suprastate authorities. On the one hand, the expression of supraterritoriality has encouraged a proliferation of direct transborder connections between local and provincial governments. At the same time, globalization has promoted a major growth of regional and transworld governance mechanisms. As a result of this multiplication of substate and suprastate arrangements alongside regulation through states, contemporary governance has become considerably more decentralized and fragmented.[5]

One aspect of this fragmentation is the rise of city-centred regions to greater prominence as economic units. For example, there is evidence that city governments engage much more actively and directly in the investment decisions of MNCs than they used to and that the role of national governments in such public/private relations is in decline. This is one of the arguments made in a widely read and controversial book by Kenichi Ohmae.[6] Consider Ohmae's description of the shifting balance of economic decision-making power between the central government of China and its emerging city-centred zones of economic expansion:

> There is no way that China, as a single nation state, could pull in the necessary resources from MNCs, multilateral lending agencies, or the taxation of its own citizens. Nor is there any way that

it could either fund or manage the needed levels, countrywide, of infrastructure development on its own. As a federation of separate, deal-making regions, however, it can—and is. A region-specific BOT (build-operate-transfer) scheme, for instance, is already harnessing foreign resources and skills to build a critical highway from Shenzhen to Guangzhou and the Three Gorges dam along the Yangtze River Chang Jiang (sic).[7]

In these ways (among others), more fluid and rapid movement of goods and capital in the international economy are promoting higher degrees of specialization in local economies. This means, first, that national economies become increasingly fictitious, in that they no longer function as aggregations of local and regional economies, a process that now increasingly occurs at the world level. Second, city-centred regions and the political authorities who operate them are becoming increasingly aware that they must act together to maximize the competitive advantage of their regions by helping the various components of the regional economy work together at the highest possible level of efficiency.

In keeping with this, location theory and the theory of comparative (or "competitive") advantage have been undergoing some major developments lately, developments that are in turn connected to forces commonly regarded as aspects of globalization. The new location theory places much emphasis on the complementarities that may exist between different cities in particular socio-economic regions, many of which span existing national boundaries. These complementarities, whose origins and consequences are becoming better understood with the aid of the new institutional economics,

---

[7] Ohmae 118. Elsewhere, Ohmae describes the changes in MNC strategies that complement the shift away from national to regional and city governments as centres of decision-making: companies no longer think in terms of national markets like France, but regional markets like Provence or Auvergne, and organize production not on the basis of national assets and endowments, but regionally specific ones, coordinated along functional rather than territorial lines. See especially Ohmae, Ch. 8.

are producing dynamic efficiencies in many rapidly growing areas of the world.[8]

Some of the interactive components that contribute to these dynamics, which are referred to as "untraded interdependencies" or "locational [positive] externalities," are the result of strategic initiatives by local governments, often without any direct involvement from central or provincial governments.[9] Production in some industries is thus migrating from more conventional locales in various countries and becoming concentrated in regions where these complementarities are significant. Ohmae, whose concept of "economies of service" is defined in much the same terms, points to numerous examples of this kind of regional specialization. In particular, he includes as Appendix C to his book the story of Penang, Malaysia, which has achieved a spectacular rate of development by facilitating a wide range of economic interdependencies centred on the production of disk-drives.

For these reasons, Ohmae argues that "national" economic performance is a fiction: "As I have repeatedly argued over the years, it was not Japan that was so stunningly competitive, but only a handful of companies led by strong individuals within those industries."[10] He even suggests that the residual economic importance of nation-states is largely a consequence of the fact that production, investment, and

---

[8] There is a large literature developing on this phenomenon; see, for example, Markus Perkmann and Ngai-Ling Sum, eds., *Globalization, Regionalization and Cross-Border Regions* (New York: Palgrave Macmillan, 2002); and Peter Maskell and Gunnar Törnqvist, *Building a Cross-Border Learning Region: Emergence of the Northern European Øresund Region* (Copenhagen: Copenhagen Business School Press, 1999).

[9] Courchene and Telmer 282-83.

[10] Ohmae 65. On the previous page, Ohmae brings the following observation into his review of the comparative advantage issue: "as Annalee Saxanian so clearly demonstrates in her book, *Regional Advantage*, Silicon Valley prospers but Boston's Route 128 declines, even though they are in the same country." Ohmae also points out that the much vaunted "Japanese" economic miracle of the 1970s and 1980s was based on the success of only five major cities.

trade statistics are recorded as national aggregates, a theme that Jane Jacobs has also visited.[11] The epiphenomenon of measurement is all that remains of national economies, at least from this perspective. To quote again from Ohmae, "the nation state has become an unnatural—even a dysfunctional—organizational unit for thinking about economic activity. It combines things at the wrong level of aggregation."[12] Of course, Ohmae's claiming this does not make it true, but the fact remains that relations of economic production, distribution, and exchange no longer conform with national territorial boundaries to anything like the extent they did for most of the past century.

Regionalism and (International) Regional Trade Associations

The final background factor to be considered here is the growing literature (most of it focused on the EU) that studies the effects of wider processes of economic and political integration on the development of stronger subnational regions. (The terminology involved in some aspects of this subject is inescapably awkward: we are trying to understand how the creation of *international* regional trade organizations such as the EU and NAFTA can promote the strengthening of *subnational* regions which, to make matters worse, can also be international—or "cross-border"—in scope.)

Many of these discussions suggest that there may be a concrete causal link between the formation of organizations, such as regional trade associations, above the nation-state and the increasing autonomy of units below it, such as states, provinces, and municipalities.

---

[11] Jacobs criticizes Adam Smith for accepting without comment "the mercantilist tautology that nations are the salient entities for understanding the structure of economic life ... In short, Smith began with what we have come to know as the gross national product and proceeded on from there." She goes on to criticize the discipline of economics for their credulity, for such a long time, "about the merit of their subject matter's most formative and venerable assumption," namely, national economies. Jane Jacobs, *Cities and the Wealth of Nations* (New York: Random House, 1984) 30-31.

[12] Ohmae 16.

For example, some have argued that Britain's entry into the EU has been a factor in the devolution of political authority to Scotland and Wales. Closer to home, the same general point has been made about the possible regionalizing effects of the FTA:

> Trade and investment flows have not grown evenly across borders. Instead, flows of goods, services, capital and people have deepened between particular areas in each country. They create new interests and sharpen regional differences ... Thus, at the same time as we see the emergence of an overarching Canada-U.S. Free Trade Agreement, we also see heightened regional differentiation within North America.[13]

Two dynamics at work here are significant for our study. The first is that the more decision-making power that provinces and municipalities assume in relation to their local economies, the less effective is the exercise of central power over the national economy. The second is that, as just noted, regional economies straddle international boundaries.

Regarding the first of these dynamics, there is no strong economic reason to resist the regional decentralization of national economies. Most advanced economies today are marked by a massive shift in production away from manufacturing and agriculture toward services, and most services are produced and consumed in the same location (that is, they are not traded at a distance). This shift accounts for the fact that, typically, over 60 per cent of economic activity today is geared to consumption within individual regions. Typically, too, an increasing proportion (often the majority) of goods that are traded outside individual regions are exported internationally, not nationally, meaning that trade within countries is in significant decline, and national economies—viewed as internal systems of exchange—are increasingly less important to the lives of most citizens.

---

[13] Stephen Blank, *The Emerging Architecture of North America* (Coral Gables, FL: North-South Center, University of Miami, 1993) 3.

In short, while economic regionalization does not directly diminish the authority of national governments, it can reduce their salience in the lives of their citizens and, over time, can erode both the capacity and the inclination of those governments to intervene in their societies in accustomed ways. For Canada, this means that the first line of defence against the encroachment of American-centred political and economic forces—the policies of the central government—is eroded. It could also mean, as it seems to be doing in some countries of the EU, that people in their regions begin to shift their expectations and possibly their identification from the national level to the level of regional intergovernmental institutions.

The direct evidence for such a shift following the adoption of North American free trade is not abundant, but a recent study of cross-border regionalism suggests that "at borders where local communities engage in transborder relations, there is a great deal more going on than many analysts have suspected and, more to the point, than either national leaders or the national press have bothered to recognize":

> In some instances, there are a myriad of examples of building trans-border "community"—an essential first step in the process of building a "North American Community" that scholar-activist John W. Wirth envisioned in [a] 1996 essay. In other instances, residents themselves seemingly desire greater and more organic cross-border "integration," as well as greater autonomy from the national government—or at least closer consultation with them by it—in affairs that affect them.[14]

Thus, the formation of cross-border economic regions (the second dynamic) is more immediately connected to the Canada-US relationship; in fact, it is a *category* of those relations and, some would add, a

---

[14] Demetrios G. Papademetriou and Deborah Waller Meyers, "Overview, Context, and Vision for the Future," in D.G. Papademetriou and D.W. Meyers, eds., *Caught in the Middle: Border Communities in an Era of Globalization* (Washington, DC: Carnegie Endowment for International Peace, 2001) 16.

category of international integration (sometimes called "micro-integration"). The most general case has been succinctly summarized in *The New Regional Economics: The U.S. Common Market and the Global Economy*: "political boundaries are not congruent with the functional regional economy."[15] As its authors explain in more detail, political jurisdictions

> are government entities created to pursue the political and public service goals of their residents. They are not economies, however. The economic region is the functional economy. Thus, a region can be said to include one economy and many jurisdictions. Economic and political boundaries do not coincide.[16]

Before turning to the two case studies that illustrate these dynamics in the Pacific Northwest and the Great Lakes region, respectively, it is important to return for a moment to make a final point about the process of micro-integration that some claim is occurring across borders in both Europe and North America. Especially in the North American context, micro-integration may have stronger potential to create political change over time than the macro-integration of the three member nations of the NAFTA, because three of the major obstacles to political integration at the continental level are not present at the level of cross-border regions.

As we saw in Chapter 6 one of the key reasons why institutional forms of political integration had a lower probability of realization in North America than they have enjoyed in Europe is that a small number of unequal partners are involved here. First, as we shall see, in at least two instances of cross-border regionalism in the Canada-US case, the number of states and provinces involved is closer to five or six, instead of only three. Second, the power differential between

---

[15] William R. Barnes and Larry C. Ledebur, *The New Regional Economics: The U.S. Common Market and the Global Economy* (Thousand Oaks, CA: Sage, 1998) 67.

[16] Barnes and Ledebur. The authors also explain that "There is no a priori reason why economic regions should conform to the political and economic boundaries of a nation. In the absence of national jurisdictions, it is almost certain that functional economic areas would spill across these economically artificial barriers" (22).

these units is significantly less pronounced than that between Canada and the US as a whole. Other things being equal, integration theory would predict that institutional forms of political integration are more likely to occur between larger numbers of more equal states and provinces than between the two countries, as such. Third, given that both Mexico and Canada have their "own" discrete border with the US, the need for "equal treatment" between these two versions of regional cross-border integration may turn out to be less pressing, especially in institutional terms, than is often required for arrangements developed among the three national governments themselves.

TWO CASE STUDIES: CASCADIA AND THE GREAT LAKES

Cascadia

"Cascadia" is not a familiar name to most Canadians east of Alberta, but it is a label with increasing currency in the Pacific Northwest. It is used by some to denote a region of North America as broad as the American states of Washington, Oregon, Idaho, Montana, and Alaska and the Canadian provinces of British Columbia and Alberta, although its core is defined as the corridor extending from Eugene, Oregon, through Seattle, Washington, across the Canada-US border to Vancouver, British Columbia. This narrower region, whose population is predicted to reach 15 million by 2010, also includes smaller border communities such as Bellingham, Blaine, and Lynden in Washington and Surrey, Langley, and White Rock in British Columbia.[17] This region is among the ten largest economic centres in the world whose economic base includes high-tech firms such as Microsoft, McCaw Cellular, and Boeing. It also features logging, fishing, farming, and tourism.

---

[17] Deborah Waller Meyers and Demetrios G. Papademetriou, "Self-Governance Along the U.S.-Canada Border: A View From Three Regions," in D.G. Papademetriou and D.W. Meyers, eds., *Caught in the Middle: Border Communities in an Era of Globalization* (Washington, DC: Carnegie Endowment for International Peace, 2001) 53.

While its origins appear to lie primarily in two decades of cross-jurisdictional cooperation in the environmental and ecology movements, Cascadia is assuming political, economic, and institutional dimensions of increasing scope and significance. Alan Artibise, writing in the mid-1990s, associates various combinations of states and provinces in the wider Cascadia region with the following regional organizations:

> ‣ the Pacific Northwest Economic Region (PNWER), consisting of politicians and officials and providing a governmental vehicle for regional economic cooperation;
> ‣ the Pacific Corridor Enterprise Council (PACE), a private (business) sector regional organization, which was formed to encourage closer business, trade, and tourism links throughout the region;
> ‣ the Cascadia Transportation/Trade Task Force, a strategic alliance formed among governments and NGOs with an interest in the I-5 corridor from Eugene, Oregon, to Vancouver, British Columbia, and a mandate to develop cross-border strategies focused on growth management, cross-border mobility, and improved regional trade and tourism lineages.[18]

As Artibise notes,

> With the passage of the Free Trade Agreement and the North American Free Trade Agreement, north-south trade links have strengthened and increased. Although much of the trade within the region is resource based, "invisible" trade in the technology sectors is increasingly important, and intraregional tourism is one of the largest sectors in the economy.[19]

---

[18] Alan F.J. Artibise, "Achieving Sustainability in Canada: An Emerging Model of Growth," in P. Kresl and G. Gapper, eds., *North American Cities and the Global Economy* (Thousand Oaks, CA: Sage, 1995) 221-22.

[19] Artibise 226.

As he goes on to say, bilateral agreements between British Columbia and Washington concerning specific environmental, economic, and transportation projects have tended to provide the core of this regional cooperation so far. Further expansion in the scope and effectiveness of future collaborative undertakings in the region depends upon "how effectively leaders on both sides can overcome differences in culture, political systems and organizational structures to create a framework for bi-national cooperation to meet specific objectives."[20]

The problems facing the formation of cross-border regions in Cascadia and throughout North America have received some very careful and informative analysis from Susan Clarke. In some respects, she shows a degree of skepticism about a rapid move toward significant levels of micro-integration along the Canada-US border:

> At the regional level in North America, the collective action problem is to promote the legitimacy of multi-level governance arrangements, to mobilize disparate interests with little common history and often conflicting interests, and to create institutional mechanisms capable of cooperation and collective representation of regional needs.

Despite the magnitude of this challenge, though, she sees signs of significant common interests among the various actors and interest groups comprising the Cascadia region:

> The commonality and interdependence of environmental interests in the Georgia Basin-Puget Sound bioregion ("one forest, one waterway, one airshed") is prompting the creation of new institutional structures to protect the quality of life and the competitiveness of the economy in "Cascadia" ... Trade within the region is strong historically but with the advent of NAFTA, the North/South trade links through Cascadia increased:

---

[20] Artibise 244.

British Columbia exports 40 per cent of its goods to the Pacific Rim and 50 per cent to the United States.[21]

In political terms, Clarke thus believes an increasingly wide and diversified coalition of actors is forming to advance the common interests of the region. However, she also notes the lack of any "glue" comparable to the resources allocated toward comparable regional initiatives within the EU,[22] as well as a lack of consensus on what problem Cascadia would solve.

In sum, Cascadia and other modes of cross-border cooperation on the west coast of North America are still a long way away from constituting a "fourth tier" of government for the continent. Still, the potential remains that, as transborder projects become further institutionalized, they will begin to influence future political outcomes and policy choices.

Ontario and the Great Lakes States

The Ontario/Great Lakes states version of cross-border regionalization is somewhat different from the British Columbia/Cascadia version. In one sense, it is less fully realized, with a smaller amount of documentary evidence of active collaboration among governments, firms, and NGOs spanning the border than is available in the literature on Cascadia. However, in another sense, the Ontario case (to the extent that it has been researched) seems to illustrate more

---

[21] Susan E. Clarke, "Regional and Transnational Regimes: Multi-Level Governance Processes in North America," paper presented at the American Political Science Association Annual Meeting, Atlanta, September 1999. In support of some of the theoretical analysis presented earlier, it is worth noting that for Clarke, "Claims that a Cascadia region could constitute a giant high-tech trading bloc exemplifies predictions that in the 21st century, economically integrated regions, rather than nation-states or individual enterprises, will be the greatest generators of wealth.

[22] For a discussion of differences between cross-border processes in North America and the EU, see Emmanuel Brunet-Jailly, "Comparing Local Cross-Border Relations Under the EU and NAFTA," *Canadian-American Public Policy*, 58 (September 2004).

powerfully than that of British Columbia what regionalization might mean for both Canada and Canada-US relations, over all.

The most prominant academic discussion of the "regionalization" of Ontario is undoubtedly Thomas Courchene and Colin Telmer's *From the Heartland to North American State*, a book we referred to above in relation to some of the general theory of economic regionalization.[23] Courchene argues that Ontario is becoming more closely integrated with proximate states of the US than with the rest of Canada. As already suggested, Courchene provides more direct evidence for the economic dimension of this change than for any associated political and institutional changes. However, the economic trend is already producing a political shift as well, primarily in the form of a new political orientation for Ontario within Canadian federalism and the province's cooling support for national economic and social policies. (Some of the data used to establish this trend will be reviewed shortly.)

Even if British Columbia's shift from an east-west to a north-south orientation in its economic and political life is (to date) more highly institutionalized than that of Ontario's, Ontario's is far more pivotal. It is commonplace to note the peripheral status of Canada's westernmost province, which is obvious geographically but is also measurable politically, socially, and economically—if not in terms of per capita income, then certainly in terms of relations with the rest of Canada. It is equally commonplace to note the historically central status of Ontario (hence, the "Heartland" in Courchene's title) at least during the second half of the twentieth century with the decline of Montreal from its former prominence. In colloquial terms, if British Columbians were to give up on the rest of Canada, most other Canadians probably would react with regret, but not despair. If Ontario were to give up on Canada, however, the rest of Canadians might be left with little to feel "Canadian" about.

Unfortunately, Courchene argues that this is exactly what is happening: Ontario is about to give up on Canada. This is not the place to recapitulate all the ways in which he expects to see this happen,

---

[23] Courchene and Telmer, Ch. 9. For ease of expression, the remainder of this chapter will refer to this volume simply as "Courchene" in the text.

but they all have their origins in trade and communications shifts away from the rest of Canada that are already well advanced. It is important, then, to catalogue at least a few of the changes Courchene cites.

First of all, in terms of provincial trade, between 1981 and 1994, Ontario's exports to the "rest of the world" (ROW)—meaning, overwhelmingly, to the US—grew by approximately $70 billion; that is, in absolute terms, it grew from $45.07 to $113.59 billion in constant 1986 dollars, while its exports to the "rest of Canada" (ROC) grew by only $7 billion from $47.04 to $54.05 billion dollars. In other words, its exports to the ROW expanded at a rate ten times that of its exports to ROC.[24] Expressed as a ratio of ROW exports to ROC exports, the change over the same period was from .96 to 2.1, meaning that the American market for Ontario exports has grown in significance from being just under the level of exports to the other Canadian provinces to being twice the level of those exports. If anything, during the years since 1994—the year NAFTA came into being—this proportion has ballooned even further, to the point where Ontario (not Japan) is the US's largest trading partner, something most Americans would be amazed to discover.

Along with fundamental trade statistics such as these come some other intriguing transactional data, all adding up to the general proposition that Ontario lies at the heart of both Canadian and American consumer and industrial markets. For instance:

▶ Two-thirds of the Canadian consumer market (about 18 million people) and half of the American consumer market (about 125 million people) are within one day's trucking of southern Ontario.

▶ Consumer markets attainable by Ontario are larger than those available to many of its American counterparts; that is, household income within 400 miles of Toronto is as high or higher than it is for Cleveland, Detroit, Boston, or New York.

---

[24] Courchene and Telmer 279, Table 9.1.

> Three-quarters of Canadian manufacturing firms and over half of American manufacturing firms are within a day's trucking of southern Ontario.

> Ontario has 22 road, rail, and port entries with major American industrial states.

> Toronto's Lester B. Pearson International Airport provides direct service to 33 American markets daily. It is the fourth largest international gateway to North America and the world's largest originator of traffic into the Unites States.

In addition, Ontario has over 1,700 firms with International Standards Organization quality certification, a number higher than any two of Ohio, Illinois, Pennsylvania, Michigan, New York, Wisconsin, and Minnesota. Finally, with a population of roughly 5.8 million in 2005 the Greater Toronto Area is now the eighth largest urban area in North America.[25]

Courchene's thesis is that these indicators, and others like them, amount to Ontario's reformation as a "region state" or economic nation-state. Moreover, it is clear from his theory and analysis that, as part and parcel of this process, Ontario is participating in a process of "micro-integration" with proximate American states. The key political implication of this transformation is that the policies and processes involved will also "alter existing regional-national linkages and identities."[26]

It is worth quoting at some length the predicted impact of this new orientation on some of the cornerstones of contemporary Canadian federalism and national life:

Students of Canadian social policy and federalism would no doubt agree that for much of the postwar period Ontario and Ontarians were more supportive of the east-west transfer system

---

[25] All data in the preceding paragraph were adapted from Courchene and Telmer 297-99, Appendix 9A (except for the population of Toronto, which was taken from <http://www.answers.com/topic/greater-toronto-area>). Courchene and Telmer's data were culled from various Ontario websites.

[26] Courchene and Telmer 287.

than were Albertans or British Columbians (or at least than were their governments). Public choice analysts would probably not attribute this to any inherent "generosity" or altruism on the part of Ontarians as compared with residents of British Columbia or Alberta. Rather, their argument would be that the "second round" spending impacts of these transfers tended to end up somewhere in Ontario, since trade flowed east-west ... With generalized north-south trade (as reflected in Table 9.1 data), however, these second-round spending impacts may now end up in North Carolina or Minnesota and not in Ontario ... Might Ontarians' tastes for east-west redistribution tend toward those of British Columbia and Alberta, where there never was any expectation that they would be the recipients of second-round spending impacts?[27]

Courchene concludes that Canadians face a new and daunting challenge to find innovative ways to ensure that the national social safety net—"the new east-west railway"—is preserved. The danger is that, instead, the web of strictly Canadian social, economic, and political "interdependencies" built around and supporting that safety net will gradually succumb to the growing economic and transactional pressures generated by the north-south trading system. Were this to occur, he worries, "we citizens in the upper half of North America would become, in effect, northern Americans."[28]

As noted earlier, Courchene makes a stronger empirical case for the economic than for the institutional and political side of his argument. However, since this book came out, other scholars have examined more closely the increasing economic and institutional integration of Ontario communities with several on the other side of the border. One of these studies (which also contains findings in relation to Cascadia) examined local activities taking place in the Detroit-Windsor and Niagara regions and discovered a wide range of public-private partnerships and private-sector, nongovernmental,

---

[27] Courchene and Telmer 288-89.
[28] Courchene and Telmer 295.

and local government initiatives.[29] More specifically, the following organizations and/or activities (among others) have a role in sorting out matters of common concern between Ontario communities and their cross-border partners: the Canadian-American Border Trade Alliance; the Eastern Border Transportation Coalition; the Canada-US BorderNet Alliance; Great Lakes United (a coalition of environmentalists, community groups, labour unions, sports organizations, and citizens); the Commercial Vehicle Processing Center; the Association of International Border Agencies; and the Great Lakes Mayors Conference. This list[30] barely scratches the surface of cross-border institutional developments. In addition to this increasingly intense buildup among subnational actors, however, the terrorist attacks of 9/11 set off a flurry of activity between numerous agencies of the two national governments as well.

TRADE *VERSUS* SECURITY

9/11 delivered the strongest single shock to the Canada-US relationship in close to 40 years. (By most accounts, the Cuban Missile Crisis of October 1962—and Prime Minister John Diefenbaker's indecisiveness over the acquisition of nuclear weapons as part of Canada's NATO and NORAD commitments shortly thereafter—represents the lowest point in the relationship in the second half of the twentieth century.[31]) The attacks in New York and Washington in themselves did not provoke animosity between Canadians and Americans or their governments; the outpouring of grief and dismay among Canadians in their immediate aftermath was intense. However, shortly afterwards it became increasingly obvious that the fallout had a very

---

[29] See Meyers and Papademetriou, "Self-Governance Along the U.S.-Canada Border" 68-76.

[30] This list is a partial and highly condensed summary of the information available in Meyers and Papademetriou, "Self-Governance Along the U.S.-Canada Border."

[31] For an excellent review of this crisis, which severely divided and ultimately brought down the Diefenbaker government, see Denis Smith, *Rogue Tory: the Life and Legend of John G. Diefenbaker* (Toronto: Macfarlane Walter and Ross, 1995) 462-80.

different appearance when viewed from opposite sides of the border: a security problem on the American side and an economic problem on the Canadian side.

Within 24 hours of the attacks, the line-ups of freight-trucks trying to negotiate border crossings into the US from Canada were over ten kilometres long, and the average time it was taking to pass through the border had increased from a fraction of an hour to as many as ten or 12 hours. The significance of this did not take long to dawn on Canadian federal, provincial, and municipal governments or on Canadians who depended directly on exports to the US for their livelihoods. In fact, it soon became clear to nearly every Canadian that they all depended, directly or indirectly, on a smoothly functioning border with the US. Everyone could do the math: roughly 45 per cent of the Canadian economy relied on export trade; roughly 85 per cent of Canadian exports were sold in the US; therefore, fully one-third of the entire Canadian economy could be severely undermined if entry to the US by truck, train, ship, and airline were to be seriously curtailed.

Meanwhile, on the American side, the absolute priority was to ensure that people and vehicles entering the US from Canada posed no possible risk of additional terrorist attacks, an objective which Canadians could fully understand. The problem was that the economic fallout from the new levels of security at the border were highly asymmetrical. Less than 20 per cent of the American economy depends on its imports, and roughly 20 per cent of that trade is with Canada, so that less than 5 per cent of the American economy is dependent on deliveries from Canada. However, in this case, the math is beside the point. Even if a much larger portion of the American economy depended on imports from Canada, it is almost certain that the American government would still give priority to the security of the border. Indeed, given that most terrorists are much less likely to consider Canada and Canadians as prime targets for their actions, the most striking imbalance between the two countries on the matter of their common border is precisely the vast difference in the *relative* importance of trade and security as national priorities following 9/11.

Hence, fears about terrorism have affected the prospects for cross-border regionalism and the progress of micro-integration in two major ways. First, intensified controls at the border most immediately and forcefully concern the communities closest to it. They act like sand in the gears of all the cross-border cooperation and interactivity outlined above. Second, and potentially more significant, once concerns about national security were thrown into the mix of issues involved in the management of the border, the balance between national and local/ regional concerns shifted dramatically back toward the national and, by extension, binational level. That is to say, micro-integration, which had been making significant progress at the level of "low politics" between political, economic, and social actors within cross-border communities, may be suspended or even reversed in deference to the "high politics" of Canada-US diplomacy concerning national interests in preventing terrorism, fighting international crime, better controlling immigration, and generally improving continental security.

In sum, the functioning of cross-border regions can be regarded as a concrete, ongoing realization of transnationalism. However, as with the case of international politics in general, the spread and intensification of transnational relations is always contingent upon the decline (or abeyance) of political realism and "power politics." In this sense, the War on Terror is bringing back to the forefront an aspect of borders that for a time seemed to be slipping out of sight, especially in the case of the border between Canada and the US. This aspect of borders reflects their ultimate status as concepts that in their practical manifestation, according to Papademetriou and Meyers, "divide communities, exacerbate differences in approach between localities and national governments, and interfere with the ability of public and private sector 'on the ground' actors to pursue their own paths toward ever greater integration."[32]

In other words, it is probably true that, as these authors argue, "national government policies toward border control tend to be inconsistent, even erratic, with patterns ranging from inattention to the 'wrong kind' of attention."[33] If so, it is also likely the case that from

---

[32] Papademetriou and Meyers, "Overview, Context and a Vision for the Future" 35.
[33] Papademetriou and Meyers 10.

the point of view of all those with a stake in an economically efficient border, recent events have tilted the scale toward the "wrong kind" of attention.

CONCLUSION

It is not the contention of this chapter that Canada is about to disintegrate or disappear. Since Confederation in 1867, the federal government has been active in constructing and sustaining an imposing set of national economic policies, along with enormous investments in transportation and communications, designed precisely to bind the country together, to resist the push and pull of the mammoth economy to the south, and to ensure the functioning of a national economy and society. There are studies suggesting that this has all worked as it was intended to work: the volume of trade among Canadian cities (as opposed to North American ones) is estimated to be roughly 12 times what it should be on the basis of the raw economic realities of population densities and distance (according to the "gravitational theory of trade").[34] It is interesting, though, that this ratio was 20 to one as recently as 1985, at the dawn of the free trade era in Canada-US relations. Apparently, then, trans-Canadian bonds are strong, but loosening, and trends are running against Canada's long-term unity and independence.

---

[34] See, J.F. Helliwell, *Globalization and Well-Being* (Vancouver: University of British Columbia Press, 2002). The wider implications of this transition are discussed in more detail in Chapter 9.

chapter 8
NORTH AMERICAN INTEGRATION
AND CANADIAN CULTURE

From economic and political issues, we will turn now to examining Canada's capacity to survive the onslaught of entertainment and cultural products emanating from the US, a challenge that John Meisel once called "escaping extinction."[1] We will do so by considering three major elements: (1) the economic fundamentals of the mass media; (2) the different industries that make up the cultural sector of a national economy; and (3) the role of government in relation to these industries. The promotion and protection of Canadian culture involves several distinct fields of enterprise and government policy toward them. These include the physical facilities and infrastructure that underlie the transmission of messages of all kinds, the service providers who use the infrastructure to deliver messages, the firms and organizations that create cultural content, and government provision and/or regulation of all the above. The politics of culture in Canada has been an almost constant source of contention because each of these activities involves various combinations of public and private interests, and conflict among these interests has been a constant.

Complicating this clash of interests is the fact that the politics of culture and identity in Canada has tended to conflate the protection

---

[1] See John Meisel, "Escaping Extinction: Cultural Defense of An Undefended Border," *Canadian Journal of Political and Social Theory* 10, 1-2 (1986): 248-65. Meisel is a highly respected Canadian political scientist and past chairman of the Canadian Radio-Television and Telecommunications Commission (CRTC).

of particular commercial and individual interests with the promotion of genuinely national interests. Over the decades, Canadians
have witnessed many businesses prosper, careers flourish, grants
spent, subsidies flow, commissions report, and regulations proliferate—all in the name of promoting a national culture that most can
only vaguely define and barely distinguish from American culture.
Increasingly of late, critics of this frenzy of spending, regulation, and
self-examination complain that Canadian culture seems to be whatever those who work in and profit from Canada's cultural industries
do to make money.

One problem for cultural protectionists is that not all Canadians
believe that the very survival of their country truly depends on such
mundane matters as the ownership of magazines, newspapers, and
television networks, or the amount of Canadian content (CanCon)
in radio and television broadcasts, theatre productions, and musical performances. It seems even less plausible to some people that
the determination and capacity of Canadians to remain politically
distinct is crucially threatened by the expansion of the Internet and
the potential fusion (or "convergence") of entertainment and information delivery systems. However, a large number of Canadians
(including a long train of royal commissions) have been persuaded
for a long time that the linkages between cultural autonomy and
national survival are real: the first public call for the creation of
a national public radio network to counter the penetration of
Canada by the rapidly expanding American radio networks NBC and
CBS was made in 1926. Consequently, a natural starting point for
our analysis is to examine the links between a distinct culture and
national independence.

NATIONAL CULTURE *versus* MASS ENTERTAINMENT

It is useful, in exploring those links, to return to Meisel's anxieties
over Canada's cultural predicament. "The greatest threat to Canada,"
he wrote, "lies in the possibility (some might even say 'probability')
that, as a result of the strong presence of American influences, our

cultural development might be stunted."[2] Because American styles, ideas, and products are never far away, he argued, there is a constant fear that Canadians' perceptions, values, ideas, and priorities will become so like theirs that Canada's distinctiveness will disappear. The key problem is not simply that Canadians are awash in entertainment products originating in the US, but more critically that Canadians' own cultural products are crowded out, to the point where most Canadians scarcely realize they even exist:

> Canada's cultural vulnerability vis-à-vis the US is manifest everywhere. Book publishing, the periodical press, film production and distribution, comic books, the record industry, theatre, dance, popular and so-called classical music—all have been dominated by foreign influences in Canada. The indigenous product has had an exceedingly hard time getting started and surviving.[3]

Emerging modes of advanced information technology (AIT), including satellites, fibre-optic cable, and the new wireless telephony and data transmission, promise no reprieve and, if anything, threaten to make things worse. In short, emerging technologies portend the emergence of North American cultural uniformity, and the question seems unavoidable (at least for Canadians) whether two separate national communities can stand for very long on the foundation of a single continental culture.

David Taras has neatly rendered the core of the dilemma Canadians face with respect to the preservation of a distinct national culture in the attic of North America.[4] He pointed out, first, that "TV, magazines and newspapers are the central nervous system of cultural transmission" and that Canada has what some scholars refer to as a "media-constructed public sphere," meaning that "the public life of

---

[2] Meisel 249.
[3] Meisel 249.
[4] David Taras, "Swimming Against the Current: American Mass Entertainment and Canadian Identity," in D.M. Thomas, ed., *Canada and the United States: Differences that Count*, 2nd ed. (Peterborough, ON: Broadview Press, 2000) 192-207.

Canada, our sense of place and of society, comes to us through the mass media." Second, however, he also reminded us that, for Canadians, the bulk of mass entertainment originates in another country, the US: "The American system is our system as well. For better or worse, Canadians have to carve out their own identity while living within an American media bubble."[5]

One of the main contributors to the enveloping strength of this foreign media bubble is the economies of scale generated by the mammoth American market for entertainment products:

> With a domestic market that is roughly 10 times the size of Canada's, American TV producers have ample opportunity to recover their costs in their home market. This allows them to dominate the international market place by selling their programs at cut-rate prices. Canadian broadcasters can buy shows "off the shelf" in Hollywood for between one-fifth and one-tenth of the cost of [domestic] production. It is far cheaper to buy an American program than it is to produce a Canadian show from scratch.[6]

American shows are also more appealing to Canadian viewers than most of the Canadian programs that do get made. This fact is confirmed annually by the frenzied competition between the CTV and Global networks to bag the hottest programs available at sales conventions held in New York and Los Angeles.[7] Canadian network executives are estimated to spend more than US$100 million during these sales competitions at which they are the second largest buyers after the American networks themselves. This practice also means that the two private Canadian networks spend a tiny fraction of their annual corporate income on the production of Canadian programming. For example, CTV's expenditure on Canadian content in 2000 was only 32.9 per cent of its total on-air revenue for that year of $497.2 million, compared with 37.1 per cent in 1998. CanWest Global, meanwhile, spent

[5] Taras 193.
[6] Taras 195.
[7] Simon Houpt and Gayle MacDonald, "'Don't Trust Anybody—Even Me,'" *Globe and Mail*, 19 May 2001: R5.

only 19.4 per cent of its of its total 2000 on-air revenue of $602.3 million on such content, down marginally from 19.8 per cent in 1998.[8] In consequence, a mere 5 per cent of Global's total audience was watching Canadian content in prime time in 1998, compared with 7 per cent in the previous year. The comparable figure for CTV was 12 per cent, down from 17 per cent in 1997.[9]

Again, economic realities dominate. According to sources quoted by Taras, American shows carried in Canada earn two dollars for every dollar spent on them, while Canadian shows earn only 62 cents for every dollar. As these numbers suggest, the privately owned Canadian networks would drop Canadian programming altogether if it were not for government funding of Canadian productions, which frequently accounts for well over 50 per cent of the costs of producing Canadian films and television series. Similar arithmetic lies behind the increasing efforts of Canadian producers to market their films and programs in the US and other foreign countries. As we shall see later, this practice tends to undermine the cultural benefits of domestic programming—such as recognizing who we are and knowing each other's stories—by encouraging producers and artists to minimize anything conspicuously Canadian in their products in order to maximize their appeal to non-Canadians.

When all is said and done, however, the Canadian audience for Canadian television production (outside the fields of sports, news, and public affairs) is very small and probably shrinking. As measured by audience share, the top 20 programs in the Toronto market in early 1998 originated in the US, and at least two-thirds of the shows watched by English Canadians are American.[10] Similar patterns of

---

[8] The author was unable to obtain equivalent numbers for more recent years. However, a recent news story showed similar patterns for Canada's private broadcasters as a whole, reporting that in 2004 they spent 27 per cent of total industry revenues on Canadian content and only 4 per cent on domestic drama, compared with expenditures of just under 18 per cent on American drama. See Antonia Zerbisias, "Spending Less on TV Drama," *Toronto Star*, 11 February 2005; accessed on 5 May 2005 on <http://www.publicairwaves.ca/index.php?page=913>. (Percentages calculated by the author.)

[9] See a report on a CRTC survey of the years 1997-2000 by Michael Posner, "CRTC to Probe Canadian Content," *Globe and Mail*, 22 February 2001: A7.

[10] Taras 198-99.

consumption (based on similar economic factors) appear in other media as well. Close to 95 per cent of movie screenings in Canada are of American-made films; over 80 per cent of across-the-counter sales of magazines are American; 70 per cent of books sold are published in the US.[11]

Assuming such cultural vehicles are in fact related to the capacity of Canadians to maintain a viable and mutually supportive political culture, statistics such as these are not reassuring. Moreover, emerging developments associated with the process of globalization—such as the trend toward conglomeration in the sports, recreational, television, publishing, movie, and music industries, along with the convergence of the television, telecommunications, and computing sectors—have the potential to make things worse, through various means of expanding the American "bubble" within which Canadians conduct their lives.

However, before drawing fatalistic conclusions on that score, it is important to clarify the dynamics of the relationship, which had Meisel so worried, between national culture and national survival.

CULTURE AND NATIONALITY

The interrelationships among the concepts of "society," "community," "nation," and "state"—not to mention the realities these concepts refer to—are highly complex, ambiguous, and politically contentious. Of course, since the rise of Quebec separatism in the 1960s, most Canadians have become familiar with a telling example of the kinds of political questions these notions can involve. Does the society formed by the people of Quebec constitute a national community, and, if so, does that community deserve the status of a nation? Further, does that national status warrant Quebec's recognition as a sovereign state? Or, to the contrary, does the presence in Quebec of

---

[11] Kevin V. Mulcahy, "Cultural Imperialism and Cultural Sovereignty: U.S.-Canadian Cultural Relations," *The American Review of Canadian Studies* 32, 2 (Summer 2000): 184.

Aboriginal peoples, anglophones, and allophones deny the francophones of Quebec the status of a distinct society? Fortunately, the work of Karl Deutsch sheds considerable light on such questions, which apply with similar force to the capacity of Canada as a whole to maintain an autonomous community, and perhaps a sovereign state, in the midst of an increasingly continental media and cultural milieu.

As already seen in Chapters 1 and 6, Deutsch is generally regarded as one of the chief advocates of a "communications" (or transactions) approach to social and political integration. In his analysis, the "stuff" of society is the interdependence, interactions, and communication among its members. The "stuff" of national *community* is an *intense level* of such interdependence, interaction, and communications *plus* the presence of collective memory, mutual sensitivity, and shared national consciousness.[12] In these terms, the determination of most Canadians to remain non-American, despite their increasing integration with American society, prevents North American society from evolving into a North American national community. However, Canadians' continued success in resisting this development may not be guaranteed, especially if the value they place on that distinct status is undermined by the increasing value they may come to place on their American connectedness.

It is useful to review briefly the role that culture and nationality played in Peter Katzenstein's application of the Deutschian model to the case of Germany and Austria (see Chapter 1):

> The cohesion that sets a group of people apart from others is defined by at least one of the following three characteristics: a high capacity for mutual cooperation, mutual predictability of behavior, and the development of mutual trust and identification.[13]

---

[12] See Deutsch, *Nationalism and Social Communication*.

[13] Katzenstein 228. He goes on to quote Deutsch's view that the key element of cultural cohesion is "the complementarity of the relative efficiency of communications among individuals—something that is in some ways similar to mutual rapport, but on a larger scale." A crude simplification of the Deutschian model might be the following (where the arrows are meant to denote the phrase "leads to"): transactions→society→community→nationhood.

As Katzenstein's study points out, however, these three factors represent a necessary, but far from sufficient condition for political unification, especially for previously separate political units. (Remember, "disjoined partners" are countries with such a degree of cultural cohesion between them that, other things being equal, one would expect them to unite.)

To this extent, then, Canada might be expected to withstand the present, or even more substantial, levels of cultural integration with the US. However, optimism on this score may be tempered by taking the Deutschian model in the other direction. If, as Meisel feared, North American cultural cohesion stands as an increasingly significant obstacle to *Canadian* cultural cohesion by preventing Katzenstein's three factors from doing their work within Canada itself, the country could be at risk of national disintegration, with absorption of all or parts of Canada into the US as an after-effect. In sum, the American cultural and media challenge to Canada's survival as such is two-fold: (1) the spread of American culture could become the foundation for Canada's political absorption by the US over time, or (2) it could displace Canadian culture to the point where the country no longer holds together. Neither fate is at all inevitable, but it seems fair to assume that either of them can only be prevented provided that sufficient levels and appropriate forms of intermediate communication are maintained.

It is true that many of the key elements of national identity come down to a sense of belonging; they forge important emotional and psychological links between an individual and her or his social setting. No individual or household in a contemporary industrial society could possibly survive without drawing upon a host of basic goods and services provided on a community-wide basis, from the delivery of water and electrical power to police and fire protection. More generally, members of a community recognize that their overall well-being and enjoyment of life depends on a continuous and highly diverse set of relations and exchanges with its other members, from conversations across the backyard fence to trips to the supermarket, attending concerts at the local high school, driving to the next town for a hockey game, and flying to another province to visit relatives.

All such activities help the individual to accumulate a sense of being a part of a discrete and distinct community of people. (This truth tends to be driven home for anyone who has tried to do such everyday things in another country, especially where a language barrier is present). It is unlikely that Canadians will ever lose this level of identification with the other Canadians around them. The problem is that this level of community can also survive even if the people concerned are no longer citizens of Canada as we know it today.

Beyond the level of the local community, it is the job of cultures, and the various media that transmit them across space and time, to create and maintain a sense of shared existence—of belonging together—among groups of individuals who may be rarely, if ever, in direct contact with one another. In recent centuries, nation-states have constituted one of the most important groups of this kind, and national cultures have evolved to provide the glue required to hold together the diverse and distant villages, towns, cities, and regions that constitute the modern state. Thus, the citizens of Sarnia, Ontario, and Surrey, British Columbia, most of whom have never met and probably never will, nevertheless all call themselves Canadian and have a roughly similar definition of what it means to be Canadian. It is at this level of maintaining a comprehensive national culture that Canada's cultural cohesion is at risk.

IDENTITY AND NATIONALITY: A CANADIAN CONUNDRUM

The development of a Canadian national culture has always been problematic, for two reasons. First, according to most accepted definitions of the term, Canada has never comprised a single nation. As the term itself implies, even when the First Nations were the sole inhabitants of what is now Canada, it was not the domain of any single community or people. The arrival of European colonists resulted, after some time and much conflict, in the consolidation of two additional national communities—English and French—on that same territory, which since have been governed together more or less harmoniously by the central government of the Canadian state. However, the persistent divide between the two founding European communities—labeled "two solitudes" by novelist Hugh MacLennan—has continuously hobbled the capacity of that state to facilitate the formation of a more or less uniform national culture similar to that of Britain, France, Germany, Japan, and other nation-states (with emphasis on the word "nation" in that term), where a significant majority of the population shares the same ethno-cultural characteristics. Second, the development of a Canadian culture has always been overshadowed by a looming external presence, first in the form of British colonial domination and later in the form of American penetration. (English) Canadian intellectual and artistic creativity has always seemed to many to be both derivative and second-rate by comparison with either its British or American counterparts. As a consequence, except for the province of Quebec, the capacity of Canadian artists and other producers of modern culture to reach an adequate audience within their own society has been diminished.

As noted, most observers deem national culture to be fundamentally about "sharing one another's stories." By this token, both the scope and the strength of Canadian national culture has been severely limited by doubts about exactly whose stories to tell: the First Nations, *les Canadiens* and now Quebeckers, the Loyalists and later English settlers, or the more recent immigrants from other parts of Europe as well as Latin America, Asia, the Caribbean, the Middle East, and Africa. Of course, in recent decades the Canadian government has tried to make a virtue out of necessity by promoting the idea of Canada as a multicultural society, in effect telling the stories of all the "hyphenated-Canadians" contained in Canada's polyglot of cultures. Canada's distinct identity is thus framed as precisely its lack of a fixed identity. Many Canadians seem happy or at least content with this solution, but others seem to regret that this cacophony of voices cannot be better orchestrated into a stronger core identity.

Meanwhile, Canadian stories tend to be drowned out by the more pervasive (or more engaging) American ones. In consequence, compared with most of the advanced industrialized world, it is not clear that Canadian existence—as a people, society, community, or country—rests on a particularly vibrant or durable cultural foundation. In other words, lacking the typical nation-state's capacity to maintain strong linkages between community and nationhood (or "national sovereignty"), Canada could be well on the way toward the status of a "virtual nation," a state without nationality. Over 30 years ago, before he became Canada's prime minister for almost two decades, Pierre Trudeau argued in favour of such a vision, decrying nationalism (especially French-Canadian nationalism) and arguing the virtues of a "civil society" in preference to a national state.[14]

There is a plausible case to be made for Trudeau's vision. In an age when culture is increasingly identified with entertainment (or "pop culture"), it may be difficult to argue that a distinctive national culture has very much to do with either preserving a nation's independence or promoting effective democratic government. After all, this is also the age of globalization, and we are often told that globalization means (among other things) the evolution of "consumer sovereignty" and the subordination of states to markets, or at least an end to the subordination of markets to states. In the present context, this can be taken to mean that one does not have to *be* anything or *belong* anywhere in order to act as a consumer of goods and services.

That said, it may nevertheless remain indispensable both to have a distinct identity and to live in a discrete location in order to exercise one's capacity as a citizen. If the national level of government and public affairs is to survive as a vibrant presence in the lives of most Canadians, it is at least arguable that it will continue to require a distinctly national culture and political community as the foundation for that nationhood. National politics is essentially the working out of a common destiny for all Canadians and managing the ways in which Canadians in their respective localities affect other Canadians' lives. However, without a common identity, there can be no common destiny, and no shared identity is possible without an effective system of national communication. In other words, the consumption of entertainment may be an individual and private good,

---

[14] See Pierre E. Trudeau, *Federalism and the French Canadians* (Toronto: Macmillan of Canada, 1968).

but the sharing of a national culture—like Taras's "media bubble"—is a public and political good.

However, even if we can establish the political case for a separate national culture, the issue does not rest there; the question remains of the extent to which a distinct national system of communications is necessary to the promotion and preservation of that national culture. So far in this discussion, no clear distinction has been drawn between, on the one hand, the forms of cultural expression involved in shaping the specific nature of the culture shared by a national community and, on the other hand, the modes of communications by which that culture is transmitted and experienced. The process of developing the precise character of a national identity—through artistic creativity or athletic competition, for example—is very different from the process of carrying that content to a national audience. Neither, though, is of any political consequence in the absence of the other. Here, too, there is a problem in determining what makes a system of communications "national." Is it the scope and structure of the physical systems over which the communications are transmitted; the ownership and operation of the networks; or the substance of the messages that are exchanged among Canadians, by whatever modes (national, continental, or global) and whoever owns and operates them?

In short, many observers have taken the view that there can be no Canadian culture without Canadian cultural and communications industries to convey it between creators and recipients. It is therefore important to understand how these industries operate, and how the government of Canada has attempted to use them in the interests of nationhood.

CULTURAL PROTECTION AND
THE COMMUNICATIONS INDUSTRY

One of the most intractable problems afflicting Canadian culture and communications is to distinguish between the promotion of the national interest in relation to culture and entertainment, on the one hand, and the protection of commercial and other private interests in cultural industries, on the other. As suggested in the introduction to this chapter, there are three functions or categories of activity involved in the creation, dissemination, and consumption of Canadian cultural and entertainment products, each of which corresponds to a separate sector of the Canadian economy. These are (1) the provision and operation of the physical infrastructure that makes possible the transmission of cultural and entertainment products; (2) the dissemination of programming; and (3) the creation of program content. This multiplicity of sectors makes it hard to sort out what the target—the media or the messages—of protective cultural policies and regulations is intended to be. On top of this source of ambiguity, there is a set of public and private interests at play in each of the three sectors. To get a better fix on the political issues that beset policy-makers and citizens in this field, it may be helpful to consider a brief breakdown of the range of sectors and interests concerned in an analogous sector, namely railway transportation.

The composition of the rail transport sector can also be broken down into three separate industries. First is the physical infrastructure, that is, the facilities that allow rail freight to travel from one part of the country to the other: the road bed, bridges, and rail lines; the switches, stations, shunting yards, and control towers; and all of the communication and operational systems necessary to move freight cars by the speediest route to the correct destinations. Second are the facilities, equipment, and personnel owned or employed by the individual railway companies (which may or may not be integrated with the companies that own the infrastructure), including the rolling stock, warehouses, and dispatch offices; the marketing and shipping agents; and the managers and administrative workers. Third are the rail transportation users, consisting mostly of freight service and shipping companies, including trucking companies that "piggyback" on trains, but which may also include goods manufacturers moving components from plant to plant or from final assembly to wholesale or retail outlets for their goods.

The communications/cultural sector is similar. The physical infrastructure comes down to the facilities owned by various communications carriers who operate different modes of broadcasting and data transmission: the communications satellites, fibre optic cables, coaxial cables, telephone lines, microwave towers, and radio transmitters that permit signals and data of all kinds to move from one place to another. Second, equivalent to the freight service providers are the broadcasting networks, cable companies, telephone companies, and data and Internet service providers. Finally, like the delivery companies, the "content" providers include the television and movie production companies; the writers, directors, technicians, and performers who work for them; and a host of firms offering goods and services over the Internet.

The Canadian government's long-standing determination to promote Canadian culture has produced a very high level of government intervention in all these broadcast and communications industries through the use of a wide variety of policy instruments. These have ranged from direct government ownership (the CBC; the National Film Board; Telesat Canada) to various forms of production and distribution subsidies (reduced postal rates for Canadian magazines; Telefilm Canada; the Canadian Television Fund) and a host of protective regulations (Canadian content requirements, foreign-ownership restrictions). In short, the seemingly simple objective of allowing Canadians to hear each other's stories has yielded over the years a massive and complex edifice of government intervention aimed at controlling Canada's mass communications. This control has been exercised both directly through government-owned and operated production and transmission systems and indirectly through regulatory restrictions on foreign-owned programming and transmission systems.[15]

In this way, the Canadian national interest in cultural autonomy has become indistinguishable from the regulatory protection of Canadian broadcasting companies, both public and private, from competition from alternative foreign-based products and services.

---

[15] According to Statistics Canada, in 1997-98, all levels of government in Canada spent almost $5.6 billion on culture, down from a peak of $5.9 billion in 1992-93, while in May 2001, the federal government announced an increase of $560 million in support of the country's cultural community. In 1997-98, "cultural businesses" consumed $1.8 billion (or 68 per cent) of the total federal cultural budget for that year, including $1.4 billion for "broadcasting." See Gayle MacDonald, "Chrétien: Culture's New Best Friend?" *Globe and Mail*, 5 May 2001: R4.

This has led some observers (most notably W.T. Stanbury) to seriously question the current balance between cultural promotion and commercial protectionism in Canadian cultural and communications policies.[16] These critics argue that the policy and regulatory apparatus built around maintaining Canadian cultural autonomy primarily protects Canadian jobs and profits in the entertainment industry with no discernible benefit to Canadians' sense of national identity (even assuming one could specify what that is).

This said, it must be made clear that Canada is by no means the only country in the world to regulate its communications and broadcasting industries. There are some universal aspects to these industries that prompt governments everywhere to maintain a watchful eye on them, at least to some degree. It will be useful, therefore, to explore briefly the types of controls that governments generally impose on firms in this sector. This will help us better understand how, in Canada's case, the need for the standard forms of regulation created the conditions for more extensive intervention in the communications and broadcasting industries.

Conventional Roles of Communications Regulation

The world over, the history of government intervention in communications and broadcasting goes back to the earliest days of telephone networks and radio broadcasting. Indeed, it seems fair to say that the communications and broadcasting industries, although in different ways, represent classic cases of the role of government and public regulation. Government regulation is generally aimed to mitigate what economists call "market failures," that is, social or economic problems that the private sector, left to its own devices, has neither the incentive nor the means to solve effectively (or at all). There are four main areas of such market failure in the field of communications.

---

[16] See, for example, W.T. Stanbury, "Regulation and Competition in Broadcasting in the Age of Convergence," in Dale Orr and Thomas A. Wilson, eds., *The Electronic Village: Policy Issues of the Information Economy* (Toronto: C.D. Howe Institute Study No. 32, 1999) 181-221.

1. Allocation of public resources. The air waves over which standard radio and television broadcasts are transmitted to their audiences constitute "common property" resources, meaning that, like the air we all breathe, they can be consumed at no cost. Such "public goods" (as they are also called) are resources that are "owned" by everybody and therefore tend to be overconsumed, leading in the case of broadcasting to the overcrowding of particular frequencies. Hence, governments all over the world exercise some kind of regulation and licensing of broadcast services to prevent the overlapping use of bandwidth and frequencies from undermining the quality of radio, television, and other wireless services.

2. Pricing of monopoly services. Because these types of service provision often tend toward "natural monopoly" (because their markets will not sustain more than one service provider in any one locality), it has been deemed necessary to rely on public regulators to impose prices and standards of service close to those that might be obtained if genuine business competition were possible.

3. Admission (or prohibition) of new entrants. Because oligopolistic competition can also arise within some imperfectly competitive markets, firms if left to themselves are likely to engage in intense competition to win outright control (and become a monopoly). This type of competition is often destructive, unstable, and otherwise detrimental to the broader public interest, leading governments to impose restrictions on producers fighting to offer the same services in the same market.

4. Promotion of community values. All countries, including both Canada and the US, try to ensure that broadcasting and communications services do not violate the values, tastes, and sensitivities of the majority of their constituents (or even of their strongly vocal minorities). Thus, private television stations and Internet service providers are constrained to avoid transmitting pornographic and/or racially offensive materials, as well as to promote community and minority broadcasting.

Given this, the government of Canada is hardly unique in exercising control over national broadcasting and communications systems. Because Canada has had no less reason than other countries to engage in the standard forms of public interest regulation, the promotion of Canadian culture was able to ride on the back of more conventional forms of regulatory intervention. However, some observers argue that Canada *is* unusual in the degree to which it attempts to determine (or, at least, constrain) the cultural content those media carry, besides regulating such matters as the pricing, structure, and "correctness" of its culture-related media. In addition, because this intervention has had the effect of reducing the number of players in any given market relative to the number of firms who were seeking to serve it, government favour was highly prized by competing private interests, which allowed the government to attach a variety of performance requirements on successful applicants for broadcast licences.

Meanwhile, as we shall see below, the emergence of digitalized storage, transmission, and retrieval of all forms of information is promoting the convergence of the broadcasting, telephone, and data transmission industries. Soon there may be only one industry where once there were three or more, which in turn means that there will be intense (and possibly destructive) competition on a sustained basis among the more successful players in each of the pre-existing industries to achieve dominance in the "commerging" market for their services. As a result, governments in advanced industrial societies now need to modulate the way players in each of these formerly separate sectors compete for one another's markets. For example, telephone companies, cable companies, and wireless Internet providers are vying to become the dominant firms in the market for Internet services in all of these areas, while Direct To Home satellites are competing with all of the terrestrial communication and broadcasting services for similar business. It is an open question whether, once merged, these media will be as susceptible to Canada's conventional modes of cultural regulation as their predecessors.

Problems Facing Canadian Cultural Regulation

Thus, the problem with Canada's customary approach to cultural promotion is that technologies change. Worse, they are beginning to change at unprecedented rates in precisely those industries that are most closely connected to the dissemination of information and culture. These technological developments, especially in conjunction with the new policy environment created by free trade, can only serve to undermine the effectiveness of cultural regulation, particularly through the process of convergence, as argued above. Specifically, five different forces seem to be at work currently to make traditional Canadian approaches to Canadian cultural protection an impractical model for the future.

1. The wedding of the digital codification of information with advanced telecommunications technologies (making up the Internet) defies control or even very effective monitoring of cross-border flows of information, data, and programming. It will not be long before a large percentage of Canadians receive their "television" programming over the Internet—as many younger Canadians already do their music programming—and the CRTC has already said it has no intention of attempting to regulate content on the web. This promises to make a complete hash out of existing CanCon regulations for television (and music) distribution (as satellite radio already seems on the verge of doing).

2. Even if conventional forms of regulation remain technically feasible, the government may be losing its political constituency for such interventions. As John Meisel astutely recognized, Canadians tend to be very attached to their almost limitless access to American television programming, and they are unlikely to accept moves by government to take it away from them or to strongly interfere with their ability to obtain it when and how they wish. It is true that there was not much public opposition to Canadian content regulations for television broadcasting and cable networks. However, the reason for this was probably that, until now, these regulations have been designed merely to add space available for Canadian content on Canadian cable packages and did not seriously limit Canadians' opportunity to watch American

programming on almost the same terms as Americans.[17] However, if the Internet provides Canadians with direct access to American programming, then blocking Canadians' access to Amercan web-sites may become the only effective way to ensure that Canadians bother with Canadian networks. It seems highly unlikely that a majority of Canadians would tolerate this degree of government interference with their use of AIT.

3. Convergent technologies are muddying even further the already murky relationship between the regulation of competition and the promotion of Canadian content, a subject covered in comprehensive detail by Globerman, Janisch, and Stanbury.[18] Conventional Canadian content requirements tend to blunt the scope and intensity of commercial competition in the Canadian market for the delivery of entertainment products and communications services, which denies Canadians the benefits of price and quality of service that such competition could otherwise bring. Whether intentionally or not, Canadian content regulations inescapably favour some forms of communications technology over others because, for example, some forms are able to accommodate Canadian content at less cost. Alternatively, insisting that all Canadian distributors—whether cable or satellite, for instance—must carry essentially the same selection of television channels artificially undermines the benefit to consumers of unrestricted competition in the packaging and variable pricing of transmission services.

---

[17] There seems to be one notable exception to this is generalization. During simultaneous cablecasts of American programs by Canadian networks, Canadian commercials are substituted for the American ones, which allows the Canadian networks to earn Canadian advertising revenue from them. This practice seems to sit fairly comfortably with most Canadian viewers except around the time of the Super Bowl, when some Canadian viewers grumble that they miss out on many of the American commercials that are created specifically for that event and have acquired "camp" status in recent years.

[18] Steven Globerman, Hudson N. Janisch, and W.T. Stanbury, "Convergence, Competition and Canadian Content," in W.T. Stanbury, ed., *Perspectives on the New Economics of Telecommunication* (Montreal: Institute for Research on Public Policy, 1996) 209-43.

4. It must be acknowledged that much of the so-called cultural regulation in this country is beginning to resemble old-fashioned job creation. There can be no question that, in some irreducible sense, the promotion of any national interest will have as a side-effect the privileging of some domestic workers (and firms) over others. However, this practice has recently come to a point where government benefits are being handed out to support the production of movies and television programs that are deliberately scrubbed clean of any Canadian references or relevance so that they can be more effectively marketed in the US and the rest of the world (where vaguely "American" or "place neutral" characteristics are deemed necessary to hold audiences). It is difficult to see the gain to Canadian unity and independence from paying Canadians to tell American stories to Americans or, for that matter, to tell the stories of nobody in particular to everybody. In fact, the only discernable effect of such policies and the programming they support is to maintain the incomes of the owners and workers involved. It can be argued that there is a national interest in preserving an indigenous capacity for the production and dissemination of entertainment since, if the industry simply vanished, there would not be any recognizably Canadian programs either, even as spin-offs. Nevertheless, as a means of ensuring the survival of a distinct Canadian culture, the argument for this practice cannot be much stronger than the argument for manufacturing Canadian running shoes, growing Canadian soy-beans, or producing Canadian antibiotics, all parts of the economy that Canadians generally seem prepared to leave to the play of market forces.

5. Finally, free trade agreements have compromised the capacity of the federal government to maintain some of the protective mechanisms it has traditionally employed to promote Canadian content. Neither the FTA nor NAFTA required Canada to abandon existing protective instruments in this area of public policy, although the potential status of any proposed new instruments under the terms of NAFTA is murky. The relevant Article (2005) of the FTA is inherently ambiguous. Its first paragraph states, in effect, that Canada retains the right to pass and enforce legislation that favours Canadian cultural products and producers and discriminates against American ones, but it is followed immediately

by another paragraph that entitles the US to retaliate against any such measures with sanctions against Canadian exports with equivalent commercial effect.

Canadians, including then Heritage Minister Sheila Copps, received a stark reminder of this rather large hole in Canada's so called "cultural exemption" during a dust-up over "split run" magazines. American publications such as *Sports Illustrated* were printing advertisements of Canadian firms in Canadian issues of their magazines that were only marginally different (except for the ads) from the versions sold in their home market, thus cutting into the revenue base of magazines based in Canada. Minister Copps tried to discourage this practice with an outright ban (Bill C-55) against Canadian advertising in any Canadian magazine with less than a minimum percentage of original Canadian content—a classic form of "CanCon" regulation. The Americans quickly responded to this action by threatening a trade war, involving duties or quotas on Canadian exports of steel (much of which is produced in Copps's home riding in Hamilton), apparel, wood, and plastics. The Canadian government basically caved in to this American pressure.[19]

For these five reasons, the days of intrusive cultural regulation appear to be numbered. Free trade agreements (including the WTO) do not appear to directly proscribe the kinds of foreign content and ownership regulations upon which Canada's protective apparatus was originally constructed. However, the spirit if not the letter of market liberalization runs directly counter to the extension of traditional forms of intervention to emerging cultural and information vehicles. In any case, it may be bending cultural nationalism to the snapping point to pretend that government support for the production of any kind of entertainment or information subject matter, simply because

---

[19] See Shawn McCarthy, "PM Moved to Stop a Trade War," *Globe and Mail*, 27 May 1999: A3; Heather Scoffield, "Publishers Greet Split-run Deal with Dismay," *Globe and Mail*, 27 May 1999. The rest of the split-run story is too long and complex to be fairly told here. See Taras 200-03.

of where it is produced and by whom, is an effective way to preserve an autonomous political community north of the US.

CANADA AND THE US AS A SINGLE SOCIETY

Of course, "culture" is not limited to creative expression, whether for pure entertainment or for higher levels of edification and intellectual stimulation. Rather, in many areas of the social sciences, culture is more generally defined as a "way of life," the sum total of the social practices that people in a given society "live out" in their day-to-day existence. In this respect, the preservation of a distinct Canadian culture may be at even greater risk than that presented by the inundation of American mass entertainment; a North American society is emerging which has the potential to fuse Canadian and American (and possible even Quebec and Mexican) cultures at this second, more pervasive level. Consequently, beyond the analysis of the cultural media presented so far, there are three other areas of North American social culture that deserve closer attention in order to more fully appreciate the forces affecting Canadian political autonomy: (1) the continental integration of AIT; (2) professional and voluntary associations; and (3) sports and entertainment networks. These three areas run closely parallel—both conceptually and functionally—to the area of mass culture and entertainment examined above, and they should be interpreted as complementary and reinforcing dimensions of the overall problem of cultural threats to Canadian survival.

Despite the parallels just noted between the cultural media and social culture, these three dimensions of social culture present some distinct conceptual challenges, and we shall pause for a moment to explore what those challenges entail. Earlier sections of this chapter focused more or less directly on Canadian policies toward the American threat to Canadian culture, which tends to place the issues involved in a nation-to-nation perspective, or at least does not call that perspective into question. The dimensions of social culture to which that focus now shifts operate largely in the private sphere, independently of intergovernmental relations (although, as argued below, they do create a number of serious political difficulties). In this respect, they raise conceptual and political difficulties that bear a close resemblance to those raised in attempts to understand the process of globalization.

Until recently, the modern nation-state was possibly best described as a "vessel" containing—or, better yet, "self-containing"—a very large proportion of the total interactions experienced on a regular basis by its citizens, individual and corporate. Just about every country engaged in international trade, of course, but the share of such international transactions in the total transactions of each country was minimal—typically around 10 per cent of national GDP.[20] Similarly, travel within national borders dwarfed the levels of travel across them. The same was true of postal traffic, telephone calls, books and newspapers read, and movies and television shows watched. In short, the demarcation of the territorial boundaries of the nation-state was almost completely congruent with the actual geographic scope of a wide range of functional activities that, in the aggregate, comprised the social, economic, and cultural life of the country.

Globalization and its cousin, international regionalization, have changed all that. There is now such an intensity and variety of flows across international boundaries that, in the estimation of a large number of observers, the very "territoriality" on which the traditional nation-state has been based for hundreds of years is no longer significant, either politically or economically. Instead, a form of "supraterritoriality" has developed in which the spatial extent of a vast amount of human interactions are no longer coextensive with the boundaries of states. Rather, such transactions have grown to encompass either entire regional groupings of states—such as the EU and NAFTA—or, in some functional areas such as finance and

---

[20] See Held et al. 169, Figure 3.3.

telecommunications, the entire world (or at least significant portions of every country in the world). As Jan Aart Scholte has explained it, this process "entails a reconfiguration of geography, so that social space is no longer wholly mapped in terms of territorial borders."[21]

Thus, returning to the notion of nation-states as vessels (and thinking of them specifically as ships, possibly passenger liners), there is more to supraterritoriality than an intensified level of exchanges passing between two or more such ships. It is rather as if—to strain the metaphor a little—multiple "ships of state" were melded together to become a multi-decked super-liner, with all the former communications between them—along with, no doubt, some unprecedented forms of interaction—being fused and overlaid with one another in a new, multidimensional network of interconnections throughout it. (This metaphor is thus in keeping with one prominent definition of globalization, which regards it as "a process whereby the world is becoming a single place).[22] From this perspective, Canada-US free trade has not merely substantially raised the intensity of economic, social, and cultural interaction between the two countries, but it is promoting the transformation of the two countries into a single society.

AIT Networks

Perhaps the most quoted sentence ever written by any Canadian is Marshall McLuhan's rather cryptic observation that "the medium is the message."[23] It is conceivable that only a Canadian could have come up with this formulation, given that, throughout the

---

[21] Scholte 16.
[22] Scholte 47-48.
[23] Marshall McLuhan with Quentin Fiore, *The Medium is the Message* (New York: Random House, 1967).

twentieth century, at least, Canadians have been preoccupied with the fear that, without "mediums" all their own, their "messages" to one to another would not get through. Canada-wide communications was deemed to require Canadian-owned, Canadian-operated, and Canadian-only communications vehicles and networks. It is not clear that this insistence was ever justified. However, Canadians may soon know whether or not it still represents a valid concern, because emerging systems of communication may turn out to be increasingly beyond national control. If this does prove to be the case, then the long-standing Canadian insistence that the "content" and the "carriers" of Canadian information must be inseparable will be harder and harder to achieve in practice.

In the days when the Canadian and most other economies were genuinely national in scope (meaning that the vast preponderance of economic exchanges occurred within, rather than across, national boundaries) it was both feasible and economically efficient to design and operate the delivery of intermediate services on a national basis as well. Canada's transcontinental railways had links to American railways, but the bulk of their traffic was between Canadian centres. Bell Canada, the dominant telephone company in Central Canada, along with the rest of the country's provincial telephone companies, all had long-distance connections with American and overseas phone companies, but their primary links were with one another. Trans-Canada Airways flew to major American and European cities, but its core business was carrying Canadians from one national airport to another.

More important than the simple fact of national traffic on these Canadian systems was that, despite their value and serviceability, links with American-based systems were not required in order to provide valuable service to Canadians. It is not clear that this continues to be true in the case of new, converging services based on AIT, or even for the current generation of rail, trucking, or air services. The provision of state-of-the-art intermediate services at internationally competitive rates may no longer be possible for Canadian service providers on a stand-alone basis; rather, their functionality and profitability may depend on their smooth and complete integration with continental networks centred in the US. If so, it is hard to know how distinctly Canadian versions of such intermediate services can survive, and what effect their disappearance might have on the survival of the Canadian political community.[24]

As we saw in Chapter 4, all of Canada's national networks of transportation and communication have been susceptible to the bypassing of their services in favour of American-based systems. Generally operating as monopolies (or, at least, as parts of duopolies) the corporate instruments of defensive expansion, such as the CPR and CBC, have relied on regulation of their respective industries by the Canadian government to protect them from such competition. Today, new competitive communications technologies based on fibre-optic transmission of digital data and signals present Canada with even more threatening versions of the problem of bypass, namely, the penetration of Canada by American-controlled courier-services, data processing services, satellite services, search engines, satellite radio, Internet-based telephone, and Internet television programming.

Will these developments bring about the complete loss of Canadian control—public or private—over either the media or the messages of telecommunications in Canada? They certainly mean that "Canadian" communications—that is, transfers of information between Canadians, in forms determined exclusively by and for Canadians—will have to compete for time and attention from packagers and transmitters of information controlled outside the country. They will thus depend on the extent to which the foreigners in control of those systems nevertheless are willing and able to offer communications vehicles capable of serving the distinct priorities and interests of Canadian users. The probable consequences of this situation do not require much imagination, because it is far from being unprecedented. Foreign-controlled distributors of movies and over-the-counter magazines offer only a tiny percentage of Canadian products as a

---

[24] There are already signs that the Internet is not friendly to some Canadian uses. Many electronic directories and search engines are devoid of direct Canadian links and content, while Canadian-owned and operated Internet service providers are struggling to offer comparable service at competitive rates to their American counterparts.

result of Canadian reliance on systems controlled outside the country to reach one another. At a deeper and more explicitly political level, similar concerns have prompted European leaders to consider the creation of a rival European search engine to Google's digitalized literary search engine, which they fear could give the US (or, at least, the owners of Google), "unilateral command of the thought of the world."[25]

Professional and Cultural Subsystems

The emerging continental structure of AIT infrastructure, moreover, is complemented by the increased integration of Canadian and American professional associations, voluntary organizations, and cultural industries. In fact, a major element of Canadian-American socio-cultural integration is the number of industrial, commercial, occupational, and professional subsystems that operate on a continental basis.[26] Many Canadians (including, of course, most Canadian academics) are directly or indirectly aware of extensive Canadian participation in American-centred professional associations, although despite this fact (or possibly because of it) the phenomenon remains a seriously understudied subject.

Even on a purely anecdotal basis, it is clear that in their working lives just about all Canadians either play some role in a subsystem operating predominantly in the US, and essentially managed from there, or make frequent contact with such subsystems in their own work and leisure. They function, in other words, as parts of North American society, that is, as members of the myriad occupational, organizational, and corporate subsystems involved in the production and distribution of nearly all the goods and services available on the

[25] See Elaine Ganley, "Europeans to Counter Google Print Project," *Associated Press*, 6 May 2005. Accessed on 8 May 2005 <http://www.post-gazette.com/pg/05126/499901.stm>.

[26] For example, Charles Pentland observed over 30 years ago that "Canadians and Americans have traditionally contributed to each other's specialized publications and belonged to each other's professional associations to a far greater extent than is the case among Europeans." *The Canadian Dilemma* (Paris: Atlantic Institute for International Affairs, 1973) 47.

continent. For example the arts, entertainment, sports, and religion all provide examples of subsystems operating to various degrees on a continent-wide basis: turn-of-the-century vaudeville, major- and minor-league football and baseball, movie-making and distribution, music production and distribution, televangelism, news production and distribution, advertising, television program production, and the design and construction of international exhibitions.[27]

The wider political significance of such continental subsystems becomes evident with the help of another conceptual tool, namely, the distinction between the national (Canadian) and the continental integration of these subsystems. If national integration is defined as the integration of various social, occupational, and cultural subsystems across Canada, and if continental integration is defined as the integration of the Canadian and American portions of such subsystems across the border, then it can be said that, for Canada, continental integration of these subsystems frustrates their national integration.

The same is not true for the US because it is easy, or at least possible, to integrate subsystems nationally at the centre of these systems, but it is very difficult to integrate them across their peripheral extremities. For all these subsystems, whether in the Canadian or the American segment of them, to "make it" is to rise to the "top" of the subsystem's hierarchy. For Canadians, but not for Americans, at some point on the "way to the top," rising stars must leave the country, because the centre of their particular subsystem is located in the US. The Canadian "bests" in various fields are never in touch with one another in their own country and rarely work together in Canada while at the top of their form. While North American subsystems are cumulative and socially integrative in the US, they are disaggregated and fragmentary in Canada; and if they contribute at all to Canadian integration, it is as part of a more inclusive process of continental integration.

---

[27] This picture emerged from detailed examinations of these activities provided in papers presented to a conference at the University of Western Ontario ("American Popular Culture in Canada: Mass Communication and Public Performance," 4-6 May 1988). These and several similar papers were later published as David H. Flaherty and Frank E. Manning, eds., *The Beaver Bites Back?: American Popular Culture in Canada* (Montreal and Kingston: McGill-Queen's University Press, 1993).

Corporate Concentration and Popular Culture

Similar structural elements can be found in cultural (or entertainment) industries. J.K. Galbraith has provided an important distinction between the "technostructure" and the "market system" as two highly contrasting dimensions of the "new industrial societies" that comprise advanced capitalism.[28] The "technostructure" (which Galbraith also refers to as the "planning sector" or the "industrial system") is essentially the world of monopolistic and oligopolistic firms, the giants of managerial capitalism that are "household names" to most Americans and Canadians. The "market system," meanwhile, is a coexisting world in which the genuinely open competition celebrated by capitalist ideology is still visible. It is a world made up of, as Galbraith puts it, the "small retail entrepreneur, repairman, independent craftsman, barber, market gardener, bookmaker," that is, a world still subject to the play of market forces.

Nearly all of the popular culture available in North America is produced and disseminated by the cultural technostructure (or the cultural segment of Galbraith's "industrial system"). That is, it comes to us by means of huge syndicates among oligopolistic or monopolistic firms and organizations, such as the alliance between professional sport and network television and, increasingly, between the music and motion picture industries. Meanwhile, in almost every one of these cultural areas, there are also the artistic, athletic, and entertainment counterparts of Galbraith's "market system": local theatre, county fairs, inter-county baseball, junior hockey, and community newspapers and broadcasting.

The Canadian cultural quandary can thus be stated as a synthesis of "systems analysis" and "market structure" perspectives. Canada,

---

[28] See John Kenneth Galbraith, *The New Industrial State* (Boston, MA: Houghton Mifflin, 1967) especially 355. The main features of the technostructure are addressed in Chapters 6, 7, and 31 of this book. Thomas McCraw makes a similar distinction between "center" and "peripheral" firms in *Prophets of Regulation: Charles Francis Adams, Louis D. Brandeis, James M. Landis, Alfred E. Kahn* (Cambridge, MA: The Belknap Press of Harvard University Press, 1984).

too, has a cultural market system. It consists of Canadian cultural activities that take place apart from continental subsystems and, hence, are "unintegrated" with them. However, they are not integrated nationally, either, so they do not constitute a "Canadian *national* culture," distinct from American culture, despite the fact that in and of themselves they are both different from and independent of American culture. To achieve "national" stature, artists, entertainers, and performers must move through the ranks of the appropriate North American subsystem, that is, move "out" of the Canadian cultural market system into the continental cultural technostructure. (Canadian students will be able to provide their own most telling instances of this phenomenon, but what comes to mind are the recent musical careers of Diana Krall and Alanis Morissette as well as the movie careers of Jim Carrey and Mike Myers.)

The problem this poses for an independent Canadian culture is that the continental cultural technostructure is based overwhelmingly on sales to the massive American market. It is therefore only marginally responsive to Canadian-oriented departures from the lowest common denominator of tastes and identification prevailing in the US. Hence, popular culture in English Canada can have only one of two forms: it is the equivalent of either county-league baseball, which is entirely Canadian but does not achieve exposure across Canada, or Blue Jays baseball, which is shared by the whole country but is as Canadian as the State of the Union Address.

CONCLUSION

Canada's status as a nation (though perhaps not as a legal nation-state) seems at risk of being undermined by the gradual erosion of its national culture at both the media and social levels. William Watson is probably right to insist that no one can predict this as anything remotely resembling a certainty and also that, in any case, the linkages between a loss of national identity and the loss of country are, generally speaking, either rarely spelled out by people who claim they exist or are simply not logical when they are spelled out.[29] At a minimum, however, Canadians seem likely to view the extinction of Canada's own culture as a significant loss to the extent that they value the integrity of Canadian public life and the survival of a meaningful level of democratic accountability in the governing of Canada and its provinces and municipalities. Even here, though, the question of what political order reigns beyond the local level is an arbitrary matter and could just as well be provincial—or even continental or global—as national in scope. For example, life today in most Canadian municipalities would probably not change very much if the various provinces were to become states of the United States of America, and it is hard to imagine that the agenda for either municipal or provincial governments would be much affected by such a change, either.

However—to pursue this hypothetical prospect a step further—nothing of Canadian national government and politics would remain, and concern about Canadian culture at a national level would be pointless. Ontarians would no longer want or need to know more about British Columbians than about Californians: what British Columbians thought and did would no longer affect Ontarians more than what Californians thought and did; in fact, it would probably matter less. California, as the most populous and productive subnational jurisdiction on the continent, would now play a significantly greater role than British Columbia in shaping the economic and political fate of the new North American polity of which Ontario would now be a part.

It is interesting in this connection that William Watson, in a chapter titled "Virtually Canadian," was largely indifferent to the possibility that Canadians might become increasingly American as a result of advanced information technologies and the content they are likely to carry. As he argued:

---

[29] William Watson, *Globalization and the Meaning of Canadian Life* (Toronto: University of Toronto Press, 1998) 223-36.

If the medium really is the message, there is little doubt that we will all be increasingly American. "They really do change your life," George Grant said of what he called "American machines," and he was right. If economic growth continues and its influence spreads, more and more of the world's citizens—and by definition all of the developed world's citizens—will live like Americans, with their cars, shopping centres, computers, high-definition TVs, VCRs and so on.... If how people live their lives *is* what counts, many of us probably *will* end up living similar lives, spending part of our time on the internet, part watching the satellite, part driving, part shopping, part travelling, and at least part (shall we say?) "interfacing" with friends, family and neighbors.

Watson goes on to question why Canadians should be concerned about such a development. He asks, "But how different would we really wish to be, even if it were possible. If, in the sense that George Grant meant, we all do become Americans, what of it?"[30]

It is important to note, however, that Watson's indifference to the loss of Canadian cultural distinctiveness is strongly associated with his belief that we are *already* identical to the Americans politically:

There is an obvious parallel in the way all Westerners—if not yet all earthlings—have accepted American political ideals ... If we really are all liberal, democratic, capitalists now—and outside China this is the only respectable political doctrine—then in a sense we *are* all Americans, since America, though by no means the sole author of liberal, democratic, capitalist ideals, has been their strongest and certainly their loudest champion.[31]

The point is that Watson's perspective, albeit in an obverse way, contributes to the case that, over time, national culture and communications are closely intertwined with the national determination to

---

30 Watson, *Globalization* 229.
31 Watson, *Globalization* 229-30.

remain politically distinct. On this score, he seems satisfied to know that "free legislatures that write countries' laws" will continue to write "slightly different code."[32]

Thus, this discussion of North American media, cultural, and social integration ties back to the dimension of political will and Canada's possible loss, especially at the elite level, of commitment to the "national project," a subject to which this discussion turns in the next chapter. Canada's earlier versions of such a commitment were, as we saw in Chapter 4, heavily weighted on the side of the political will to exploit a prospective national economy, a will that may well be vanishing among Canada's business community. Just when the need for determined application of traditional policy instruments is rising, the willingness to bear additional costs and forego valuable benefits for the sake of nationally based systems of transportation and communications may be sinking below even the levels that once sustained more viable instruments. It is possible to build a country around a railroad. Canadians proved it. It may or may not be possible to maintain a country around six or seven international airports.

---

[32] Watson, *Globalization* 231.

chapter 9
FREE TRADE AGREEMENTS AND CANADIAN
SOCIAL POLICIES, ATTITUDES, AND VALUES

One of the primary concerns of Canadians who opposed free trade with the US was its possible impact on Canada's social safety net. Providers of Canada's large array of health and social programs made up a large portion of the groups supporting the Pro-Canada Network and the Council of Canadians in their fight against the agreement. They feared that opening the border would motivate Canadian firms to relocate in the US because of the lighter tax burden associated with American social welfare programs. They were also concerned that those employers who did not relocate would nevertheless tend to press for policy harmonization, "meaning a weakening of Canadian health, child care, employment insurance and pension standards, as well as a shift away from government intervention in the areas of regional development, agricultural policy, workplace safety and equal pay." Moreover, this cluster of anxieties—labelled the "social programs challenge"—was the most effective argument in the anti-trade campaign.[1]

In sum, many Canadians opposed free trade with the US because they believed that it would bring about a convergence of social programs in the two countries, most often by bringing Canadian standards down to the American level. This chapter reviews the evidence for the extent to which this is happening (1) by setting out briefly

---

[1] Bashevkin 111.

what NAFTA says about social policy and the delivery of social programs; (2) by summarizing the contending arguments and evidence
that several Canadian scholars have assembled in making the cases
for and against the idea that Canadian and American social policies
are converging under the free trade regime; (3) by reviewing what
some observers point to as the "commercialization" of public policy under free trade; and (4) by identifying the major differences in
Canadian and American values that seem to account for prevailing
differences in their social policies. We will conclude with an overall
assessment of the probability that those differences will persist or,
rather, be eroded by the free play of market forces.

NAFTA AND CANADIAN SOCIAL POLICIES

The logical place to begin a discussion of the effect of free trade on
Canadian social policies is to examine what NAFTA actually says
about social policies and programs and the extent to which articles
of the agreement actually constrain what governments can and cannot do on behalf of their populations. (The NAFTA provisions on
this subject are essentially the same as those introduced earlier in
the FTA.) In the present context, the principal question to be asked
about those provisions is whether or not, assuming Canadians continue to demand more interventionist social legislation from their
governments, NAFTA prevents or limits their governments' possible
responses to those demands.

Lipsey, Schwanen, and Wonnacott firmly insist that nothing in
NAFTA imposes constraints on national governments, calling it a
"misconception" that the agreement "encroaches on Canada's ability to pursue a wide range of domestic policies." Specifically, they
note that NAFTA does not prevent the Canadian government from
"adopting any tax or social policy it chooses."[2] This certainly appears

---

[2] Lipsey, Schwanen, and Wonnacott 164.

to be the case. For example, Article 1101, Paragraph 4 of Chapter 11, on investments, reads as follows:

> Nothing in this Chapter shall be construed to prevent a Party from providing a service or performing a function such as law enforcement, correctional services, income security or insurance, social security or insurance, social welfare, public education or public training, health, and child care, in a manner that is not inconsistent with this Chapter.

There is some reassurance in this wording, but some observers believe that the "investors' rights" provisions elsewhere in Chapter 11 still have the potential to constrain future government actions in some areas of social policy, including health and the environment. These provisions give investors and *potential* investors the right to take a government to dispute resolution if they believe a policy adopted by that government is denying them a commercial benefit by acting in violation of the agreement. This may mean that the investor is effectively in a position to sue the government for financial compensation equivalent to the income it would have received if the government's policy had not prevented it from undertaking a particular investment.

The precise legalities of this possibility are beyond the scope of this discussion, but—as we shall see in the next section—most commentary concerning the issue of investor rights comes down to the following: NAFTA does not require governments to abandon any social policies currently in place, including the delivery of health and other social services through Canadian government-owned monopolies. However, should the federal or provincial governments begin to privatize the delivery of some of these services, then the national treatment and investor rights provisions of the agreement circumscribe the ability of these governments to place restrictions on competitive private provision. For instance, if several Ontario municipalities decide to privatize their municipal water systems, they could not prevent multinational corporations from bidding for contracts to provide them. The same would apply to privatized health services and private colleges and universities.

It seems reasonably clear that Canada's social programs are well protected from dismantling by NAFTA, and none of them has undergone a direct attack based on the agreement. However, this has not prevented a debate in the social policy literature over the potential for free trade both to undermine Canada's existing social policies over time and to prevent Canadian governments from undertaking major new policies in the future. In particular, specialists remain divided on whether or not Canadian and American social policies have converged, or are destined to converge, in the free trade era.

FREE TRADE AND SOCIAL POLICY CONVERGENCE

It is now over 15 years since the FTA came into force, and assessments are mixed concerning the extent to which the fears of social policy convergence under the new free trade regime have proven to be well founded. One of the greatest difficulties in framing firm conclusions about the effects of free trade on social programs is that there are several contending explanations for whatever "convergence" may be observed between Canadian and American social policies. Writing on this subject in the mid-1990s, Keith Banting points to at least four possible reasons for such convergence:

1. Convergence as a result of parallel domestic factors: the two countries face similar problems, experience similar domestic political responses to them, or learn from each other's experience.
2. Convergence as a direct result of economic integration: as free trade critics feared, Canadian policies—such as higher corporate taxes—might be altered out of a fear that firms would leave the country.
3. Convergence as an indirect result of economic integration: if free trade should negatively affect Canada's economic performance, social spending could suffer; or, similarly, if economic integration were to lead over time to convergence in the two na-

tional cultures, thus reshaping Canadian political preferences, differences in social programs might narrow over time.

4. Convergence as a result of wider global integration: Canada and the US could both be responding to widespread changes in the global economy and a widely shared policy agenda at IGOs.[3]

In an attempt to determine the degree of convergence both before and after the FTA was introduced, Banting compares Canadian and American social programs, specifically concentrating on four policy areas: unemployment insurance; child benefits; public assistance; and poverty, inequality, and redistribution. The details of his review of the evidence on convergence will not be reviewed here, but his conclusions are succinctly stated: "Convergence was limited to two of the programs ... child benefits and unemployment insurance." Moreover, "it is clear that convergence in these two programs did not flow unambiguously from closer integration of the Canadian and American economies."[4] Rather, as he points out, the narrowing of the gaps with respect to these programs was significantly affected by American, not Canadian, decisions, and he found it is difficult to argue that free trade with Canada was driving changes in American policy. In addition, a close look at the child benefits and unemployment insurance cases does not suggest that changes in Canadian policies are exclusively the result of bilateral economic integration either. Parallel domestic trends in the two countries seem much more responsible for convergence in child benefits. Similarly, domestic conservatism, fiscal constraint, and labour market pressures seem more responsible for changes in the Canadian unemployment insurance program, although here "concern for economic competition between the two countries may have been part of the calculus in Canada."[5]

On balance, then, Banting does not see a very strong link between increasing economic integration between Canada and the US and

---

[3] Keith Banting, "Social Policy in a North American Free Trade Area," in Charles Doran and A.P. Drischler, eds., *The New North America: Cooperation and Enhanced Interdependence* (Westport, CT: Praeger, 1996) 94-95.

[4] Banting 105.

[5] Banting 106.

increasing similarities in the two countries' approaches to social welfare. As a consequence, despite their promotion of closer economic
ties, he concludes that free trade agreements have made little contribution to the integration of social policies. However, other Canadian
social policy analysts point to a different, more ideological link between free trade agreements and associations and a decline in government provision of social welfare. James Rice and Michael Prince, for
example, see globalization and North American market liberalization
as shifting the existing balance between social and economic policy
decidedly in the direction of economic policy. As they point out:

> During the building of the postwar welfare state, social policy
> was commonly distinguished from economic policy in terms of
> its goals of building identities and fostering community and [so
> cial] integration, as well as making changes in the structures of
> society and the distribution of market-generated incomes.[6]

While serving distinct goals, the social welfare system and the
economic market-place have been linked in a mutually reinforcing
manner through the Keynesian philosophy of public finance that
dominated the countries of the industrialized world during most of
the post-Second World War period. That is, social spending served
to stabilize national economies, while the redistribution of income
promoted economic growth by increasing consumer demand.

More recently, Rice and Prince argue, "social policy and the welfare state are being pitted against economic policy and the market,
heightening the tension between the two sides."[7] Like globalization
generally, free trade agreements such as the FTA and NAFTA aggravate and deepen this tension, as international market liberalization
is granted a higher priority than any single nation's social contract.
Not only that, the reigning economic principle of competitiveness
is transforming "safety nets" into "springboards"; that is, welfare

---

[6] James J. Rice and Michael J. Prince, *Changing Politics of Canadian Social Policy*
(Toronto: University of Toronto Press, 2000) 130.
[7] Rice and Prince 130.

systems are moving away from an emphasis on social protections to an emphasis instead on retraining and advancement. In their words, "the new conception of the welfare state thus reframes the role of social policy as being a handmaiden to economic development and labour market adjustment."[8] Because this principle, under conditions of globalization, is becoming so pervasive across most of the capitalist world, most welfare states are disengaging from their previous social contracts in similar ways, and it is this disengagement that is producing greater uniformity among national approaches to social policy.

However, Banting remains sceptical about how far this process of standardization of social policies is likely to go. In a nice turn of phrase, he invokes "the tenacity of national differences in social affairs," to suggest strongly that domestic politics can be expected to continue to give distinctive national shape to social policy, despite the movement toward trade agreements and market liberalization generally.[9] Moreover, he argues this position even more forcefully in a later study conducted with two fellow political scientists, George Hoberg and Richard Simeon. Paying particular attention to several areas of social policy as well as to environmental policies, they conclude that there has been very little convergence between Canadian and American policies in these areas since the adoption of the FTA in 1989.[10] Moreover, with regard to the notion that market liberalization must, as some would put it, "shrink that state," they cite several studies to the effect that, in Canada itself or across the Organization for Economic Cooperation and Development (OECD), average corporate taxation rates have not converged at lower levels than several decades ago and have not become more uniform.[11]

Hoberg, Banting, and Simeon do not deny that "international pressures of many sorts have a critical effect on Canadian policy and on governments' capacity to address these matters," but they are keen to argue "that crude generalizations about the impact of globalization on policy autonomy are not very helpful."[12] In particular—as we saw

---

[8]   Rice and Prince 142.
[9]   Banting 109.
[10] Hoberg, Banting, and Simeon, Ch. 9.
[11] Hoberg, Banting, and Simeon 288.
[12] Hoberg, Banting, and Simeon 290-91.

Banting argue above—they emphasize the need to recognize that such international constraints (1) vary across sectors, time, and countries; (2) should not be confused with policy convergence as a result of common domestic pressures, emulation, learning, or the transfer of ideas; (3) may promote a "race to the top" as well as a "race to the bottom"; (4) are counterbalanced by powerful forces sustaining policy difference and divergence, such as path dependency and social entrenchment; (5) are best seen as costs to be weighed rather than as walls or straightjackets; and (6) are often chosen by domestic policy-makers rather than imposed from without.[13]

Despite the strength of the argument and evidence that Hoberg, Banting, and Simeon marshal in support of these propositions, the potential for policy convergence as an outcome of trade liberalization is greater than they allow, for reasons that will be set out in the last section of this chapter. In the meantime, let us look at the effects of the free trade orientation to government itself.

THE "MARKETIZATION" OF GOVERNMENT

So far in this discussion of social policy under free trade, a prominent theme has been the tendency of market liberalization to "shrink the state." Another theme in the literature, however, is not simply that governments have abandoned a variety of fields to the play of market forces, but also that even in the fields they continue to occupy, they have begun to "mimic" the market. This has led to the popularization of some new terminology for contemporary government, including such phrases as "competitive governments," "entrepreneurial government," and the "competition state." This development reflects the growing presence of market-like behaviour within the state apparatus

---

[13] Hoberg, Banting, and Simeon 291. It is worth noting that these authors do acknowledge the potential constraining effects of Chapter 11 on environmental regulation: "Chapter 11 investor suits—an apparently unforeseen implication for regulators—could pose a significant constraint on policy autonomy if it is interpreted expansively" (285).

itself, a process that may be described as the "commodification" or "marketization" of the state *per se*.[14]

The main focus of the "competition state" (to pick one of these new phrases) is the promotion of economic activities that will make firms and sectors located within individual states more competitive in world markets, rather along the lines of arguments about city-regions presented in Chapter 7. Philip Cerny describes the new role for government this way:

> Rather than providing public goods or other services which cannot be efficiently provided by the market—in other words, rather than acting as a "decommodifying" agent where market efficiency fails—the state is drawn into promoting the commodification or marketization of its *own* activities and structures.[15]

This, of course, can be regarded as an extreme version of the growing imbalance between social and economic markets discussed by Rice and Prince, and in fact they too complain about the "marketization" of social policy and even of cultural policy.

In fact, Rice and Prince provide a brief summary of several examples of this process, which are even further summarized (and paraphrased) here:

▶ the downward adjustment of working conditions in the public service to match those in the public sector;

▶ a trend toward "technological liberalism" in the new agenda for curriculum reform in education, involving measuring performance, ranking schools, and acquiring corporate donations for activities and facilities, along with an emphasis on preparing a highly skilled and competitive work force;

---

[14] Philip Cerny, "Globalization, Governance and Complexity," in J. Nederveen Pieterse and B. Parekh, eds., *Decolonization of Imagination, Culture, Knowledge and Power* (London: Zed Books, 1995) 196-97.

[15] Cerny 205; emphasis in original.

▶ an increasing tendency to regard immigrants as imported "human capital," accompanied by increasing misgivings about the impact of immigrants on job creation, social programs, and public services;

▶ a strong priority on trade promotion in foreign policy and international assistance, with development aid attuned to national economic goals and commercial interests;

▶ an increasing emphasis on breaking dependency on welfare, "making work pay," and encouraging self-reliance, with more stringent work obligations directed at able-bodied applicants and clients, including training courses for single mothers with young children.[16]

Of course, after years of government deficits during the 1960s and 1970s, not all these items will be seen as entirely negative by a large number of Canadians. But that is not the point. The real point of a list such as this is to consider whether or not, in the eyes of most Canadians, the pendulum may be swinging too far back toward the market and away from the kind of state that Canadians have traditionally invested with many of their political, social, and moral values.

CANADIAN AND AMERICAN VALUES: SIMILAR, DIFFERENT, OR CONVERGING

Hoberg, Banting, and Simeon conclude that the preservation of Canada's distinctive social policies ultimately depends on the democratic assertion of the different values that Canadians generally hold. In other words, the avoidance of Canada's social policy convergence with the US depends ultimately on Canadians' political will to remain different from Americans on this score. If this is true, we must have a clear picture of which values are most central to this desire and how likely they are to survive the free trade environment. As we

---

[16] Rice and Prince 151-52.

saw briefly in Chapter 1, there is some dispute among contemporary observers regarding the degree to which Canadian and American values are distinct and even more contention over whether they may be becoming more or less so with time.

Two books, in particular, stand out in this respect and, interestingly, contradict one another on some key dimensions of their Canada-US comparisons: *Regions Apart*, by Edward Grabb and James Curtis, and *Fire and Ice*, by Michael Adams. Grabb and Curtis make the case that there are two very different subregions of Canada and the US—Quebec and the American south—and that the existence of these subregions distorts undifferentiated surveys of Canadian and American values and leads them to understate the extensive similarities between the two societies. In particular, English Canada and the northern American states are quite similar to one another, a similarity that stems from their common colonial heritage:

> Although northern Americans are certainly different from English Canadians in some areas, most notably their approach to religious and moral issues, these two sub-groups usually exhibit much the same attitudes, orientations and behaviours, whether the topic is child-rearing values, feelings about economic crime, experience with many non-violent crimes, the acceptance of individualistic beliefs, levels of self-confidence and assertiveness, participation in various forms of civil dissent, or involvement in voluntary-association activity. Therefore, even as these two regions have changed over time, absorbing an increasing number of immigrants from all over the world in the past two hundred years, we can still find good evidence to support the view that both English Canada and the northern United States continue to represent two kindred, if somewhat distinct, branches from the Old English tree.[17]

Grabb and Curtis thus directly contradict Adams, who argues that Canadians "embrace a different hierarchy of values. Moreover, the

---

[17] Grabb and Curtis 251-52.

differences ... are increasing rather than decreasing with economic integration."[18] Most significantly, like Kim Nossal's integrationists discussed in Chapter 1, Adams holds out the possibility of

> economic integration and strategic interdependence without the loss of cultural integrity and political sovereignty. This, I would argue, is because Canada's founding values, historical experiences, and political institutions are very different from those in the United States and have a greater influence on Canadians' contemporary values than the much vaunted forces of globalization.[19]

Grabb and Curtis strongly disagree with this assessment, particularly with respect to the notion that Canada and the US have "very different" founding values. To the contrary, they describe as largely a myth the belief that Canada inherited a "Tory touch" from the United Empire Loyalists who moved to Canada during and after the American War of Independence, claiming that, at best, this might describe certain members of the elite in the Canadian colonies who were British-born and had upper-class backgrounds:

> Otherwise, the loyalist refugees ... seem to have evinced the same "Anglo-American" values and way of life as those that were exhibited by the population of the early United States ... [I]t appears that a similar mix of local communalist ideas, coupled with a belief in some limited forms of liberty, legal equality, popular sovereignty, and pluralism, were probably at work in both of these parts of North America during the era of the Revolution and the loyalist exodus.[20]

We will not undertake to establish which of these two interpretations is the correct one. Both arguments are largely beside the point

---

[18] Adams 142.
[19] Adams 143.
[20] Grabb and Curtis 86. It is worth noting that Grabb and Curtis also provide a detailed and quite convincing critique of Adams's findings and interpretations; see 269-71.

for our discussion because neither gives sufficient weight to at least two other factors. The first is the very substantial differences between the two economies that evolved in the separate parts of North America, as outlined in Chapters 3 and 4. The second is the consequence that flowed from the very fact of separate, but adjacent, sovereignties on the continent. The possibility that their independent existence would not be respected by the US created in and of itself a defensive dynamic to the politics of the British North American provinces that gave a distinct cast to the political economy of the smaller polities and subsequently to Canada. This distinct status on the continent ensured that *political* (as opposed to cultural) differences were bound to develop between the populations of the two countries, even if the people who lived in provinces that were to become Canada were exact clones of their American cousins (which, in any case, was decidedly not true for the substantial portion of them who were French-speaking).

THE CANADIAN ECONOMIC ELITE

For this reason, one other factor requires our attention, namely, the question of whether or not Canada's economic and political elites remain as committed as they once were to Canada's independent status. Grabb and Curtis point out that, historically and at present, "a significant gap can occur between elite beliefs or priorities and those of the general population."[21] This proposition is confirmed by an important and detailed study of the structure of elite and public opinion in Canada conducted during the late 1970s and early 1980s.[22] This investigation reveals (along with much else) substantial differences among corporate elites, on the one hand, and labour and academic elites, on the other, with regard to such issues as the overall effect of foreign investment on the Canadian economy. Here, although 59 per cent of corporate executives regard it as "mostly good," only 11 per

---

[21] Grabb and Curtis 259. See also their elaboration on this fact, 259-62.
[22] Michael Ornstein and H. Michael Stevenson, *Politics and Ideology in Canada: Elite and Public Opinion in the Transformation of a Welfare State* (Montreal and Kingston: McGill-Queen's University Press, 1999).

cent of trade union leaders, 30 per cent of academic leaders, and 0 per cent of farm leaders share that favourable opinion.[23] Similar differences in perspective are also evident with regard to the desirability of a "left-wing foreign policy" for Canada.[24]

Moreover, although it is difficult to document the case definitively, it seems probable that the gap between the Canadian business elite and general public has widened since the advent of free trade and especially since 9/11 has raised the level of business anxiety over the efficiency of the Canada-US border. (The gap between the opinions of Canada's business leaders and the general public on the question of Canada's lack of participation in the 2003 invasion of Iraq provide a clear example of this.) One reason for this divergence is that the workings of the North American economy under free trade have generally produced—or at least have coincided with—socio-economic trends that most business people approve and many among the general public do not, such as nearly stagnant real incomes for most working people, deteriorating public services, and seemingly interminable impasses on a growing list of trade issues for which free trade was initially sold as the solution. Another reason is that free trade has promoted the integration of the Canadian and American business communities themselves. As it was both designed and predicted to do, the reduction of trade and investment barriers has multiplied and intensified interconnections among business people in the two countries, and that interconnectedness is almost certain over time to produce a greater conformity of outlook toward both business itself and the political environments within which it operates.

However, it should be noted that one recent and careful examination of the interconnectedness of the Canadian and American business elites contradicts this interpretation.[25] William Carroll's study, based almost exclusively on a meticulous investigation of Canada's interlocking corporate directorships, sees fewer linkages between

---

[23] Ornstein and Stevenson 350, Table 9-3.
[24] Ornstein and Stevenson 359-61 and Table 9-6.
[25] William K. Carroll, *Corporate Power in a Globalizing World: A Study in Elite Social Organization* (Don Mills, ON: Oxford University Press, 2004) especially Ch. 6.

Canadian and American firms, relative both to the levels found in the past and to the levels now existing between Canada and the broader global business community. Carroll himself expresses some surprise at this discovery, but he nevertheless does a pretty good job of explaining it.

Carroll first points to the rationalization of intercorporate structures and operations that also figured prominently in the account here of the adoption of free trade (see Chapter 5). In the immediate post-Second World War phase of international business operations in North America, according to Carroll, the ties between American parent companies and their Canadian subsidiaries relied more heavily than they typically do today on director-level ties between executives. Second—and related to a similar process of rationalization—is the reduction in the status of many Canadian subsidiaries from, essentially, a proxy national firm to a more narrowly defined operational unit, where managerial rather than executive ties are more critical. Finally, for very large and highly globalized American firms, interconnections have become so complex in aggregate that interlocking directorships have been outgrown, and other forms of integrated management, encouraged by information technologies, have developed as substitutes for them.[26]

In short, business practices have moved beyond the overlapping boards of an earlier day. However, none of these developments need be taken as evidence that high-level business people in Canada and the US are any less fused together than they used to be, and some suggest that some forms of fusion may have intensified. The issue then becomes one of the degree to which the community of interests and identity among Canadian and American business elites has deepened to the point that the Canadian portion has essentially given up on Canada as a political value. If so, a secondary issue arises concerning the extent to which the Canadian economic elite can lead the rest of the country in the direction of more complete political integration with the US. Part of this assessment must include an appreciation of the differences that currently exist between elite and public opinion.

---

[26] Carroll 124.

The main point is how much the orientation of Canadian business has changed in the neo-conservative and free trade era. Free trade would not have come about if dominant Canadian business interests had not abandoned their traditional insistence on the preservation of a national economy and embraced instead the free trade option. However, matters have moved well beyond that initial repudiation of national protectionism. Today, Canadian business not only places a higher priority on market forces than on state intervention, it is beginning to place a higher priority on the American than on the Canadian market. Where foreign direct investment flows were once almost entirely one way—from south to north—they recently have evened out, and during the past year or so they have begun to flow more heavily from north to south. Thus, according to DFAIT, the compound annual growth rate of outward Canadian foreign direct investment into the US has risen from 0.35 per cent in 1989-94 to 16.38 per cent in 1994-2002. Meanwhile, the comparable figures for inward American investment into Canada have fallen from 26.33 per cent to 16.63 per cent.[27] This growing desire of Canadian businesses to penetrate the American (and other foreign) markets with invest-ments, rather than simply exports, means that they have taken on an even greater hostility to what remains of Canadian protectionism.

Knowing that investor access to foreign markets is generally available only on a reciprocal basis, a substantial proportion of the Canadian business community now lobbies the Canadian govern-ment to make the country more open than before to trade in services (for example) so that it can more effectively acquire more open access for similar investments in other countries. As a result, according to Stephen Clarkson, "Now thinking of Canada more as a home than as a host country for foreign investment, Ottawa's trade officials wel-comed the tough rules that the United States wanted to impose on the world."[28] Having grown to enjoy their recent status as free trad-ers, Canadian business people now fancy themselves as footloose

---

[27] DFAIT, *NAFTA @ 10: A Preliminary Report* (Ottawa: Minister of Public Works and Government Services Canada, 2003) 31, Table 2.4.1.
[28] Clarkson 119.

international investors.[29] Moreover, this reorientation of Canadian business toward foreign markets in preference to the national market creates some new opportunities for clashes of perceived self-interest between economic elites and the general public on a range of issues.

There is already evidence of such a clash. In a speech before the Canadian Club in early 2001, Frank L. Graves, the president of Ekos Research Associates, reported on poll results that indicated very different attitudes among different categories of Canadians with respect to both the Canada-US relationship and the pace and direction of social change. For example, private-sector elites and the general public expressed substantially different levels of interest in becoming more like the US. Only 14 per cent of the general public wished this to happen, as opposed to 37 per cent of private-sector elites.[30] Regarding the integration question specifically, more direct evidence of the attitudes of Canadian business people toward Canada-US integration exists in a report by the Public Policy Forum.[31] Generally, the business executives interviewed increasingly perceive the physical border between the two countries as "a nuisance from a business perspective" and are concerned that Canada's foreign policy is frequently out of alignment with its trade policy: "A number of industry representatives contend that Canadian policy positions have been taken in the past without regard for their implications or impact on Canadian trade and have frequently irritated our American neighbours."[32] A case in point is business apprehension over the position Canada has taken on the American National Missile Defense system. As one interviewee put it, "Canada should recognize that Homeland Defence is a priority in the U.S. It should stop irritating the U.S. with its foreign policy or otherwise think about an alternative trade policy, if one exists out there."[33]

---

[29] The growing extra-North American linkages of many Canadian firms are consistent with this interpretation. See Carroll, Ch. 10.

[30] Frank L. Graves, "Identity, Globalization and North American Integration: Canada at the Crossroads," speaking notes for an Address to the Canada Club, Ottawa, 16 January 2001, 11.

[31] Public Policy Forum, *Background Report: the Views of Canadian Industry and Business Associations on Canada-United States Economic Integration*, October 2000.

[32] Public Policy Forum 36-37.

[33] Public Policy Forum 37. Another was quoted as saying, "We are on the same continent and facing the same threats."

In contrast to this is the general outlook of the Canadian public toward the US. Especially in early 2003 after the American attack on Iraq, Canadians revealed some deep concerns about the US's foreign policy direction, along with some scepticism over the value of their relationship with Americans. In particular, an extensive May 2003 poll of Canadians' attitudes toward the US reveals that the American attack on Iraq may have stirred up some conflicting emotions among Canadians and led some of them to re-evaluate their views of their powerful neighbour.[34] In the first place, 81 per cent of them said "No" and only 17 per cent said "Yes" when asked whether, if they had the chance, they would like to live in the US. (Slightly fewer—74 per cent—of Canadians between the ages of 18 and 24 said "No" to this question.) At the same time, 52 per cent said that they thought that over time the two countries were becoming more alike, with only 15 per cent saying they thought the countries were becoming less so (and roughly 30 per cent saying they saw no change one way or the other). Very few Canadians thought that Canada should copy the way the US runs its economy, by a margin of 79 to 14 per cent. Meanwhile, substantial majorities of Canadians admired—and thought that their own country should aspire to achieve—the US's economic opportunities for its people and levels of scientific and technological innovation.

Some ambivalence was also evident in the fact that 82 per cent of Canadians polled expressed a generally favourable view of the US (with only 16 per cent unfavourable), but fewer than 50 per cent were favourable toward President George W. Bush and his administration's policies toward the environment and nuclear proliferation. One notable exception to this was relatively strong Canadian support

---

34 See The Pew Research Center for the People and the Press, "War With Iraq Further Divides Global Publics," *Views of a Changing World 2003*, 3 June 2003. The Pew Global Attitudes Project surveyed 16,000 people in 20 countries (including Canada) and the Palestinian Authority in May 2003. The author was invited by the CBC to comment on the Canadian results on a sequence of local morning radio shows and, as part of this, received over 75 pages of raw data on those results as an e-mail attachment. All of the data reported in this and the following paragraph were obtained from this source. A copy of the Center's report, which does not contain all of the Canadian results, may be accessed at <http://people-press.org/reports/display.php3?ReportID=185>.

(60 per cent) for the US in relation to the issue of terrorism. The low level of support for President Bush himself is probably related to Canadians' wariness of the increasing tendency of the US to adopt a "go it alone" approach to foreign policy, with 68 per cent choosing to describe the Americans as "arrogant" and 65 per cent explicitly agreeing with the statement that "The United States now feels it is the only superpower in the world and they can do what they like." Despite this, solid majorities (of 66 per cent and 72 per cent, respectively) felt that the US is a force for good in the world and a beacon of hope and opportunity, despite the fact that 40 per cent felt that American economic policies make Canada poorer (as opposed to 31 per cent who thought they made Canada richer).

The new orientation of Canadian business toward the foreign instead of the national market thus creates some new opportunities for clashes of self-interest between economic elites and the general public on a range of issues. The growing business interest in a global level playing field translates into pressure on government for a relandscaping of the Canadian field in directions a majority of Canadian people may not desire. To the extent this happens, the Canadian public interest and business interests will be in conflict. Again, this clash of economic and social values is unlikely to occur as starkly or as broadly in the US, given that the global level playing field is more likely to resemble the American status quo than the existing equilibrium in most other countries. However, setting aside the details of specific conflicts over tangible costs and benefits, a more general effect of the new Canadian business agenda is likely to surface as a widening divergence between the attitudes, values, and opinions of the Canadian socio-economic elite, on the one hand, and the general public, on the other hand.

MUTUAL TRUST AND CANADA-US INTEGRATION

It is now time to revisit some of the broader theoretical and analytical considerations that bear on the relationship between fundamental social values and political outcomes, including institutional change.

The Deutschian approach to political integration includes the compatibility of core values and regards the degree of mutual trust between national populations as a critical intervening variable in the
relationship between increased transactions and public support for
both closer economic ties and, ultimately, political integration. In a
major application of this analytic framework, Inglehart, Nevitte, and
Basañez summarize these vital linkages very helpfully:

> Deutsch argued that high levels of transactions between peoples
> (the movement of peoples, cross-border commerce, and com-
> munication flows) encourage similarities in main values. Simi-
> larities in main values interact and are conducive to greater mu-
> tual trust between different peoples. Higher levels of trust, in
> turn, encourage greater cooperation and economic integration.
> And economic integration, Deutsch concludes, is conducive to
> greater political integration.[35]

In other words, economic and political integration should ultimately
be regarded as part of a process of social learning in which whole peoples can experience fundamental reorientations toward one another,
as a wide range of mutual interactions leads them to see one another
as increasingly predictable, positively responsive, and trustworthy.[36]
Perhaps the most dramatic historical instance of such a process of
reorientation is the transformation in mutual regard between the
French and the Germans over the decades following the Second World
War. In 1950 they distrusted each other deeply as a consequence of
having been on opposite sides of that war but by 1980—following 30
years of intensified transactions and increasingly formalized political cooperation—they found each other among the nationalities they
trusted most.[37]

Closer to home, where mutual trust between Canadians and
Americans has been relatively high throughout the twentieth century (partly because they were both on the same side of three major

---

[35] Inglehart, Nevitte, and Basañez, 6.
[36] Inglehart, Nevitte, and Basañez 7.
[37] Inglehart, Nevitte, and Basañez 8.

wars that took place during it), the strongest empirical demonstration of the validity of the Deutschian model is to be found in the links between the levels of Canadians' and Americans' trust in one another and their respective support for closer economic ties, as well as the links between support for stronger economic ties and support for political integration (defined as support for "doing away with the border").[38] In addition, it is entirely consistent with the same model that the Canadian and American decisions in 1988 to consolidate their economic relationship in a more formalized legal and institutional arrangement followed at least two decades of increases in a wide range of commercial and social transactions.

However, John Helliwell has recently reminded us that mutual trust, like the intensity of material transactions, tends to be significantly higher within national boundaries than across them.[39] He believes this partly explains why nation-states still matter in an age of increasing global interdependence and why, in consequence, national policies should not be too far disassociated from their domestic constituency and frame of reference (such as those mandated by trade treaties, for instance). In his analysis, the "border effect" (according to which, for a variety of reasons, economic exchanges tend to take place more easily within national boundaries than across them) tends to trump the "gravity theory of trade" (according to which economic exchanges between regional centres tends to increase directly with their size and inversely with the distance between them). That is, for example, there is much more trade between Toronto and Vancouver than between Toronto and Los Angeles despite that fact that the distance in each instance is roughly comparable, but the size of the Los Angeles-centred market is much larger than the Vancouver-centred market. Even after the tangible and direct economic effects of national boundaries—such as tariff charges and nationally protective regulation—are reduced to zero, their intangible and indirect effects—such as social and legal practices, as well as shared attitudes—still matter, and matter a lot.

---

[38] Inglehart, Nevitte, and Basañez 166-67, Figures 6.5 and 6.6.
[39] Helliwell.

The reason that national boundaries can have significant economic effects, even after they have ceased to interfere directly with
commercial transactions, is that personal interconnections of practically all kinds are significantly denser within nation-states than between them. The explanation for this is "social capital," a result of
the greater familiarity of the institutions, social norms, and personal
characteristics one shares with one's own compatriots.[40] At an informal level, this is a product of the frequency of interpersonal contact,
which tends to decline with distance as a function of cost and with
borders as a function of differences in national policy. At another
level, formal institutions supplement and/or substitute for the frequency of interpersonal contact, including

> laws and the administration of justice, the design and imple-
> mentation of standards, and the efficiency and quality of es-
> sential services, including (especially) health and education but
> also including the classic utilities—water, heat, light, power, and
> communications.[41]

In sum, according to Helliwell, distinct national characteristics matter and are probably more resistant to the supposedly corrosive effects
of international transactions and interdependence than the hyper-
globalists would otherwise lead us to expect.

If this is true, then just as the border effect may be said to trump
the gravity theory of trade, it is possible that the density of social
capital may impede the mutual social learning that underlies the
Deutschian model of political integration. It is important therefore, to underscore three key points about the current direction of
Canadian attitudes and values relating to Canada-US integration that
were discussed in the previous section. First, it is highly probable that
in Canada the effects of Deutschian social learning have been undermining the border effect for at least half a century, at least with respect to the norms, predictability, and mutual responsiveness of its

[40] See Helliwell 31 and 37.
[41] Helliwell 35.

business elite. As we saw in some of the data presented above, the current attitudes of this group toward a number of issues show signs of assimilation—or at least of strong similarity or compatibility—to those of its American counterpart. It is intriguing to note that almost 40 years ago, the prominent Canadian sociologist, John Porter, was greatly perplexed by the question of whether or not the "foreign resident directors of the dominant corporations" in Canada should have been included in his definition of the Canadian economic elite.[42] In the end, he decided such inclusiveness was not warranted in his study of the relationship between the economic elite and the Canadian social structure because few foreign resident directors belonged to that structure.

Even more noteworthy, however, was Porter's failure, even in the early 1960s, to identify any significant differences between Canadian and American business people in his socio-political analysis of Canadian society. In a line of analysis that resonates with Helliwell's, he argued:

> Corporations ... are governed by human beings who behave in accordance with a set of institutional norms—those of corporate capitalism. To argue that national sentiments and the "national interest" would supplant the historical and inexorable norms of capitalist enterprise is to reveal an ignorance of the capitalist economy.[43]

In other words, the social capital of the Canadian and American business communities is largely indistinguishable. "Because the nationalities of actors in the system have no place in the instrumental norms of capitalism ... it is difficult to see how nationality affects the behaviour of those who govern a capitalist economy."[44] In short, it would not surprise Porter to see that, once the logic of capitalism

---

[42] John Porter, *The Vertical Mosaic: An Analysis of Social Class and Power in Canada* (Toronto: University of Toronto Press, 1965) 273. Porter devoted eight pages of a 43-page chapter to working the problem out.

[43] Porter 269.

[44] Porter 269-70.

comes to dictate that borders must disappear altogether, most Canadian business people would happily embrace the disappearance of Canada.

Even if matters have not come to this, it seems reasonable to conclude that, as a consequence of more than half a century of extensive foreign direct investment in the Canadian economy, much of it concentrated in the largest firms in many key sectors, the business community in Canada may currently represent the highest existing level of cross-border social and professional integration between the two communities. As one example of this, cross-border linkages within transnational corporations appear to be affecting the structure and performance of industry associations in Canada. According to one study:

> A generation ago, most industry associations were composed of Canadian companies that operated primarily in Canada. In our survey, over half the associations told us that the majority of their members (and frequently their most important members) are actually American companies—or at least multinational companies whose headquarters are based in the U.S.—operating in Canada.[45]

Moreover, this change is seen to be altering the dynamics and even the very role of these associations, as "Canadian industry associations insist they now spend as much time explaining Canada and Canadian government to their members, who come from the U.S., as they do explaining their industry to government."[46]

This evolution of a form of continental social capital can be predicted, according to a version of integration theory, to develop into a precondition for political integration and an erosion of the border effect. At the same time, and precisely for this reason, it can be predicted to separate the bulk of the Canadian business community from Canadians generally on the proper course for the Canada-US

---

[45] Public Policy Forum 20.
[46] Public Policy Forum 21.

relationship. The future prospects for the deeper integration of the continent may thus be framed as the ultimate outcome of a collision between the North American social capital developing jointly within the Canadian and American business communities, on the one hand, and the historically accumulated, national social capital shared (respectively) by the Canadian and American publics, on the other.

VALUE CONVERGENCE AND POLICY HARMONIZATION

The form of international political integration that is taking place between Canada and the US is not about "doing away with the border" or fusing the two countries into a new state. In effect, the high levels of mutual sensitivity, cross-border cooperation, and policy coordination that Deutsch associated with a "pluralistic" security community (as opposed to the full transfer of sovereignty characteristic of an "amalgamated" security community) amount to political integration as policy harmonization.[47] Presumably, the level of mutual trust and the degree of value convergence associated with this form of political integration can be lower than that associated with political unification.

For this reason, we will conclude with a closer look at Hoberg, Banting, and Simeon's arguments that Canada's "capacity for choice" (or policy autonomy) has not been seriously affected by trade liberalization, since this is essentially an argument that policy harmonization is not taking place and need not take place.[48] If they are correct, one of the core components of my argument is largely undermined. Fortunately, there are some strong reasons to doubt either the validity or the applicability of their conclusions.

First of all, there is a vast and still growing literature on the ways and extent to which globalization is bringing about massive adjustments in state policies almost everywhere, and it is not implausible to suggest that Canada-US relations over the past 20 years or so

---

[47] Karl W. Deutsch, *The Analysis of International Relations*, 3rd ed. (Englewood Cliffs, NJ: Prentice Hall, 1988) Ch. 19.
[48] Hoberg, Banting, and Simeon.

represent a microcosm of the process of globalization. Key indicators of both include increasing flows of trade and investment (including in the service sector); highly integrated capital markets; a high incidence of fully networked international firms; high levels of travel for business, education, tourism, and family reasons; and large flows of information and entertainment products. Of course, no *volume* of literature can establish the absolute truth of any scientific explanation, but there are so many academic studies showing that globalization is having significant impact on state autonomy that they cannot be ignored.[49] It seems extremely implausible that governments in Canada have remained immune to these effects, or that the FTA and NAFTA have done nothing to deepen and augment them.

Second, without pretending to refute or overturn Hoberg, Banting, and Simeon's findings, the fact that they find little convergence in social and environmental policies directly attributable to international constraints may be largely a product of the policy fields they examine and therefore may not be very representative of larger realities. After all, pro-free traders assured Canadians that their social policies were exempt from trade agreements, and the environmental side agreement to NAFTA is limited to the monitoring of respective national legislation. Among the wider realities that do not agree with their findings are various industrial policies, such as regulations specifically singled out in NAFTA as candidates for harmonization and standardization under the auspices of the agreement's multiplicity of working groups and committees. In many instances (as discussed in Chapter 6), these agencies are made up of both government officials from the three member countries along with representatives of multinational firms, and the new or revised regulations they arrive at become the law of all three countries. One may claim that there is no harm in such procedures, but one cannot easily claim that they represent autonomous policy processes.

---

[49] For a valuable review of some significant contributions to this literature, see Gil Gunderson, "Review Essay: Democratic Government in the Age of Globalization?" *Public Organization Review: A Global Journal* 3 (December 2003): 421-29. One sentence in this review reads: "The great fear is that the quest for capital accumulation in economic globalization has been assisted and directed by ruling elites to the detriment of the nation-state" (422).

Finally, there is the more comprehensive manner in which economic integration alters the players and modes of Canada's domestic policy processes. International economic integration—including that embracing the North American continent—is at least as much about investment as it is about trade, and foreign direct investment in particular is not simply about flows of capital but rather structures of power. International business firms are hierarchical structures concerned with making decisions within and influencing decisions without the organization. Canada is host to many subsidiaries of American-based firms, and the government of Canada interacts with a lot of them every working day. Not only that, but many observers are beginning to believe that Chapter 11 of NAFTA has extended the rights of such foreign-based multinationals *vis-à-vis* Canadian governments beyond those available to any Canadian company or, indeed, any Canadian citizen. Among these rights is the capacity to take such governments before international tribunals to either overturn or receive financial compensation for any law that impedes their ability to realize their expected profits from any existing or *intended* business investment.[50]

In sum, Hoberg, Banting, and Simeon seem to ignore the possibility that North American economic integration has changed the structure of economic and political power in Canada and that this new structure of power may be less conducive to the realization of democratically determined policy choices that the majority of Canadian citizens prefer. They come close to recognizing this as an abstract possibility, but it plays no part in their analysis of the scope for autonomous choice in the "New North America." They write:

> Relationships [among causes of convergence] become ambiguous, especially when the analysis incorporates the potential indirect effects of economic integration. If economic integration leads over time to greater cultural integration and convergence

[50] Stephen McBride, "Quiet Constitutionalism in Canada: The International Political Economy of Domestic Institutional Change," *Canadian Journal of Political Science* 36, 2 (June 2003): 265-66.

in values on either side of the border, then domestic pressures may be less separate than they appear. As well, international economic constraints can operate by altering the distribution of influence among different domestic actors, which may be hard to discern.[51]

In sum, there may be more convergence of values taking place across the Canada-US border than most Canadians realize, especially among the business communities of the two countries, and the "distribution of influence among domestic actors" may be detracting from the capacity of the rest of Canadians to promote politically the kind of future the majority of them wish they could choose. That loss of capacity is precisely what this study takes to be political integration.

---

[51] Hoberg, Banting, and Simeon 254.

chapter 10
chapter 10
CANADA-US RELATIONS IN THE
TWENTY-FIRST CENTURY: THE EMERGENCE
OF NORTH AMERICAN POLITICS

This chapter places the Canada-US relationship in the broader context of each country's overall foreign policy, and its main focus is on international relations since the end of the Cold War. At the same time, it examines the effects of globalization on Canada-US relations and on international relations generally over the past 20 years. In particular, the first section reviews what some observers have labeled a shift from "world politics" toward "transnational relations" as the dominant model of recent international relations and considers the extent to which that move may parallel a shift in relations from "Canada-US diplomacy" to "North American politics." The second section examines how a decline in Canada's traditional intermediary role may be responsible for this shift, while the third considers how this change has been accompanied by a similar decline in the significance of traditional security concerns, including the dictates of "power politics." Here, it is argued that the significance of foreign policy independence has been downplayed in favour of the benefits of interdependence and economic issues such as trade and investment. All these changes have served to tie Canada and Canadian foreign policy more tightly to North America and simultaneously to loosen its connections with the wider international community, trends that accelerated after 9/11.

FROM WORLD POLITICS TO TRANSNATIONAL RELATIONS

For over 50 years, world politics was consumed by the rivalry between the United States of America and the Union of Soviet Socialist Republics. As intense as their rivalry was, the two superpowers managed to contain the life-and-death character of this struggle below the level of military warfare. Most observers believe that this mutual avoidance of conventional military hostilities was a result of the mortal fear on both sides that any such engagement might escalate to an all-out nuclear exchange.

Despite this mutual restraint, power politics dominated the relationship between the American and Soviet alliances and also the relations within each alliance. Although the mechanisms of control differed within the two blocs (as the alliances were often called), the relations the US had with its alliance partners—as well as with most of the Third World—were bound up in one way or another with the central preoccupation of American foreign policy: to contain any expansion of Soviet power and to match if not surpass the Soviet Union in world power. This policy promoted a more or less explicit "with us or against us" attitude on the part of the US in relation to most countries outside the Soviet bloc.

Because the Cold War was ultimately all about power politics of this kind, the "Realist" school of international relations became one of the most prominent orientations of both practitioners and scholars of national foreign policies and world politics. Realism subscribes to the view that calculations of national power pervade international diplomacy; hence, national security is the central consideration in most international relationships. Another important Realist assumption is that states act as unitary agents, meaning that the conduct of foreign policy is rarely an issue for national political debate and that internal (or "domestic") processes generally have little to do with states' external behaviour. This implies that foreign policy is decided at the highest levels of government and involves a small group of central political actors. Such centralized decision-making reflects the fact that foreign policy is meant to promote the security interests of the state as a whole, rather than the special interests of corporations, labour unions, farmers, or any of the special interests that normally participate in the formulation of domestic policies.

Given that it is meant to depict Realism in international relations, the world politics model (WP) is centrally concerned with relations among national governments—commonly referred to as "states"—and usually governments at the highest level. These interstate relations may be conducted multilaterally through IGOs such as the GATT, the G7, or the UN. However, it is assumed by the WP model that IGOs have no consequential powers beyond what the major states in the system are prepared to grant them. Moreover, private international activities, such as trade and investment, are rarely drawn into the picture and tend to be treated as subordinate to primary security objectives. For example, throughout the Cold War, the predominant share of international financial assistance (as well as private investment flows) were extended to allied or friendly countries but withheld from allies of the Soviet Union and even many non-aligned states.

In contrast to WP is the transnational relations model (TNR), which places much more emphasis on the economic and social relations among states, stressing economic interdependence and the potential for cooperation as well as conflict in the international system of states. It correspondingly gives greater weight and recognition to internal political processes and domestic actors, as well as subnational governments (such as provinces) and lower level national government officials and agencies. MNCs (increasingly referred to as "transnational corporations" or "transnational enterprises") figure largely in the TNR model, especially the networks of interaction between parent firms in one country and subsidiaries in others. Similarly, IGOs and NGOs, such as Greenpeace and Amnesty International, also figure more prominently in TNR than WP and are assumed to represent genuine constraints on the behaviour of national governments.

Yet another way of picturing the differences between WP and TNR is to consider the degree of interpenetration that goes on among states in the political economy and society of the post-Cold War period. It is consistent with Realist assumptions to depict the states in the international system as largely impermeable units, exposing a "hard shell" to other states and interacting with one another rather like billiard

balls on a pool table. The interpenetration of their respective societies is largely ignored. It is hard to come up with a contrasting image
that captures the essence of TNR. Instead of balls knocking into one
another, it is rather like circles representing individual countries su-
perimposed on a dense web or latticework of lines depicting interrelationships of all kinds connecting the domestic society of each state
with that of all the others (perhaps with some lines penetrating other
circles meant to stand for IGOs and NGOs).

National governments still have a place in TNR, and lines might still
be drawn to represent the traditional diplomatic relations between governments. Even here, however, variations on WP need to be added. For
example, TNR depicts various *levels* of government, with not only provinces and states playing a part but also *subgovernmental* agencies and departments of national governments. Thus, members of the CRTC might
represent Canada at meetings of the International Telecommunications
Union (along with representatives of Bell Canada), or National Energy
Board officials might negotiate with officials of the American Federal
Energy Regulatory Commission over the construction of a new power
transmission line between Quebec and New York.

With TNR in mind, it is possible to highlight a number of differences between the Cold War and post-Cold War eras that have promoted
parallel changes in the Canada-US relationship. (Similar contrasts
were drawn in Chapter 2 between Phases II and III of these relations.)
The first is that, through much of the 1970s and 1980s, the two models
co-existed, whereas after the Cold War, WP pretty much faded into
insignificance (at least temporarily). That is, WP was appropriate for
the relations between the two major East and West blocs. At the same
time, however, TNR became an increasingly accurate way to represent international relations within the West, especially relations between Canada and the US. In fact, one of the first major studies of
TNR was published as early as 1974 and, interestingly enough, was
heavily based on an analysis of Canada-US relations.[1]

---

[1] Annette Baker Fox, Alfred J. Hero, and Joseph S. Nye, Jr., eds., *Canada and the
    United States: Transnational and Transgovernmental Relations* (Madison, WI: World
    Peace Foundation, 1974).

A second and related difference is that, when the Soviet Union disappeared, thus ending the deep divisions that had dominated world politics for half a century, the geographic scope for TNR expanded. That is, the kind of relationships that had come to characterize the internal workings of the West were now in a position to spread across the entire world. Indeed, one way of thinking about globalization is to consider it as the expansion and intensification of TNR and the gradual enlargement of the domain of international capitalism centred in the US. In 1993, during one of his first speeches on foreign policy, newly elected American President Bill Clinton spoke of "enlarging the world's community of market democracies."[2] While it was little remarked upon at the time, this speech—coming as it did only a few short years after the Berlin Wall was torn down—can be taken as an abrupt turn in American foreign policy from an era of containment to one of enlargement, from confining the Soviet Union within its share of the world to spreading American predominance across the entire world. TNR, which had once played a role in consolidating American power in the West alone, now became a hallmark of the US's global reach.

THE DECLINE IN CANADA'S INTERMEDIARY ROLE

The fundamental shift in the global power structure from bipolar rivalry to unipolar dominance has greatly altered the context for the conduct of Canadian foreign policy. As discussed in Chapter 2, Canada's foreign policy throughout the Cold War was generally marked by mediation. This role typically did not take the legal/technical form of intervening in ongoing negotiations between two sides to a dispute and helping them reach an agreement, but was rather more like getting between the parties to a brawl to prevent them from killing one another. Since the end of the Cold War, Canada is discovering that—in a world with only one side—there is not much call for

---

[2] Bill Clinton, "Confronting the Challenge of a Broader World," UN General Assembly, New York, 27 September 1993.

getting between parties to a conflict. The disappearance of the Soviet Union has not brought an end to international conflict, but it has significantly reduced the capacity of civil wars and local international conflicts to escalate into more dangerous confrontations between nuclear powers. In a world of one superpower, there may be no "in between."

The shift from a bipolar to a unipolar global structure has therefore brought about a major reduction in the scope for what Canada has traditionally done best internationally. It has seriously undermined Canada's claim to a distinct role in the world and thereby reduced much of its previous foreign policy independence. Canadian independence was once bolstered by doing important things in the world that the US needed to be done but, in the context of Cold War power relations, could not do as effectively on its own. Canada also took advantage of the fact that, if it was to act as an effective intermediary, the country could not be seen simply as a minion of American foreign policy or a servant of American national interests. It achieved some prominence as a country that, while an American ally that would never deliberately seek to undermine American interests, nevertheless maintained a "mind of its own" in world affairs. Other countries, including the US, valued and generally respected Canada's contributions along these lines to the UN and other IGOs.

There were three major areas in which Canada exercised its function as an intermediary in world politics and played out its role as a "middle" power. The first, as already suggested, was to act as an international peacekeeper aimed at keeping the US and the Soviet Union—as well as their "proxies" or "client states"—at a safe distance from one another even as they competed for spheres of influence throughout the Third World. The second was to act as an "interpreter" in trans-Atlantic relations between the US and its major Western European allies. The third was to act as both an interpreter and a conciliator in relations between the Third World and the West.

Regarding peacekeeping, there can be little doubt that Canada made a significant contribution to the ability of the superpowers to avoid situations that might escalate into a Third World War. There is no question that mutual nuclear deterrence was the primary factor restraining the US and the Soviet Union. However, throughout the

Cold War era, exactly where one superpower's sphere of influence began and the other's left off remained imprecise. Worse, in some areas such as the Middle East, several countries always appeared to be "up for grabs," since many countries in the Arab world were not perceived as firm members of either camp. As a consequence, any localized conflicts had the potential to draw the superpowers into the contest on opposite sides, opening the possibility of a direct military confrontation between them. Practically no one contemplated that such a battle between Soviet and American troops could be prevented from escalating into a world war, possibly involving attacks with nuclear weapons.

It was this fear of superpower confrontation that prompted Canada and other middle powers to devise the mechanisms of injecting "neutrals"—"non-combatants" is probably a better term—into regional conflicts to help the regional players involved come to a resolution of their local differences before the superpowers succumbed to the temptation to intervene on opposite sides. In this sense, UN intervention was designed as a significantly less dangerous substitute for mutual and peremptory intervention by the two superpowers. Examples of such interventions are the Suez Crisis of 1956, the Congo Crisis of 1961-63, and the Yom Kippur (Arab-Israeli) War of 1973. (The Cyprus peacekeeping operation of over 30 years duration had a similar logic, but in this case the fear was mutual intervention by Greece and Turkey on opposite sides of a civil war between Greek and Turkish Cypriots, which had the potential to escalate into a broader war between two NATO allies.)

Meanwhile, confusion has developed over the emergence of "peacemaking" following the end of the Cold War. The Gulf War of 1991, the ten weeks of aerial bombardment of Serbia by NATO forces in the spring of 1999, the bombardment and invasion of Afghanistan following 9/11, and the US-led invasion of Iraq in March 2003 are the leading examples of this new variety of international intervention. Canada made only a limited contribution to the Gulf War, which was overwhelmingly an American military campaign; however, Canada was, next to the US, one of the most active bombers of Serbia and contributed ground and naval forces to the American effort against hostile forces in the Afghan campaign. These interventions have to be regarded as departures from the classic peacekeeping model, mostly because these acts of military coercion had only tenuous links with the UN, and service in them is better regarded as an extension of membership in NATO and Canada's allegiance to the US than as an expression of Canada's traditional UN peacekeeping commitment. As one observer has phrased this difference, Canada is now making more "green helmet" (NATO) than "blue helmet" (UN) commitments, and green helmet commitments seem to be more about shoring up its partnership with the US than keeping faith with its long-standing tradition of international peacekeeping.[3]

In sum, the peacekeeping function has been drastically altered as a consequence of the end of the Cold War. Moreover, the number (and type) of countries providing soldiers for recent UN missions has also changed substantially, with former middle powers such as Canada doing less and countries of the Third World, such as Nigeria and Bangladesh, doing much more.[4] Indeed, some of Canada's most recent contributions to the UN have involved the RCMP rather than the armed forces, a sign perhaps that the next phase of UN "peacekeeping" will be in the form of an international extrapolation of "aid to the civil power" rather than the prevention of wars between states.[5] It may also be a sign that, in the post-Cold War era, revolutions and civil wars may be the major threats to international stability. This could become uncomfortable for many Canadians, because

---

[3] Joel J. Sokolsky, "The Bilateral Security Relationship: Will 'National' Missile Defense Involve Canada?" *The American Review of Canadian Studies* 32, 2 (Summer, 2000): 236.

[4] Former Canadian peacekeeping commander Lewis MacKenzie has pointed out that in the ranking of nations contributing to UN peacekeeping missions, Canada has gone from number 1 in 1993 with close to 5,000 troops deployed to number 36 with a mere 300 Canadians in such service. See Lewis MacKenzie, "Mission: Remaking the Military," *Globe and Mail*, 21 April 2005: A19.

[5] Aid to the civil power is essentially a government's use of military forces for domestic rather than external security. The extreme form is calling in the army to put down local insurrections or to help restore order during large and violent demonstrations. Recent use of the Canadian armed forces to provide emergency services during floods, ice-storms, and blizzards is a more benign example. The War Measures Act of 1970 and the Oka Crisis of 1990 are also familiar cases to Canadians.

the source of such instability is often the desire of national majorities to throw off the repressive rule of economic and political elites who are well connected to international capitalism. Canadians may or may not be pleased to support military action that essentially consolidates existing economic and political power structures, especially if they perceive that such actions promote the interests of the US and its partners in the global economy rather than protect human rights.

It may seem strange to suggest that a country—Canada or any other—could adopt the role of intermediary between the US and its strongest allies, the European members of NATO. However, British wartime prime minister, Winston Churchill, may have provided a clue to the plausibility of this function when he once described the US and Britain as two great peoples "divided by a common language." This comment suggests that even very good friends and allies can still have differences over how best to promote their common interests. It also hints that any two countries may occasionally find it difficult to interpret precisely and accurately what the other is saying and doing in international affairs. It is for both these reasons that Canada has periodically found itself interpreting the US to its allies in Europe, especially Britain and France, and conversely interpreting the Western Europeans to the Americans.

Canada has some obvious pedigree for this role. For one thing, of all the allies of the US, it is the only one with historical, cultural, and linguistic links to *both* Britain and France. For another, Canada occupies an intermediate position in relations between the US and the rest of NATO. It is like the US in that it is the only other non-European member of the alliance (except Turkey). Sharing a continent with the US, Canada can appreciate better than the Europeans how the world looks from North America. At the same time, it is closer to the Europeans in being—like all of them—a follower of the US's lead and shares with them the need to balance specific national interests involved in any particular item on the alliance agenda against their longer term interest in maintaining the solidarity of the alliance, which requires deferring to the priorities of the ultimate guarantor of every member's security. Once again, however, some of the distinctiveness of this Canadian disposition has become less salient in the strategic environment of the post-Cold War period. As with the global structure of power, the emerging power structure in the West seems to leave no more "in between" for Canada to occupy.

Lastly, Canada's Cold War foreign policy also sought to play an intermediary role between the West and the Third World, with roughly equal emphasis on the British Commonwealth and *la Francophonie*, whose memberships constitute a representative sample of First World and Third World nations, and universal IGOs within the UN system. Once again, some peculiarities in Canada's economic, political, and historical place in the world supported an effective performance of this role. For one thing, Canada was a developed country, a member of the club of the world's largest economies, but was neither a superpower to be distrusted as a potential meddler nor a former imperial power to be resented and feared for its "neo-colonial" tendencies. For another, the Canadian economy, despite its impressive aggregate strength, shared some of the common structural weaknesses of Third World economies. Canada, too, had relied for economic development on the export of raw materials to more advanced industrial powers, as well as on foreign direct investment and technology from those powers. Finally, Canada had itself once been a colony of not one, but two former European empires and still experiences anxieties about possible economic subordination to the US, the most dynamic economy of the postwar era.

Moreover, by taking its seat in the Organization of American States (OAS) in 1989, Canada signaled that economic interests were beginning to displace diplomatic interests as the primary motors of its foreign policy and that its immediate neighbourhood was of greater importance to it than the world community as a whole. Although the list of goals motivating Canada's foreign economic policy agenda has not shifted greatly, the venue for the pursuit of those objectives certainly has. The kinds of foreign assistance, private investments, development initiatives, and trade relations that Canada used to pursue with the developing countries of the Commonwealth can be pursued as actively and beneficially with the developing countries of the Americas, but they are unlikely to serve as an equivalent counterweight to the pull of the country's bilateral relationship with the US.

Since the early nineteenth century—the days of the Monroe Doctrine—the western hemisphere has been essentially an American economic empire. In its relations with the countries of the Caribbean
and Central and South America, Canada will essentially be doing
with and for them what it tries to do for itself: finding a way to cope
with American supremacy in the hemisphere. In a sense, therefore,
Canada's role in the Americas still may be predicated on the need
and desire for independence from the US, but the Canada-US relationship will remain the definitive factor in all the issues it will have
to address. Canada's policies toward the region are likely to serve as
an extension of, rather than an independent counterweight to, its
relationship with the US. Now that President George W. Bush has
received "fast-track" negotiating authority from Congress to pursue
a Free Trade Area of the Americas, pressures along this fault-line in
Canada's policies toward the Third World are only likely to increase.

HOMELAND SECURITY AND THE FUSION OF
CANADIAN AND AMERICAN FOREIGN POLICY

Previous to 9/11, it was frequently observed that, with the disappearance of the Soviet Union, the US no longer faced any serious threat
to its security and lacked a credible single adversary. As one observer
put it, the US is now faced with "threats without enemies." Accordingly, many Canadian analysts explored the ways in which Canada's
relations with the US were adjusting to that fact. After 9/11, some
reconsideration of these propositions is necessary. Certainly most
Americans believe they face an enemy, either specifically in the form
of al Qaeda terrorists, the "Axis of Evil" condemned by President
George W. Bush, or Islamic extremism. However, as we saw in the
Introduction, much of the supposedly new security is not new at all,
but merely a crystallization and intensification of concerns that had
been accumulating strength over the previous decade. Indeed, terrorism was at the top of most lists of "threats without enemies"; the
threat, though, lacked today's personification and precise focus.

Since 9/11, several important books have been published expressing deep concern about the effect of the War on Terror and President George W. Bush's new security doctrine on Canada's foreign policy independence.[6] While differing in emphasis, all agree that the challenge of maintaining an independent Canadian foreign policy—and, indeed, the problem of maintaining a Canadian foreign policy that continues to reinforce Canadian independence over all—is a significant challenge. This is not only because of new kinds of pressures emanating from south of the border, but also because of some of the global changes discussed above as well as some changes within Canada itself. Underlying all these discussions is a new, starker version of the "autonomy prosperity trade-off" with which this book opened. The core issue is how Canada can maintain and effectively utilize room for manoeuvre in relation to the rest of the world while, at the same time, reassuring the US that an open northern border is not an unacceptable risk to its security.

By these accounts, Canadians face an "impossible trinity" in its foreign policy by which only two out of three major objectives can be reached: (1) expending sufficient financial and human resources to ensure that Canada contributes its "fair share" to North American security in order to make Americans feel safe in maintaining an open border with Canada and in order to prevent them from doing so entirely themselves, and in their own way; (2) as a counterweight to that highly integrative agenda, expending sufficient resources to both upgrade Canada's pursuit of its own extra-North American agenda and at the same time pursue key domestic policies that also contribute to a distinct national identity; and (3) avoiding budget deficits.[7] While none of the books referred to adopt the impossible trinity framework, it nevertheless provides a perspective on where they place their respective emphasis and priorities.

---

[6] See Lloyd Axworthy, *Navigating a New World: Canada's Global Future* (Toronto: Knopf Canada, 2003); Andrew Cohen, *While Canada Slept: How We Lost Our Place in the World* (Toronto: McClelland and Stewart, 2003); Jennifer Welsh, *At Home in the World: Canada's Global Vision for the 21st Century* (Toronto: HarperCollins, 2004); Clarkson; and Drache.

[7] In economics, the "impossible trinity" represents the inevitable trade-off between the three monetary policy goals of exchange rate stability, national monetary policy autonomy, and capital mobility, such that only two of the three goals can be realized at the same time.

Andrew Cohen makes perhaps the most explicit call for a greater financial investment in Canada's military and security establishment, foreign aid, and international diplomatic presence. It is not clear whether he would sacrifice balanced budgets in order to obtain his other two recommended goals, namely, carrying our proper share of the burden of North American security and of undertaking an expansive "new Canadian internationalism."[8] However, it is obvious that considerably more expenditures across a broad front would be required for Canada to experience again anything like what he terms "the Golden Age" of Canadian diplomacy during the Cold War. It is worth noting, in this connection, that Cohen's diagnosis of the reasons for Canada's loss of place in the world is primarily domestic: a dissipation of political will and a misallocation of resources by successive Canadian governments.

Stephen Clarkson also attributes much of the Canadian dilemma to domestic sources, in particular what he sees as the triumph of American-style neoconservatism in Canada in the free trade era. However, he is also mindful of the structural power of the US, which seems to make the political climate within that country a durable and powerful determinant of Canada's range of foreign and domestic policy options in the aftermath of 9/11. Speaking of the threats to an independent Canadian foreign policy represented by Canada's unavoidable engagement with the US's homeland security agenda, which he describes as a "lurch from Lloyd Axworthy's human security agenda toward a globally networked, continentally implemented anti-terrorist state," Clarkson sees little scope for independent Canadian action unless "reason forced Americans to accept less than 100 per cent security."[9]

Lloyd Axworthy, though, feels that, even in the face of a US preoccupied with continental security, there remains room for an independent Canadian foreign policy focused on providing leadership to the rest of the world in the service of a broad human security agenda.

---

[8]   Cohen 200-03.
[9]   Clarkson 405.

Here, the key components lean less toward financial resources, as Cohen would have it, and more toward a clarity of purpose requiring full public debate of options and priorities among Canadians and a recognition that many other countries find themselves in more or less the same position of feeling pressures on their independence either from the US itself or from their own larger and sometimes domineering neighbour.[10] However, in making this case, Axworthy comes close to invoking his own version of Cohen's Golden Age of Canadian diplomacy by proposing a re-energized multilateralism for Canada based on the philosophy, essentially, that when Canada gives initiative to the world, it usually gets a counterweight to American dominance.

Again, it is difficult to say how the Axworthy agenda would "cost out" as a matter of national finances, but as Jennifer Welsh points out, when he advanced similar ideas as Minister of Foreign Affairs he was often criticized "by some for resorting to self-righteous moralism and by others for trying to wage foreign policy on the cheap."[11] Certainly Axworthy's "human security" and "soft-power" approaches to international diplomacy do not entail the tangible increases in defence spending that we saw Granatstein call for in the Introduction,[12] or even the firm priorities placed on that and additional forms of spending outlined by Andrew Cohen. There is, instead, much talk of shared principles, international networking, and leading by example.[13] However, as Welsh recognizes, "the areas amenable to innovative diplomacy have probably narrowed" and Canada's role as a "serial joiner" of international organizations and campaigns is probably numbered.[14]

Nevertheless, like Axworthy, Welsh sees power in the "demonstration effect" on other, like nations of getting a clear fix on a set of precisely framed priorities and acting on them. However, the fiscal imbalance side of the impossible trinity may be peeking through her

---

[10] Axworthy 91-92.
[11] Welsh 182.
[12] Granatstein, "A Friendly Agreement in Advance."
[13] See Welsh, Ch. 6 and *passim*.
[14] Welsh 157 and 159.

notion that some of the goals she recommends might be better advanced not just by "Canada with a capital C," but also by individual Canadians. She expressly rejects the idea that this lets the government off the hook for devoting tangible resources to a new direction in foreign policy, but she comes close to sharing Axworthy's emphasis on networking and the potential role of AIT in new forms of international citizenship. One has to wonder if this kind of recommended shift in priorities is not at least an implicit recognition that the more concrete, tangibly supported strategies recommended by Cohen will not survive competition in Ottawa over fiscal priorities.[15]

Daniel Drache, meanwhile, may have originated a way of escaping, or at least softening, the sharpness of some of the hard choices implicit in the foregoing discussion. Of all these authors, his analysis comes closest to replacing the fiscal deficit with the democratic deficit as the third side of the impossible trinity. That is, he believes strongly that the key Canadian issues driven by the new American security agenda are much more substantially political than economic ones and that to date the Canadian government has failed to place the full implications of the new security version of the Canada-US border clearly before the public as political choices. Instead, spooked by dire warnings from the country's business elite about the economic costs of a failure to adopt the new American security agenda, the Canadian government has failed to articulate and defend Canada's own national interests bearing on the border: "Canada's political class would prefer to operate by stealth and make agreements for the new economic and security agenda with US officials outside the glare of public scrutiny."[16]

Moreover, according to Drache, this political accommodation at the top is belied by a grassroots affirmation of Canadian differences: "There is a constituency outside of the business community that is

---

[15] Denis Stairs once encapsulated Canada's distinguishing characteristics as "Medicare at home and peacekeeping abroad." See *isuma: Canadian Journal of Policy Research* 1, 1 (Spring, 2000): 14. Following Andrew Cohen, Canadians may now have to contemplate changing that formulation to "Medicare at home; peacekeeping abroad—pick one."

[16] Drache 115.

comfortable with being offside. Canadians are not ready to accept a role as deputy sheriff in the coalition of the obedient."[17] The issue then becomes which stance toward the US—integration by stealth or conspicuous displays of distance—has the greater support in the Canadian national political system, which in turn seems to depend on the extent to which economic elites continue to more or less control the Liberal and Conservative parties (which they may find harder to do with new restrictions on corporate financing of political parties). As Axworthy points out, however:

> attacks on the legitimacy of the Canadian nationalist stance involve powerful forces not only in business but in the media and academic world. Too many of our elite structures define the Canadian interest primarily as following the American lead without question. The stronger the pull toward American integration, the more insistent they are that we simply bow to the inevitable, ignoring the oft-stated preference by most Canadians for keeping our own identity.[18]

It is true that two major Canadian decisions since 9/11—Prime Minister Chrétien's refusal to join the "coalition of the willing" in invading Iraq and Prime Minister Martin's refusal to endorse and take part in a joint system of missile defence—seem to belie the power of Canadian business to drive the Canadian political system in the direction of their favoured outcomes. However, each of these decisions was taken under conditions of extraordinary political accountability for both leaders. Chrétien made his decision during a provincial election in Quebec and had grounds to fear that joining the US in an attack on Iraq could turn the tide in that election toward the Parti Québécois, thus giving a boost to the nationalist forces in that

---

[17] Drache 113.
[18] Axworthy 88. Earlier in his book (85), Axworthy describes how shaken John Turner was upon meeting several of his old Bay Street acquaintances at an Ontario ski resort shortly after his 1988 fight against the FTA as leader of the Liberal party. He told Axworthy, "These guys don't believe in Canada any more."

province he had been fighting against during his entire political career. Martin made his decision as leader of a precarious minority government, well aware of both a loss of support to the Bloc Québécois in Quebec over the sponsorship scandal and of strong Canadian nationalist sentiments in his caucus, particularly in Ontario where the Official Opposition seemed poised to gain seats. It is consistent with the overall argument presented in this book to observe that what matters most to the future of the Canada-US relationship is not what happens under exceptional political conditions in national politics, but rather what happens routinely.

There has been much to observe about what, under more normal political conditions of Liberal majority government, can transpire between Canada and the US in the post-9/11 environment. In fact, it is becoming difficult to keep track of all the Canadian changes in policy and practice that have taken place over the past four years in order to accommodate American security priorities. As Lloyd Axworthy points out:

> The Canadian government has already signed a comprehensive border agreement that incorporates a thirty-point action plan covering everything from immigration to infrastructure, customs control and schemes for detecting suspicious persons seeking refugee asylum. There is no doubt that some of these measures are necessary. They lead inexorably, however, to a greater harmonization of key policies.[19]

As if taking a cue from Axworthy's projection of further policy harmonization to come, the Canadian Council of Chief Executives, in April 2004, issued a discussion paper outlining the Canadian policies they would like to see in the service of a closer Canada-US partnership, including (among others) harmonized tariff-rates; joint review of regulatory differences; a combined energy strategy and resource

---

[19] Axworthy 103-04. Axworthy goes on to add at the beginning of his next paragraph, "The opaque nature of the cooperation is also a worry." Cf. Clarkson's overview of Canadian policy changes during the first year of so after 9/11 in Clarkson 401-05.

security pact; a reform of trade remedies, including "joint institutional arrangements, competition policy, regulatory convergence and multilateral institutions"; fully interoperable armed forces and North American defence institutions; and "a private sector advisory group to support its new Cabinet Committee on Canada-United States Relations."[20]

As important as such detailed changes may be (especially in the aggregate), it is crucial to place all such specifics in the context of the broader Canada-US relationship and of its place in the even broader context of American relations with the rest of the world. In sharing a continent with the US, Canada now shares much of the new American security agenda, a fact that tends to "keep us closer to home" in international affairs. Moreover, Canada is not a major player in world politics, and its diplomacy cannot truly make much impact on American actions and policies one way or another. If Canada's position is substantially different from that of the US, the latter can pretty much ignore it without sacrificing its own effectiveness. On the other hand, if Canada is in agreement with the goals and means of American policy, Canadian support adds little of consequence. One of the few levers Canada can manipulate in its relations with the US in this area is the US's own commitment to multilateralism (assuming it ever returns to pre-9/11 levels). Canada can take advantage of the desire of the American government to maintain a consensus and to build a coalition of states around some of its major initiatives in world affairs, such as the campaign against Serbia and a possible appeal to the UN for help in stabilizing postwar Iraq. However, an American desire for multilateral endorsement cannot be taken for granted, especially on matters of high politics, as their pursuit of National Missile Defence and defiance of most of their allies over the war against Iraq clearly illustrate. In any case, as both the 1991 Gulf War and the bombing of Serbia also indicate, when the US has sought

---

[20] Canadian Council of Chief Executives, *New Frontiers: Building a 21st Century Canada-United States Partnership in North America* (April 2004): 28-29; available at <http://frwebgate2.access.gpo.gov/cgi-bin/waisgate.cgi?WAISdocID=84732836637 4+0+0+0&WAISaction=retrieve>.

a multinational coalition to join its initiatives, Canada is one of its most loyal and uncritical followers.

The whole question of how the Canada-US relationship affects and is affected by the policies of both countries toward the rest of the world is, in 2005, very much in flux, and it remains to be seen what balance will be struck in a post-Iraq global environment between established traditions and new directions in this increasingly difficult aspect of it.

CONCLUSION

We saw at the beginning of this chapter that TNR represents in part a fusion of domestic and international politics, of internal and external relations. In a similar manner, a form of North American politics is developing out of the fusion of Canada-US relations with the national and international politics of both countries. The wider context for this development is fusion on an even grander scale of the American and the world economies (which is one way of viewing globalization). Of course, this also implies a merger of the American and Canadian economies. From a Canadian national perspective, the melding of the country's economy with that of the US is producing new combinations in the content and conduct of Canadian foreign policy. One aspect of this is tighter coordination of the Canada-US relationship with Canada's overall foreign policy. In many respects, Canadian foreign policy is "coming home" to North America and the western hemisphere. This development parallels the extent to which Canadian foreign policy overall is becoming derivative of, rather than a counterweight against, its primary relationship with the US.

The trend toward keeping Canadian foreign policy closer to home can be summed up as a shift in the country's status from "valued critic" to "junior partner." This shift has been accompanied by yet further fusions of Canada's foreign economic with its diplomatic interests, of its international with its domestic interests, and even of its foreign and domestic policy decision-making. To the extent that the world becomes a single market, and as economic interests become the country's highest priority, there is a blurring of the line between domestic and foreign interests and therefore between foreign and domestic policies.

What all this merging adds up to is a decline in the importance of foreign policy to Canadian independence of the US. Former Prime Minister Pierre Trudeau once famously compared Canada's position in North America to that of a mouse in bed with an elephant: the mouse did not necessarily get squashed, but it had to be constantly wary of every twitch and grunt of the huge beast beside it.[21] By this analogy, Canada's Cold War foreign policy as described in this chapter might see the mouse as averting injury by slipping out of bed and doing a little community service. The role of "fixer" in the international community had the virtue of placing some distance between Canada and the US through teaming up with others and being of use to others.

The current trend in the deployment of Canada's armed forces both symbolizes and adds substance to these more general developments. During the Cold War, Canada's commitments to multilateral defence through NATO and to universal peace and security through the UN had both served as a counterweight to its commitment to continental defence through its membership in NORAD and numerous other continental defence arrangements. Each of these institutional venues marked a different degree of Canadian autonomy from (or, conversely, dependence upon) the US. In NORAD, Canadian autonomy was lowest and its dependence highest. Within NATO, autonomy was higher and dependence lower because, while still relatively small in membership and dominated by the US, that organization was at least multilateral. Within UN peacekeeping operations, undertaken in cooperation with countries from all over the world and often on terms specifically excluding the US, autonomy was highest and dependence lowest. Recently, however, in the face of what Dymond and Hart have labeled "the fading salience of club memberships as foreign policy attributes and assets,"[22] Canada has moved away from participation in

---

[21] Speech before the National Press Club, Washington, DC, 25 March 1969. See John Robert Colombo, *Famous Lasting Words: Great Canadian Quotations* (Toronto: Douglas and McIntyre, 2000) 81.

[22] Bill Dymond and Michael Hart, "Canada and the Global Challenge: Finding a Place to Stand" (Toronto: C.D. Howe Institute Commentary No. 180: March 2003) 14.

NATO- and UN-sanctioned deployments and toward more substantial involvement in American-led peacemaking initiatives overseas, cooperation with its Homeland Defence initiatives, and extending NORAD-style collaboration to it naval and ground forces.

Moreover, during the Cold War, the services that Canada performed on behalf of the world community were complemented by two of the key elements in Canada's bilateral relationship with the US itself. Here, Canada had the primary objective of maintaining its independence despite the closeness of the economic, social, and cultural dimensions of the relationship. A vital component of this overall strategy was to persuade the Americans that they had a stake in Canada's independence. As mentioned earlier, this was done during the Cold War in two different but mutually reinforcing ways. First, Canada was able to perform some tasks in international affairs that were helpful (or at least not damaging) to Americans' foreign interests, but which they could not do as effectively on their own, such as cooperating with non-aligned countries on development and stability issues. Second, Canada could perform the delicate task of acting as a trusted and friendly critic of American foreign policy. Again, Canada never attacked the fundamental objectives of American policies and rarely condemned the means chosen to achieve those objectives. However, it did occasionally point out that some American actions were contrary to its own interests in the longer term.

In short, Canadian dissent from American foreign policy was generally constructive and valued by most administrations in the US. Moreover, American critics of American foreign policy were often pleased to see one of its allies taking the administration to task on grounds similar to their own. This pattern was repeated in the American political debate over the possibility of invading Iraq. As we saw earlier in this chapter, the end of the Cold War had already begun to diminish the scope for the performance of this role, and the intensification of the threat of terrorism is (so far) reducing it even more. Globalization has promoted an identity of international interests between the two countries even further.

At the same time, to the extent that economic interests have come to dominate both the American and Canadian definition of their national interests, there is less basis than there once was for a distinct foreign policy for Canada. In the common promotion of peace and prosperity through the institutions of global governance, the country has shifted in status from a valued critic and independently helpful actor to a junior partner. Canada, too, acts as though the expansion of the world's community of market democracies is practically the only game to be played in the greater world, and in any case our continental economic interests are vastly more important to the country than any of its overseas economic interests. As a consequence, Canada has come home.

CONCLUSION:
DOES CANADA STILL MAKE SENSE?

Canada's origins as a nation-state lie in the superimposition of British institutions on the French fur trade in North America. The generation that brought British institutions, customs, and values to the northern half of the North American continent were, essentially, British Americans who refused to sever their ties with the Crown at the time their fellow colonialists revolted. After 1867, continuing ties to Britain, plus the forging of a national economy by means of Prime Minister John A. Macdonald's National Policy, enabled the federation of the British North American colonies to remain an independent political community despite increasingly close economic relations with the US throughout the twentieth century. In the late 1980s, the national policy model, which had been looking rather threadbare for several decades, was formally abandoned through a free trade agreement with the Americans, and Canada-US economic interdependence became even more pronounced. In the meantime, global economic interdependence was also on the rise, leading numerous analysts to predict the end, or at least a major transformation, of the nation-state. If in fact the threat of obsolescence hangs over the nation-state, it is hard to imagine any country more exposed to this threat than Canada. Indeed, we may already be, in Sylvia Ostry's phrase, a "virtual nation." All this confronts Canadians—perhaps especially younger Canadians—with a serious political issue: is the survival of Canada as a distinct and autonomous political community still possible, and what should be done to ensure it?

William Watson has brought an interesting analytical perspective to this question. In concluding his study of the impact of globalization on Canada, he posed the question, "Do countries still make sense?"[1] More specifically, economist that he is, he devoted a section of his conclusion to the question, "Are countries cost-effective?" and applied the tools of public choice to finding an answer. Watson begins by pointing out that all political communities confront four different kinds of "costs of governance": signalling, mobility, coordination, and administration.[2] The point of his approach is to determine whether the cost of government rises or falls at different levels (and sizes) of jurisdiction: city-state, nation-state, or world government. (A comparable mode of analysis is undertaken by macro-economists who attempt to determine the "optimal currency area," that is, the level—and hence size—of jurisdiction that can best issue money and regulate the cost of borrowing through a central bank.)

In broadly comparing the costs of "micro-states" *versus* "macro-states," the first issue Watson raises is whether or not there are economies of scale in government. If there are, then "bigger is probably better, at least as far as administrative costs are concerned."[3] Like business overhead costs, many of the costs of government—such as, for example, designing a taxation system and the forms that go with it—are fixed, and so the per unit cost of the "production" of government goes down as the number of citizens served goes up. Therefore, the administration of most government programs is more efficient with 100 million citizens than with 1 million. Signalling, however, works better the smaller (or lower) the jurisdiction. For most Canadians, it is easier to get to City Hall than to Parliament, and even for most Ontarians, Queen's Park is probably more accessible than Parliament in Ottawa. In the more likely case of phone calls and e-mail

---

[1] Watson, *Globalization* Ch. 20.

[2] Watson, *Globalization* 247-48. The meaning and importance of these concepts should become clear in the ensuing analysis. However, brief definitions are as follows: signalling is a cost borne by citizens in trying to get their viewpoint and/or grievances heard by those in authority; mobility is the opportunity for citizens to move from one jurisdiction to another when they become dissatisfied with their current one; coordination is a cost borne by governments out of the need to dovetail the activities of different jurisdictions; and administration is a cost borne by governments in conducting their own policies.

[3] Watson, *Globalization* 248.

messages, both are likely to get through more easily to a city council-lor than to a cabinet minister. On the other hand, as an illustration of the point just made about economies of scale, national politicians and governments are in a better position to conduct opinion polls of their national constituency than a small municipal government might be of its local one.

Mobility definitely improves with the number of jurisdictions in that it increases variability in the way governments get things done. In the limiting case, if there were a world government, there would be no way to leave its jurisdiction. By contrast, the 50 American states offer a very wide range of state laws affecting the way of life of their citizens. Existing nation-states, too, can be thought of as competing for citizens, or at least for some categories of workers, and refugees can be described as "voting with their feet" as they escape oppres-sion or poverty by moving to countries that promise greater freedom and/or a higher standard of living. Closer to home, the multiplicity of provincial and territorial jurisdictions allows Canadians to move to places where the cost-benefit ratio represented by different mixes of tax levels, government services, and employment prospects is most favourable.

Finally, off-setting the benefits of mobility, the cost of coordinating the actions of different governments definitely goes up as the num-ber of jurisdictions increases. As Watson notes, solutions to environ-mental problems would probably be more effective and less costly to reach through a world authority than through years of negotiations among more than 190 sovereign nations, as the struggle to achieve and implement the Kyoto Protocol attests. More generally, Watson invites us to imagine how complicated the business of international governmental organizations would become if it had to be conducted among 2,000 members rather than 200.[4] Negotiating agreements among a multiplicity of nations takes time and resources, and the monitoring and enforcement of agreements goes up with the number of nations covered by them.

---

[4] Watson, *Globalization* 249.

After weighing all these factors, Watson asserts that the nation-state level of government is optimal for most purposes and is likely to remain so despite a number of technological changes that could affect its relative efficiency in different ways, such as reducing signalling costs and increasing economies of scale. He also suggests that nation-states such as Canada, by spreading risk across regions with different but complementary economic profiles, provide a form of economic insurance that smaller units cannot. However, the finer details of his argument are not directly relevant to this discussion. The mere fact that Watson can demonstrate that individual countries *generally* still make sense does not firmly establish the particular case that *Canada* still makes sense. Most of his arguments support the conclusion that *some* level of government between the city-region and the world-state is rational on a cost-effective basis. However, the creation of a "United States of North America" is as strongly justified on the basis of his arguments as the continuation of Canada as such, because it too would stand in an intermediate position between the local and the global. As interesting (and as important) as it is, Watson's analysis does not justify conclusively that Canadians should rationally seek to remain citizens of the Canadian nation-state they now have, rather than seek to join with the Americans (and possibly Mexicans) in creating a continental nation-state.

Of course, any question of Canada disappearing is beside the point if either of two conditions continues to hold: first, if enough Canadians continue to insist on maintaining their sovereign status, and, second, if the Americans were to refuse to have us. To begin with the second of these conditions, Canadians should not assume that a majority of Americans would support the absorption of Canada into the US or the construction of some continental superstate on the foundation of NAFTA. Most Americans are significantly to the right of most Canadians on a number of key political issues, such as health and social policies, drug control, gun control, and foreign policy. Those Americans who know anything about Canada at all are aware of these differences and would not be keen to see close to 30 million "liberals" added to the election rolls in the US or to see each of the ten provinces (let alone the three territories) allocated their share of senators and representatives in Congress. At the same time, there is unlikely to be much American support for ceding their country's sovereignty to an EU-style supranational government for North America, although some "policy wonks" in Washington are beginning to float the idea of a more highly institutionalized NAFTA.

As for the first condition—Canadians' continued determination to remain separate and sovereign—there seems no clear evidence that Canadians are ready to give up on their country any time soon. However, the fact that Canadians are unlikely to sacrifice their sovereignty is no guarantee that they will continue to insist on genuine independence. In fact, the clearest political challenge to Canada is not that it might lose its status as a nation-state, but rather that its possession of that status will become increasingly hollow with respect to the substance of government policies. Canadians, in other words, are at lesser risk of losing their country than of losing their political autonomy. Their insistence on being separate—of remaining "disjoined" from the US—may turn out to be stronger than their determination to remain qualitatively different from the US. They may never support "doing away with the border" in large numbers, but a majority may cease to care whether or not two genuinely different societies exist on either side of it. For example, there was general public support for the policy changes Canada was required to adopt to ensure a freer border in the aftermath of 9/11.

INTEGRATION BY STEALTH:
CONTINENTAL FREE TRADE AND CANADIAN DEMOCRACY

As this book has argued, when Canada signed the FTA and later NAFTA, it was essentially undertaking a long-term commitment toward various forms of policy harmonization with the US. In this respect, the Canadian government has not been very forthcoming with its public when it comes to the politics of trade liberalization (in itself a serious lapse in democratic accountability). The official line on trade agreements tends to reject or simply ignore two of their critics' most persistent and forceful complaints: first, that they are more about investment and the rights of corporations than they are about trade, and, second, that, as such, they have the potential to bring about significant changes in national politics and government policies.

From the beginning, during the debates in Canada surrounding the FTA, including the 1988 "free trade election," the Progressive Conservatives and their allies in the Canadian business community and economics profession insisted time and again that a free trade agreement with the US would have no significant political consequences and that economic integration could not possibly lead to political integration. Now the Liberals, along with the *same* allies in the Canadian business community and economics profession, are insisting that free trade has not done so nor is in the process of doing so. The problem with these arguments is that the past dozen years have produced considerable evidence to the contrary. International "trade" agreements inescapably and undeniably entail changes in national policies; that, especially in their investment related provisions, is precisely what they are designed to do.

Canada's political, economic, and academic elites are thus at a fateful fork in the road of deeper economic integration and must choose one of two political directions. They can acknowledge—finally—that the benefits of trade liberalization are only obtainable at the price of autonomy in significant domains of domestic social, economic, cultural, and possibly even foreign policy. Alternatively, they can continue to insist that trade agreements are about nothing beyond the exchange of goods and the allocation of resources and cannot cause any government in Canada to do anything it would not otherwise prefer to do. To take the former course is to embrace democracy by acknowledging frankly and openly that economic integration entails major political adjustments and by engaging in an open and accurately informed debate with the Canadian public on the merits of the unavoidable trade-offs between economic benefits and political autonomy. To take the latter course is to pervert democracy by understating, if not falsifying, the true political implications of the terms and conditions of trade agreements and to risk the spread of a sense of frustration, alienation, and betrayal among large numbers of Canadians.

Despite the drama created by media coverage of occasional demonstrations against the spread of market liberalization (such as the
protests against the Free Trade Area of the Americas agreement in
Quebec City), only a minuscule percentage of Canadians have ever
taken political action against free trade. To the contrary, opinion
polls tell us that a significant majority of Canadians have come to
support being part of NAFTA in principle, and a plurality of them
believe that the overall effects of NAFTA have been favourable.[5] However, similar polls suggest strongly that a majority of Canadians (to
date) have done exactly what their elites, as argued above, have consistently wanted them to do, namely, to associate free trade agreements simply and exclusively with the reduction of trade barriers.
When large numbers of Canadians associate free trade agreements
closely with things they do not regard positively, such as the possible
erosion of Canadian social policies or increased foreign ownership of
Canadian business, the proportion of them who endorse such agreements is noticeably weaker or at least more qualified.[6]

In fact, it appears that the global trade liberalization agenda en-
counters greater and greater scepticism, if not outright opposition,
the more that international trade agreements and associations are

---

[5] See Media Release Center, "Support for North American Free Trade Agreement
(NAFTA) Still Strong With 64% Support," Public Release, Ipsos-Reid, 4 February
2001. The release points out that "this is down from its highest level of support
(70%) in October 1999 but well ahead of an Ipsos-Reid poll of February 1999 that
showed only 46 percent in favour of the initiative." The release also reports that 40
per cent of Canadians believe that the country has benefited since being part of the
agreement, as opposed to 32 per cent who believe it has been hurt and 23 per cent
who believe it has had no impact.

[6] Despite overall support for NAFTA, 84 per cent of Canadians surveyed by the
Canadian Centre for Research and Information on Canada (CRIC) said that they
would place restrictions on American investment in Canada to prevent investors
from taking control of Canadian companies. (This was up ten percentage points
from 1964, when the same question was put.) As CRIC points out, these respondents
seem to be ignorant of the fact that any such (new) restrictions would contravene
the FTA and NAFTA, a fact which tends to confirm the point made here that most
Canadians who support so-called free trade agreements are generally not aware
that they are about much more than simply trade relations. See Canadian Centre
for Research and Information, "Trade, Globalization and Canadian Values" CRIC
Papers, Montreal (April 2001): 15.

perceived to impinge on domestic social, labour, and environmental policies, and the more that intergovernmental decisions in these fields are perceived to favour the interests of corporations at the expense of populations at home or abroad, especially in the Third World. Matthew Mendelsohn and Robert Wolfe make essentially this point in a carefully researched and argued survey of Canadian attitudes toward free trade over time. They observe that "[d]omestic framework policies are now at the heart of the trade agenda" and note, further, that recent opposition to the WTO and the ongoing free trade agenda is largely focused on the domestic impact of market liberalization:

> [t]he WTO has come to be seen by some activists as globalization incarnate because trade is the vector that brings policies in different countries into conflict, and when the WTO mediates such conflict, it can be portrayed as favouring multinational enterprises. The WTO may become even more of a lightning rod for concerns about globalization because it seems to displace parliament from its role with regard to formerly domestic decisions about the environment, human rights and many other policy domains—telecoms, competition, health, education, magazines, asbestos, beef hormones, and others.[7]

It seems highly probable that, as NAFTA's working groups and other institutions begin to affect national policies in many of these same fields and in similar ways, a growing number of Canadians will begin to associate free trade with two things they may very well not like: first, their own disenfranchisement, and, second, a decline in the capacity of their governments to help Canadians help one another, as Mendelsohn and Wolfe put it.[8]

Canadians are not the only ones to face the corrosive effects of economic integration on the democratic accountability of their

---

[7] Matthew Mendelsohn and Robert Wolfe, "Probing the Aftermyth of Seattle: Canadian Public Opinion on International Trade, 1980-2000," School of Policy Studies Working Paper 12 (Kingston, ON: Queen's University, December 2000) 14.

[8] Mendelsohn and Wolfe 15.

governments. As Ian Clark has argued persuasively, globalization is not *promoting* state transformation, it *is* state transformation. Jennifer Welsh apparently agrees:

> Globalization isn't something that happens to us as a result of changes in the world. Rather, as Deputy Minister of Foreign Affairs Peter Harder explains, it is "something we do to ourselves, as a matter of explicit national policy."[9]

Moreover, as one aspect of this transformation process, states are becoming less democratic and accountable to voting majorities and the demands of domestic groups. In Clark's view, the persistence of what he calls "the Great Divide"—essentially the clear-cut distinction between the "internal" domain of national politics and the "external" domain of international politics that anchors the international relations paradigm—continues to obscure the impact of globalization on democratic nationhood. Analysis conducted in the framework of the Great Divide, he writes,

> ... maintains that the democratic shortcomings of the contemporary state have arisen because of the growth of globalized forces that disempower it from outside. As a result, its democratic procedures barely conceal the nakedness within. If the situation is to be retrieved, the scope of democratic accountability must be extended beyond the state so that it matches the global reach of the influences that wash up on its shores. Such an analysis fails to take due account of the reciprocal manner in which democratic deficits on the inside have been the necessary accomplices of globalization.[10]

It remains to be seen how much "internal state transformation" Canadians will prove willing to embrace as the political pressures for

---

[9] Welsh 238.
[10] Ian Clark, *Globalization and International Relations Theory* (Oxford: Oxford University Press, 1999) 165-66.

continental market liberalization grow in scope and intensity. With the anomalous exceptions of the Iraq War and missile defence, Liberal governments since 1993 have seemed readily prepared to accommodate most American demands for policy harmonization, whether expressly in relation to increased North American security or more subtly and less conspicuously through the efforts of NAFTA's committees and working groups. The Conference Board of Canada has expressed doubts about the track record of such institutions in promoting the harmonization of regulations and standards, but it also recommends that their role be expanded and efficiency be enhanced to do just that.[11] It also observed that the effectiveness of such committees and working groups was contingent upon greater input from industry, a sentiment that parallels a recent recommendation from the Canadian Council of Chief Executives that the federal government establish "a private sector advisory group to support its new Cabinet Committee on Canada-United States relations."[12]

In all of this, Canada continues to undergo both an internal shift in the balance between Katzenstein's "co-pressures" and "counter pressures" bearing on political integration with the US and does so in the midst of an external shift in the structure of the international political system from bipolarity to unipolarity and the assertion of America's hyperpower status. His model thus predicts higher levels of what was described in Chapter 1 as "purposeful coordination of political behaviour in the achievement of common tasks," particularly if Canada's economic and political elites continue to press for change in that direction and if the Canadian party and electoral systems continue to produce governments with larger parliamentary presence than their share of electoral support warrants.

---

[11] See Conference Board of Canada, *In Search of a New Equilibrium in the Canada-U.S. Relationship*, Report (February 2005) 36. It is worth noting in this context that Miles Kahler, in his *International Institutions and the Political Economy of Integration* (Washington, DC: The Brookings Institution, 1995) anticipates that, in the absence of more highly articulated international institutions along the lines of the EU, "substantial asymmetries in bargaining power could be predicted to result in harmonization to the more powerful partner's standards" (15).

[12] Canadian Council of Chief Executives 29.

Current signs are that the minority Liberal government of Paul Martin is not fully disposed to endorse the pro-integration agenda of Canadian business, although that could change rapidly if the Liberals return to majority status. At the same time, the Official Opposition appears to stand for closer relations with the US. On balance, therefore, it would be rash to predict that Canada's young adults will live to see their country disappear, but—as this book has tried to demonstrate—they may well witness the end of democratic accountability of their governments and, with that, the gradual disappearance of the differences between themselves and their cousins to the south. Through a process of political drift, they may become, despite their preferences to the contrary, northern Americans.

BIBLIOGRAPHY

Abbott, Frederick M. *Law and Policy of Regional Integration: the NAFTA and Western Hemispheric Integration in the World Trade Organization System.* Dordrecht, NL: Martinus Nijhoff Publishers, 1995.

Adler, Emanuel, and Michael Barnett, eds., *Security Communities.* Cambridge: University of Cambridge Press, 1998.

Adams, Michael. *Fire and Ice: The United States, Canada and the Myth of Converging Values.* Toronto: Penguin Canada, 2003.

Aitken, H.G.J. "Defensive Expansionism: The State and Economic Growth in Canada." In W.T. Easterbrook and M.H. Watkins, eds., *Approaches to Canadian Economic History.* Toronto: McClelland and Stewart, 1967.

——."The Midwestern Case: Canadian Gas and the Federal Power Commission." *Canadian Journal of Economics and Political Science* 25, 2 (May 1959).

Anonymous. "A History of the Mails." *Records of the Post Office* Vol. 3296. Ottawa, ON: National Archives of Canada, n.d. [probably 1861].

Appendini, Kirston, and Sven Bislev, eds., *Economic Integration in NAFTA and the EU: Deficient Institutionality.* New York: St. Martin's Press, 1999.

Artibise, Alan F.J. "Achieving Sustainability in Canada: An Emerging Model of Growth." In P. Kresl and G. Gapper, eds., *North American Cities and the Global Economy.* Thousand Oaks, CA: Sage, 1995.

Axworthy, Lloyd. *Navigating a New World: Canada's Global Future.* Toronto: Alfred A. Knopf Canada, 2003.

Banting, Keith. "Social Policy in a North American Free Trade Area." In Charles Doran and A.P. Drischler, eds., *The New North America: Co-operation and Enhanced Interdependence.* Westport, CT: Praeger, 1996.

Barnes, William R., and Larry C. Ledebur. *The New Regional Economics: The U.S. Common Market and the Global Economy.* Thousand Oaks, CA: Sage, 1998.

Barry, Donald. "The Road to NAFTA." In D. Barry, ed., *Toward a North American Community?* Boulder, CO: Westview Press, 1995.

——. ed. *Toward a North American Community?* Boulder, CO: Westview Press, 1995.

Barry, Norman. "Dutch Join French in Rejecting EU Constitution." Foundation for Economic Education (2 June 2005). Accessed at <http://www.fee.org/vnews.php?nid=6944>.

Bashevkin, Sylvia B. *True Patriot Love: The Politics of Canadian Nationalism.* Toronto: Oxford University Press, 1991.

Bensel, Richard Franklin. *Yankee Leviathan: The Origins of Central State Authority in America, 1859-1877.* New York: Cambridge University Press, 1990.

Blank, Stephen. *The Emerging Architecture of North America.* Coral Gables, FL: North-South Center, University of Miami, 1993.

Blank, Stephen, and Jerry Haar. *Making NAFTA Work: U.S. Firms and the New North American Business Environment.* Coral Gables, FL: North-South Center Press, 1999.

Brunet-Jailly, Emmanuel. "Comparing Local Cross-Border Relations Under the EU and NAFTA." *Canadian-American Public Policy* 58 (September 2004).

Cameron, David R. "Post-Modern Ontario and the Laurentian Thesis." In Douglas M. Brown and Janet Hiebert, eds., *Canada: the State of the Federation 1994.* Kingston, ON: Institute of Intergovernmental Relations, 1994.

Canada. *Summary of Canadian International Trade.* Ottawa, ON: Statistics Canada, December 1988.

Canadian Centre for Research and Information. "Trade, Globalization and Canadian Values." *CRIC Papers.* Montreal, April 2001.

Canadian Council of Chief Executives. *New Frontiers: Building a 21st Century Canada-United States Partnership in North America* (April 2004). Accessed at <http://frwebgate2.access.gpo.gov/cgi-bin/waisgate.cgi?WAISdocID=847328366374+0+0+0&WAISaction=retrieve>.

Carroll, William K. *Corporate Power in a Globalizing World: A Study in Elite Social Organization*. Don Mills, ON: Oxford University Press, 2004.

Castro-Rae, Julian. "Toward Single North American Polity? The Effects of NAFTA on Mexican and Canadian Domestic Policies." In C.C. Paraskovopoulos, R. Greenspun, and G.E. Eaton, eds., *Economic Integration in the Americas*. Cheltenham: Edward Elgar, 1996.

Cerny, Philip. "Globalization, Governance and Complexity." In J. Nederveen Pierterse and B. Parekh, eds., *Decolonization of Imagination, Culture, Knowledge and Power*. London: Zed Books, 1995.

Clark, Ian. *Globalization and International Relations Theory*. Oxford: Oxford University Press, 1999.

Clarke, Susan E. "Regional and Transnational Regimes: Multi-Level Governance Processes in North America." Paper presented at the American Political Science Association Annual Meeting, Atlanta, September 1999.

Clarkson, Stephen. *Uncle Sam and Us: Globalization, Neoconservatism and the Canadian State*. Toronto: University of Toronto Press, 2002.

Clement, Norris C., et al. *North American Economic Integration: Theory and Practice*. Northampton, MA: Edward Elgar, 1999.

Clinton, Bill. "Confronting the Challenge of a Broader World." UN General Assembly, New York, 27 September 1993. Accessed at <http://frwebgate2.access.gpo.gov/cgi-bin/waisgate.cgi?WAISdocI D=847328366374+0+0+0&WAISaction=retrieve>.

Cohen, Andrew. *While Canada Slept: How We Lost Our Place in the World*. Toronto: McClelland and Stewart, 2003.

Colombo, John Robert. *Famous Lasting Words: Great Canadian Quotations*. Toronto: Douglas and McIntyre, 2000.

Condon, Bradley J., and Tapen Sinha. *Drawing Lines in Sand and Snow: Border Security and North American Economic Integration*. Armonk, NY: M.E. Sharpe, 2003.

Conference Board of Canada. *In Search of a New Equilibrium in the Canada-U.S. Relationship*, Report (February 2005); available at <http://www.conferenceboard.ca/boardwiseii/temp/BoardWise2F CNIPFGBJHIGHBDNACJALDKI20058311856/709-05%20New%20 Equilibrium%20US%20Canada%20rpt.pdf>.

Cooper, Andrew F. "Canadian Foreign Policy after September 11: A Preliminary Analysis." Paper presented to the Annual Conference of the Canadian Political Science Association, Toronto, 31 May 2002.

Cooper, Richard N. *The Economics of Interdependence: Economic Policy in the Atlantic Community.* New York: McGraw-Hill, 1968.

Courchene, Thomas J., and C.R. Telmer. *From Heartland to North American Region-State: The Social, Fiscal and Federal Evolution of Ontario.* Toronto: University of Toronto Press, 1998.

Creighton, Donald. *Toward the Discovery of Canada.* Toronto: Macmillan of Canada, 1972.

de Grandpré, A. Jean. "Adjusting to Win." Interview. *The Canadian Business Review* 16, 4 (Winter 1989).

Deutsch, Karl W. *The Analysis of International Relations,* 3rd ed. Englewood Cliffs, NJ: Prentice Hall, 1988.

———. *Nationalism and Social Communication: an Inquiry into the Foundations of Nationality.* 2nd ed. Cambridge, MA: The M.I.T. Press, 1966.

DFAIT (Department of Foreign Affairs and International Trade, Canada). *NAFTA @ 10: A Preliminary Report.* Ottawa: Minister of Public Works and Government Services Canada, 2003.

Dobson, Wendy. "Shaping the Future of the North American Economic Space: A Framework for Action." *C.D. Howe Institute Commentary* No. 162, April 2002.

Doern, Bruce, and John Kirton. "Foreign Policy." In G.B. Doern and B. Tomlin, eds., *Border Crossings.* Toronto: Oxford University Press, 1996.

Doern, G. Bruce, and Brian Tomlin. *Faith and Fear: The Free Trade Story.* Don Mills, ON: Stoddart, 1991.

Doran, Charles F. *Forgotten Partnership: U.S.-Canada Relations Today.* Baltimore, MD: Johns Hopkins University Press, 1984.

Drache, Daniel. *Borders Matter: Homeland Security and the Search for North America.* Halifax, NS: Fernwood, 2004.

Dunning, John H. *Alliance Capitalism and Global Business.* London: Routledge, 1997.

Dymond, Bill, and Michael Hart. "Canada and the Global Challenge: Finding a Place to Stand." Toronto: *C.D. Howe Institute Commentary* No. 180, March 2003.

Easterbrook, W.T. *North American Patterns of Growth and Development: The Continental Context*. Toronto: University of Toronto Press, 1990.

Egnal, Marc. *Divergent Paths: How Culture and Institutions Have Shaped North American Growth*. New York: Oxford University Press, 1996.

Flaherty, David H., and Frank E. Manning, eds., *The Beaver Bites Back?: American Popular Culture in Canada*. Montreal and Kingston: McGill-Queen's University Press, 1993.

Fox, Annette Baker, Alfred J. Hero, and Joseph S. Nye, Jr., eds. *Canada and the United States: Transnational and Transgovernmental Relations*. New York: Columbia University Press, 1976.

Fox, William T.R. *A Continent Apart: The United States and Canada in World Politics*. Toronto: University of Toronto Press, 1985.

Galbraith, John Kenneth. *The New Industrial State*. Boston, MA: Houghton Mifflin, 1967.

Ganley, Elaine. "Europeans to Counter Google Print Project." *Associated Press*, 6 May 2005. Accessed on May 8, 2005 <http://www.post-gazette.com/pg/05126/499901.stm>.

Garreau, Joel. *The Nine Nations of North America*. Boston, MA: Houghton-Mifflin, 1981.

George, Peter. *The Emergence of Industrial America: Strategic Factors in American Economic Growth Since 1870*. Albany, NY: State University of New York Press, 1982.

Glazebrook, G.P. de T. *A History of Transportation in Canada*. Foreword, H.A. Innis. Toronto: The Ryerson Press, 1938.

Globerman, Steven, Hudson N. Janisch, and W.T. Stanbury. "Convergence, Competition and Canadian Content." In W.T. Stanbury, ed., *Perspectives on the New Economics of Telecommunication*. Montreal: Institute for Research on Public Policy, 1996.

Goldfarb, Danielle. "The Road to a Canada-U.S. Customs Union: Step-by Step or in a Single Bound?" C.D. Howe Commentary No. 184, June 2003.

Government of Canada. *Foreign Direct Investment in Canada*. Ottawa: Information Canada, 1972.

Grabb, Edward, and James Curtis. *Regions Apart: The Four Societies of Canada and The United States*. Don Mills, ON: Oxford University Press, 2004.

Granatstein, J.L. "A Friendly Agreement in Advance: Canada-US Defense Relations Past, Present and Future." *C.D. Howe Commentary* 166 (June 2002).

——. *Yankee Go Home? Canadians and Anti-Americanism.* Toronto: HarperCollins, 1996.

Graves, Frank L. "Identity, Globalization and North American Integration: Canada at the Crossroads." Speaking notes for an Address to the Canada Club, Ottawa, 16 January 2001.

Gruber, Lloyd. *Ruling the World: Power Politics and the Rise of Supranational Institutions.* Princeton, NJ: Princeton University Press, 2000.

Gunderson, Gil. "Review Essay: Democratic Government in the Age of Globalization?" *Public Organization Review: A Global Journal* 3 (December 2003): 421-29.

Haas, Charles. *Comparative Politics: Domestic Responses to Global Challenges.* 2nd ed. St. Paul, MN: West, 1997.

Haas, Ernst B. *Beyond the Nation-state: Functionalism and International Organization.* Stanford, CA: Stanford University Press, 1964.

——. *The Uniting of Europe: Political, Social, and Economic Forces, 1950-1957.* Stanford, CA: Stanford University Press, 1968.

Hampson, Fen Osler, and Maureen Appel Molot. "Does the 49th Parallel Matter Any More?" In Maureen Appel Molot and Fen Osler Hampson, eds., *Vanishing Borders: Canada Among Nations, 2002.* Don Mills, ON: Oxford University Press, 2000.

Handelman, Stephen. "The Rise of North America Inc.: A Perspective from the United States." *isuma: Canadian Journal of Policy Research* 1,1 (Spring 2000): 19-20.

Harris, Richard G., and David Cox. *Trade, Industrial Policy and Canadian Manufacturing.* Toronto: Ontario Economic Council, 1984.

Held, David, Anthony McGrew, David Goldblatt, and Jonathan Perraton. *Global Transformations: Politics, Economics and Culture.* Stanford, CA: Stanford University Press, 1999.

Helliwell, John F. *Globalization and Well-Being.* Vancouver, BC: University of British Columbia Press, 2002.

Higginbotham, John, and Jeff Heynen. "Managing Through Networks: The State of Canada-US Relations." In David Carment, Fen Osler

Hampson, and Norman Hillmer, eds., *Canada Among Nations 2004: Setting Priorities Straight*. Montreal and Kingston: McGill-Queen's University Press, 2005.

Hoberg, George, Keith G. Banting, and Richard Simeon. "The Scope for Domestic Choice: Policy Autonomy in a Globalizing World." In George Hoberg, ed., *Capacity for Choice: Canada in a New North America*. Toronto: University of Toronto Press, 2002.

Houpt, Simon, and Gayle MacDonald. "'Don't Trust Anybody—Even Me.'" *Globe and Mail*, 19 May 2001: R5.

Hymer, Stephen. *The International Operations of International Firms: A Study of Direct Investment*. Cambridge, MA: MIT Press, 1976.

Inglehart, R.F., N. Nevitte, and M. Basañez. *The North American Trajectory: Cultural, Economic and Political Ties among the United States, Canada and Mexico*. Hawthorne, NY: Aldine de Gruyter, 1996.

Innis, Harold A. *The Fur Trade in Canada: An Introduction to Canadian Economic History*. Rev. ed. Toronto: University of Toronto Press, 1956.

——. "The Importance of Staple Products in Canadian Development." In Daniel Drache, ed., *Staples, Markets and Cultural Change: Selected Essays*. Montreal and Kingston: McGill-Queen's University Press, 1995. Originally appeared as "Conclusion" in Harold A. Innis, *The Fur Trade in Canada*. Rev. ed. Toronto: University of Toronto Press, 1956.

——. "Transportation as a Factor in Canadian Economic History." In Daniel Drache, ed., *Staples, Markets and Cultural Change: Selected Essays*. Montreal and Kingston: McGill-Queen's University Press, 1995.

——. "The Unused Capacity as a Factor in Canadian Economic History." In Daniel Drache, ed., *Staples, Markets and Cultural Change: Selected Essays*. Montreal and Kingston: McGill-Queen's University Press, 1995.

Jacek, Henry J. "Unequal Partners: The Historical, Political, Economic and Cultural Dimensions of The Austrian-FRG/Canadian-U.S. Dyads." In Harold von Riekoff and Hanspeter Neuhold, eds., *Unequal Partners: a Comparative Analysis of Relations Between Austria and the Federal Republic of Germany and Between Canada and the United States*. Boulder, CO: Westview Press, 1993.

Jacobs, Jane. *Cities and the Wealth of Nations*. New York: Random House, 1984.

Jones, Robert A. *The Politics and Economics of the European Union*. Brookfield, VT: Edward Elgar, 1996.

Kahler, Miles. "Preface: Changes in the Government of Nations." *International Institutions and the Political Economy of Integration*. Washington, DC: The Brookings Institution, 1995.

Katzenstein, Peter J. *Disjoined Partners: Austria and Germany since 1815*. Berkeley, CA: University of California Press, 1976.

Kaufman, Jason. "Origins of the Asymmetric Society: Freedom of Incorporation in the Early United States and Canada." Paper presented to a seminar sponsored by the Centre for American Studies, University of Western Ontario, 4 April 2005, mimeo.

Keohane, Robert O., and Stanley Hoffmann. "Conclusions: Community Politics and Institutional Change." In William Wallace, ed., *The Dynamics of European Integration*. London: Pinter Publishers for the Royal Institute of International Affairs, 1990.

Keohane, Robert O., and Joseph S. Nye. *Power and Interdependence: World Politics in Transition*. Toronto: Little, Brown and Co., 1977.

Kirton, John. "Promoting Plurilateral Partnership: Managing United States-Canada Relations in the Post-Cold War Period." *American Review of Canadian Studies* 24, 4 (Winter, 1994).

Konrad, Victor. "Borderlines and Borderlands in the Geography of Canada-United States Relations." In Stephen J. Randall and Herman W. Konrad, eds., *NAFTA in Transition*. Calgary, AB: University of Calgary Press, 1995.

Koring, Paul. "Task Force Urges Joint Security Perimeter." *Globe and Mail*, 14 March 2005: A1.

Krasner, Stephen. *Sovereignty: Organized Hypocrisy*. Princeton, NJ: Princeton University Press, 1999.

Langille, David. "The Business Council on National Issues and the Canadian State." *Studies in Political Economy* 24 (Autumn 1987): 41-85.

Laxer, James. *The Border: Canada, The U.S. and Dispatches from the 49th Parallel*. Toronto: Doubleday Canada, 2003.

Leblanc, Daniel. "Ailing Forces Get Big Boost." *Globe and Mail*, 24 February 2005: F2.

Levitt, Kari. *Silent Surrender: the Multinational Corporation in Canada.* Toronto: Macmillan, 1970.

Lipsey, Richard G., Daniel Schwanen, and Ronald J. Wonnacott. *NAFTA: What's In, What's Out, What's Next.* Toronto: C.D. Howe Institute, 1994.

MacDonald, Gayle. "Chrétien: Culture's New Best Friend?" *Globe and Mail,* 5 May 2001: R4.

MacKenzie, Lewis. "Mission: Remaking the Military." *Globe and Mail,* 21 April 2005: A19.

MacLaren, Roy. "The Three Amigos Have Work To Do." *Globe and Mail,* 30 May 2005: A13.

Mancke, Elizabeth. "Early Modern Imperial Governance and the Origins of Canadian Political Culture." *Canadian Journal of Political Science* 32, 1 (March 1999): 3-20.

Maskell, Peter, and Gunnar Törnqvist. *Building a Cross-Border Learning Region: Emergence of the Northern European Øresund Region.* Copenhagen: Copenhagen Business School Press, 1999.

McBride, Stephen. "Quiet Constitutionalism in Canada: The International Political Economy of Domestic Institutional Change." *Canadian Journal of Political Science* 36, 2 (June 2003).

McCarthy, Shawn. "PM Moved to Stop a Trade War." *Globe and Mail,* 27 May 1999: A3.

McCarthy, Shawn, and Campbell Clark. "Canada Will Make Its Own Laws, PM Vows." *Globe and Mail,* 20 September 2001.

McCraw, Thomas. *Prophets of Regulation: Charles Francis Adams, Louis D. Brandeis, James M. Landis, Alfred E. Kahn.* Cambridge, MA: The Belknap Press of Harvard University Press, 1984.

McDougall, John N. *Fuels and the National Policy.* Toronto: Butterworths, 1982.

———. *The Politics and Economics of Eric Kierans: A Man for All Canadas.* Montreal and Kingston: Queen's University Press, 1993.

McKinney, Joseph A. *Created from NAFTA: The Structure, Function, and Significance of the Treaty's Related Institutions.* Armonk, NY: M.E. Sharpe, 2000.

McLuhan, Marshall, with Quentin Fiore. *The Medium is the Message.* New York: Random House, 1967.

Media Release Center. "Support for North American Free Trade Agreement (NAFTA) Still Strong With 64% Support." Public Release. Ipsos-Reid, 4 February 2001.

Meisel, John. "Escaping Extinction: Cultural Defense of An Undefended Border." *Canadian Journal of Political and Social Theory* 10, 1-2 (1986): 248-65.

Mendelsohn, Matthew, and Robert Wolfe. "Probing the Aftermyth of Seattle: Canadian Public Opinion on International Trade, 1980-2000." School of Policy Studies Working Paper 12, Queen's University, December 2000.

Meyers, Deborah Waller, and Demetrios G. Papademetriou. "Self-Governance Along the U.S.-Canada Border: A View From Three Regions." In Demetrios G. Papademetriou and Deborah Waller Meyers, eds., *Caught in the Middle: Border Communities in an Era of Globalization.* Washington, DC: Carnegie Endowment for International Peace, 2001.

Molot, Maureen A. "The Political Implications of North American Capital Flows." In John H. Pammet and Brian W. Tomlin, eds., *The Integration Question: Political Economy and Public Policy in Canada and North America.* Don Mills, ON: Addison-Wesley, 1984.

Mulcahy, Kevin V. "Cultural Imperialism and Cultural Sovereignty: U.S.-Canadian Cultural Relations." *The American Review of Canadian Studies* 32, 2 (Summer 2000): 181-206.

Murphy, Jamie. "Hanging Out the Welcome Sign." *Time,* 24 December 1984. Accessed at <http://www.time.com/time/archive/preview/0,10987,951396,00.html>.

North, Douglass C., Terry L. Anderson, and Peter J. Hill. *Growth and Welfare in the American Past: A New Economic History.* Englewood Cliffs, NJ: Prentice Hall, 1983.

North, Douglass C., and Robert Paul Thomas. *The Growth of the American Economy to 1860.* Columbia, SC: University of South Carolina Press, 1968.

Nossal, K.R. "Economic Nationalism and Continental Integration." In Denis Stairs and Gilbert R. Winham, Research Coordinators, *The Politics of Canada's Economic Relationship with The United States.* Vol. 29. Royal Commission on the Economic Union and Development Prospects for Canada. Toronto: University of Toronto Press, 1985.

——. *The Politics of Canadian Foreign Policy.* 3rd ed. Scarborough, ON: Prentice Hall, 1997.

Ohmae, Kenichi. *The End of the Nation-State: The Rise of Regional Economies.* Toronto: The Free Press, 1995.

Ornstein, Michael, and H. Michael Stevenson. *Politics and Ideology in Canada: Elite and Public Opinion in the Transformation of a Welfare State.* Montreal and Kingston: McGill-Queen's University Press, 1999.

Ostry, Sylvia. *The Post-Cold War Trading System: Who's on First?* Chicago, IL: University of Chicago Press, 1997.

Papademetriou, Demetrios G., and Deborah Waller Meyers. "Overview, Context, and Vision for the Future." In Demetrios G. Papademetriou and Deborah Waller Meyers, eds., *Caught in the Middle: Border Communities in an Era of Globalization.* Washington, DC: Carnegie Endowment for International Peace, 2001.

Pastor, Robert A. *Toward a North American Community: Lessons from the Old World for the New.* Washington, DC: Institute for International Economics, 2001.

Pentland, Charles. *The Canadian Dilemma.* Paris: Atlantic Institute for International Affairs, 1973.

Perkmann, Markus, and Ngai-Ling Sum, eds., *Globalization, Regionalization and Cross-Border Regions.* New York: Palgrave Macmillan, 2002.

Pew Research Center for the People and the Press. "War With Iraq Further Divides Global Publics." *Views of a Changing World 2003,* 3 June 2003. Accessed at <http://people-press.org/reports/display.php3?ReportID=185>.

Porter, John. *The Vertical Mosaic: An Analysis of Social Class and Power in Canada.* Toronto: University of Toronto Press, 1965.

Posner, Michael. "CRTC to Probe Canadian Content." *Globe and Mail,* 22 February 2001: A7.

Public Policy Forum. *Background Report: the Views of Canadian Industry and Business Associations on Canada-United States Economic Integration.* October, 2000.

Raboy, Marc. *Missed Opportunities: The Story of Canada's Broadcasting Policy.* Montreal and Kingston: McGill-Queen's University Press, 1990.

Raustiala, Kal. "Rethinking the Sovereignty Debate in International Economic Law." *Journal of International Economic Law* 6, 4 (December 2003).

Rice, James J., and Michael J. Prince. *Changing Politics of Canadian Social Policy.* Toronto: University of Toronto Press, 2000.

Ritchie, Gordon. "Who's Afraid of NAFTA's Bite?" *Globe and Mail,* 15 February 2005: A21.

Rugman, Alan M., and Michael Gestrin. "NAFTA's Treatment of Foreign Investment." In Alan M. Rugman, ed., *Foreign Investment and NAFTA.* Columbia, SC: University of South Carolina Press, 1994.

Rugman, Alan M., John Kirton, and Julie A. Soloway. "Canadian Corporate Strategy in a North American Region." *The American Review of Canadian Studies* (Summer 1997): 199-219.

Safarian, A.E. *The Performance of Foreign-Owned Firms in Canada.* Montreal: Private Planning Association of Canada, 1969.

Scholte, Jan Aart. *Globalization: A Critical Introduction.* New York: Palgrave, 2000.

Scoffield, Heather. "Publishers Greet Split-run Deal with Dismay." *Globe and Mail,* 27 May 1999.

Sell, Susan K. "Structures, Agents and Institutions: Private Corporate Power and the Globalization of Intellectual Property Rights." In R.A. Higgott, G.R.D. Underhill, and A. Bieler, eds., *Non-State Actors and Authority in the Global System.* New York: Routledge, 2000.

Sharp, Mitchell. *Which Reminds Me ... A Memoir.* Toronto: University of Toronto Press, 1994.

Shore, Sean M. "No Fences Make Good Neighbors: The Development of the US-Canada Security Community, 1871-1940." In Emanuel Adler and Michael Barnett, eds., *Security Communities.* Cambridge: University of Cambridge Press, 1998.

Sloan, Elinor. "The Road from September 11: Canada-US Defence Relations in the Terrorist Era." In David Carment, Fen Osler Hampson, and Norman Hillmer, eds., *Canada Among Nations 2004: Setting Priorities Straight.* Montreal and Kingston: McGill-Queen's University Press, 2005.

Smith, Denis. *Rogue Tory: the Life and Legend of John G. Diefenbaker.* Toronto: Macfarlane Walter and Ross, 1995.

Smith, Peter H. "Decision Rules and Governance." In Peter H. Smith, ed., *The Challenge of Integration: Europe and the Americas*. New Brunswick, FL: University of Miami, North-South Center, 1993.

Sokolsky, Joel J. "The Bilateral Security Relationship: Will 'National Missile Defense' Involve Canada?" *The American Review of Canadian Studies*, 32, 2 (Summer, 2000).

Stairs, Denis. "Liberalism and the Triumph of Efficiency in Canada-US Relations." *isuma: Canadian Journal of Policy Research*, 1,1 (Spring, 2000): 11–16.

Stanbury, W.T. "Regulation and Competition in Broadcasting in the Age of Convergence." In Dale Orr and Thomas A. Wilson, eds., *The Electronic Village: Policy Issues of the Information Economy*. Toronto: C.D. Howe Institute Study No. 32, 1999.

Stevenson, Garth. *The Politics of Canada's Airlines from Diefenbaker to Mulroney*. Toronto: University of Toronto Press, 1987.

Taras, David. "Swimming Against the Current: American Mass Entertainment and Canadian Identity." In D.M. Thomas, ed., *Canada and the United States: Differences that Count*. 2nd ed. Peterborough, ON: Broadview Press, 2000.

Thompson, John Herd, and Stephen J. Randall. *Canada and the United States: Ambivalent Allies*. Montreal and Kingston: McGill-Queen's University Press, 1994.

Trudeau, Pierre Elliott. *Federalism and the French Canadians*. Toronto: Macmillan of Canada, 1968.

——. Speech before the National Press Club, Washington, DC, 25 March 1969.

Urquhart, M.C., and K.A.H. Buckley, eds., *Historical Statistics of Canada*. Toronto: Macmillan, 1965.

Vanssay, Xavier de, and Edelgard Mahant. "Three's Company and Fifteen's a Union: The Comparative Political Economy of NAFTA and the European Union—Integration or Liberalization?" In Till Geiger and Dennis Kennedy, eds., *Regional Trade Blocs, Multilateralism, and the GATT: Complementary Paths to Free Trade?* London; New York: Pinter, 1996.

Vogel, Steven K. *Freer Markets, More Rules: Regulatory Reform in Advanced Industrial Countries*. Ithaca, NY: Cornell University Press, 1996.

Wallace, Iain. *A Geography of the Canadian Economy.* Don Mills, ON: Oxford University Press, 2002.

Walley, John, with Colleen Hamilton and Roderick Hill. *Canadian Trade Policies and the World Economy.* Toronto: University of Toronto Press, 1985.

Watson, William G. "Canada-U.S. Free Trade: Why Now?" *Canadian Public Policy* 13, 3 (September, 1987): 337-49.

Watson, William G. *Globalization and the Meaning of Canadian Life.* Toronto: University of Toronto Press, 1998.

Weber, Max. *The Protestant Ethic and the Spirit of Capitalism.* Trans. Talcott Parsons with a forward by R.H. Tawney. London: G. Allen and Unwin, 1930.

Weingast, Barry. "The Economic Role of Political Institutions: Market Preserving Federalism and Economic Development." *Journal of Law, Economics and Organization* 4, 1 (December, 1994): 1-31.

Weintraub, Sidney. *NAFTA at Three: A Progress Report.* Washington, DC: Center for Strategic and International Studies, 1997.

Welsh, Jennifer. *At Home in the World: Canada's Global Vision for the 21st Century.* Toronto: HarperCollins, 2004.

Williams, Glen. *Not for Export: Toward a Political Economy of Canada's Arrested Industrialization.* Toronto: McClelland and Stewart, 1983.

Winham, Gil R., and Heather A. Grant. "NAFTA: an Overview." In D. Barry, ed., *Toward a North American Community?* Boulder, CO: Westview Press, 1995.

Wolfe, David A. "Economic Growth and Foreign Investment: A Perspective on Canadian Economic Policy, 1945-1957." *Journal of Canadian Studies* 13, 1 (Spring, 1978): 3-20.

World Bank. *Total GDP 2004.* Accessed at <http://www.worldbank.org/data/databytopic/GDP.pdf>.

Zerbisias, Antonia. "Spending Less on TV Drama." *Toronto Star,* 11 February 2005. Accessed 5 May 2005 at <http://www.publicairwaves.ca/index.php?page=913>.

INDEX

accelerated depreciation allowances, 127–28

Adams, Michael, 35, 281

advanced information technology (AIT), 239, 258, 260–63

Afghanistan, 15, 305–06

agriculture, 84, 104

airlines, 119–20, 167, 261

American Civil War, 68, 89, 93n12, 100

American War of Independence, 55, 56, 68, 89, 109, 114, 118, 321

anti-dumping provisions, 147n4, 168

anti-terrorism measures, 13–15, 66–67, 142, 309
    Canadian support for, 288–89
    cross-border ties and, 233-36
    interoperability and, 190

Arctic nuclear threat, 58–59

armed forces, 66–67, 310–12. *See also* defence

Artibise, Alan, 226

"at the border" trade restrictions, 64, 147, 180n7

attitudes. *See* values

Australia, 104, 153, 186

automobile industry, 122–23, 153–54, 166

autonomy. *See* political autonomy

autonomy/prosperity trade-off, 16–20, 310

Auto Pact, 154

Axworthy, Lloyd, 18, 311–12, 314, 315

Banting, Keith, 274–75, 278

"behind the border" trade restrictions, 147, 180n7

Berlin Wall, 62

bilateral arrangements, 60, 146, 191–92, 203n19, 227

Bill C-55, 257

border, 18, 213–14, 225, 294, 313
    agreement, 315
    attitudes about, 195
    business and, 154, 284
    control of, 41, 67
    open, 15–16, 19–20
    political integration and, 295
    security, 13–15, 17, 18, 45, 310, 313
    smart, 19, 233–36

border effect, 291–92, 294

"Border Papers," (C.D. Howe Institute), 16–17, 20

branch plants, 123. *See also* subsidiaries

Breadbasket, 213–14

Britain, 53, 113–14, 222, 307